SUNDAY BEST

8O GREAT BOOKS FROM

A LIFETIME OF REVIEWS

JOHN CAREY

YALE UNIVERSITY PRESS
NEW HAVEN AND LONDON

All essays and reviews originally published in the *Sunday Times*

First published in paperback in 2023

Copyright © 2022 John Carey

For information about this and other Yale University Press publications, please contact:
U.S. Office: sales.press@yale.edu yalebooks.com
Europe Office: sales@yaleup.co.uk yalebooks.co.uk

Set in Adobe Caslon Pro by IDSUK (DataConnection) Ltd
Printed in Great Britain by Clays Ltd, Elcograf S.p.A

Library of Congress Control Number: 2023935507

ISBN 978-0-300-26668-9 (hbk)
ISBN 978-0-300-27302-1 (pbk)

A catalogue record for this book is available from the British Library.

10 9 8 7 6 5 4 3 2 1

SUNDAY BEST

JOHN CAREY is emeritus professor at the University of Oxford. His recent titles include *100 Poets: A Little Anthology* and *A Little History of Poetry*. Carey has been reviewing two books per month for the *Sunday Times* since the mid-1970s.

Contents

SCIENCE

CONTENTS

MEMOIRS

CONTENTS

ANTHROPOLOGY

CONTENTS

BIOGRAPHY

LITERATURE

BACK TO NATURE

MIND BENDERS

VEGETABLE GARDENING

ACKNOWLEDGEMENTS

I am deeply grateful to Julian Loose, who has been my editor for many years and whose idea this book was. I owe thanks, too, to Andrew Holgate, literary editor at the *Sunday Times*, who has helped me in tracking down the reviews reprinted here. I am also grateful to previous literary editors who chose books for me that they knew I would be pleased to review. They date back to the 1980s, and are John Whitley, John Walsh, Harry Ritchie, Claire Tomalin, Penny Perrick, Geordie Greig, Caroline Gascoigne and Susannah Herbert. I owe each of them a great deal.

As ever, my wife Gill has been my wisest critic.

INTRODUCTION

S *unday Best* is a sequel to *Original Copy: Selected Reviews and Journalism, 1969–1986.* I must have clocked up getting on for a thousand reviews since 1986, and reading through them to decide which should go into a new selection might have been a daunting task. In fact, it was a pleasure to be reminded of books that I had truly prized, and the ones that brought back the happiest memories were the ones I chose for this collection.

Of course, I re-read *Original Copy* before choosing pieces for this new collection, and to be honest I found its constant point-scoring a bit overdone. Perhaps I have managed to grow up in the interim, but anyway I no longer feel the compulsion to be funny or caustic all the time. The pieces in this new collection are not chosen because they are funny but because they can open new lives and new perspectives for the reader.

A survivor from *Original Copy* retained here is *Vegetable Gardening* (1980). I have kept it because it has attracted some hostile attention over the years. I have also reprinted here my two favourite pieces from *Pure Pleasure: A Guide to the 20th Century's Most Enjoyable Books* (2000). *Pure Pleasure* was an idea hatched by Geordie Greig (then literary editor at the *Sunday Times*) and I assembled it by going through my shelves, choosing books that spanned the century, from Conan Doyle's *The Hound of the Baskervilles* (1902) to Graham Swift's *Last Orders* (1996), and writing 1,000 words on each. The pieces appeared in the paper weekly and attracted a lively postbag from readers, many of them discontented with my suggestions and proposing their own.

Their comments revealed to me what an interesting selection of readers regularly scan the books pages in the national newspapers. Letters started to arrive soon after my first column had hit doormats. The ones I liked best were chatty and nostalgic, recapturing those special moments of discovery that give perspective to life and that only the bookish can have – for example, 'Thank you for sending me back to a book I first read in a tent in Saudi-Arabia, 23 December 1947'. Others were more critical. Why, I was asked, had I not included in my choice of the century's fifty best books Yutang Lin's *Gay Genius*, or Kurban Said's *Ali and Nino*, or Jean-Pierre Greenlaw's *The Coral Buildings of Suakin*, or K. Dhondup's *The Water Horse and Other Years: A History of 17th- and 18th-Century Tibet*? Because I had never heard of them was, of course, the answer, and I was made to feel that I belonged to a real community of readers with fields of knowledge far outside my own scope.

Among my most popular choices was Thomas Hardy's poetry. One reader who applauded it was a poet himself and he sent me a copy of his first collection. Bulgakov's *A Country Doctor's Notebook* was popular too. A retired professor of English, grateful for the introduction, rated it 'quite unparalleled'. Keith Douglas's *Alamein to Zem Zem* produced the most exciting letter of all. 'I met Douglas in Alexandria shortly before Alamein when he was engaged to my cousin Milena Pegna'. The writer went on to explain that Milena, whose breaking off of her engagement to Douglas inspired some of his finest poetry, was not the 'siren' some have made out, but a gentle, sensitive girl who did not feel ready for marriage. I have included my review of *Alamain to Zem Zem* in this collection.

But enough of retrospect. I should add that I have changed the layout of this new collection. Whereas *Original Copy* poured out its reviews on the page helter-skelter, this book gathers them under headings – 'Science', 'Literature', and so on – hoping the different sections will strike sparks off each other.

But why read book reviews? The obvious answer is that too many books are published for anyone to read for themselves, so some kind of filter is needed, and book reviews provide it. To my knowledge the first person who became aware of the explosion of print culture was the seventeenth-century bibliomaniac Robert Burton, author of *The Anatomy of Melancholy*. He really did try to read, or anyway dip into, everything that had been published both in English and Latin before his arrival on earth. Since then, the torrent of printed books has redoubled year by year. Reading book reviews is a way of keeping your chin above the flood – or, to put it another way, keeping in touch with the current of ideas during your lifetime.

But there is something else that I try to think of when starting out on a book review, and it is from a more serious source than Burton. When Milton wrote *Areopagitica* in 1644 he was protesting against the idea that books should have to be licensed by the Parliamentarian government before they could be published. He wrote:

> For books are not absolutely dead things, but do contain a potency of life in them to be as active as that soul whose progeny they are; nay, they do preserve as in a vial the purest efficacy and extraction of that living intellect that bred them ... As good almost kill a man as kill a good book. Who kills a man kills a reasonable creature, God's image; but he who destroys a good book, kills reason itself, kills the image of God, as it were, in the eye ... A good book is the precious life blood of a master spirit, embalmed and treasured up on purpose to a life beyond life.

That may seem a stratospheric height from which to look at the book reviews that I write, week by week. And it is. But it is a reminder that what you do when you review someone else's book is intensely important to them. It can blight a budding career; it can make you an enemy for life; it can inflict a wound that will never heal. I was reminded of this by something that happened recently. When the poet and author Clive James was dying, his publisher bussed a group of his friends over to Cambridge, where he held court. For a man who had come out of hospital only the previous day, and was mortally ill, he was astonishingly animated. He reminisced about his life in books, and a discussion evolved. I had hugely praised his *Unreliable Memoirs*, which is one of the funniest books I have ever read. But I was uncomfortably aware that I had given a needlessly rancorous review to his first book *The Metropolitan Critic*, which I hoped Clive had forgotten. He had not. I could see that he was mischievously edging towards it as he talked, and I blurted out some feeble plea, 'Oh Clive, please don't mention that!' – or words to that effect. Tom Stoppard was in the audience and intervened, rightly, to say Clive should finish his story. But mercifully he relented. Later his widow told me that he could have quoted the offending review word for word.

A different kind of advice I'd give to reviewers is to keep a copy of anything you consider really outstanding. When I started reviewing poetry for Karl Miller at the *Listener*, a BBC weekly, now defunct, the first batch of books I was sent contained a pamphlet published by Queen's University of Belfast and titled *Eleven Poems* by an unknown poet called Seamus Heaney. I thought it astonishingly good and called it 'masterly' in my review. But I did not keep the pamphlet. Or perhaps some wise person stole it. Now a copy of *Eleven Poems* would fetch more than £2,000. Not that I would sell it. But it would be a memento of the moment a new poet burst upon the world, and how often does that happen?

4

I must stop, for I want this to be a short Introduction. But two more words of advice to reviewers. One, never review a book by someone you know personally. Two, never review a book you do not think worth reviewing. *Bon voyage!*

John Carey
Oxford, 2022

CULTURAL HISTORY

The Mediterranean in History
edited by David Abulafia, 2003

This looks like a coffee-table book but is something a lot more interesting. David Abulafia, professor of Mediterranean history at Cambridge University, has gathered an international team of scholars, each of whom contributes a chapter about a different historical period, starting with the geological upheavals that first formed this small, landlocked sea, with its jagged north coast and smooth south one. The illustrations are magnificent and not just decorative but mesh intelligently with the text. The emphasis is on how the exchange of commodities and ideas across the sea developed, rather than on the history of the societies along its shores.

As Oliver Rackham points out in the first chapter, the Mediterranean has, for its size, an extraordinary variety of landforms, from snowy mountains to 'several small, curious and beautiful deserts'. This has proved the key to its history, for it made internal trade imperative, as it would not have been in an ecologically uniform region. The islands, too, are miniature continents, with their own geologies and cultures. Crete, for example, has alps, jungles, arctic wastes and tropical gorges.

Prehistoric Crete had animals found nowhere else, including an elephant the size of a calf and a miniature non-aquatic hippopotamus.

The only native Mediterranean food plants are olives and a few legumes, and this also made trade vital. Wheat and barley came from the Near East, and the vine from central Europe. Most of what we think of as Mediterranean food arrived courtesy of the Arabs. The first European lemons were grown in Muslim Spain. Limes, artichokes, aubergines, bananas, watermelons and the hard wheat from which couscous and pasta are made all came from the Islamic world. Without Islam, no spaghetti.

Abulafia is effusively pro-Mediterranean, celebrating it as 'the cradle of Western civilisation'. The three great monotheistic religions – Judaism, Christianity and Islam – began there, he points out. The alphabet we use was invented by the Phoenicians. Other civilised amenities traceable to the region include the dinner party, pioneered by the Etruscans; the shopping mall, dating from sixteenth-century Aleppo; and the bikini, clearly depicted on a Roman mosaic from Sicily, which shows young women working out in a gym with dumbbells.

However, you cannot help noticing, as you turn the pages, a formidable list of human institutions, first developed in the Mediterranean, that the world would have been better without. It was the cradle of tyranny. The 'great kings' of the Bronze Age built their empires on subjection and slavery, surrounding themselves with an aristocratic élite, and importing from the East the regalia of kingship – thrones, footrests, sceptres, gold and purple vestments – that have remained standard items of royal flummery and the wonder of goggle-eyed crowds to the present day.

It was also the cradle of religious massacre. Developing three separate monotheistic religions turned out, from a purely evolutionary viewpoint, not to have been such a bright idea. From the seventh century on, bitter and merciless warfare between Muslims and Christians was waged virtually nonstop. Atrocities on both sides beggar belief. One Christian emperor of Byzantium in the eleventh century sent home

14,000 prisoners of war blinded, presumably to emphasise the superiority of his faith. The clash of religions inspired the first weapon of mass destruction, Greek Fire, invented by a seventh-century Syrian. A mixture of quicklime, petroleum and sulphur, it was a kind of proto-napalm that ignited on contact with water, and allowed the Byzantine navy to incinerate Muslim fleets.

The Mediterranean was also the cradle of organised crime. Piracy had already become a profitable institution in pre-Roman times. The Romans' ruthless policy of executing pirates and destroying their coastal settlements made the seas safe for nearly 1,000 years. But with the fall of the empire pirates once again became the terror of every merchant and seafarer. In the Middle Ages, when half the Mediterranean was in Muslim and half in Christian hands, piracy was organised along religious lines, with each side plundering the other's shipping. By the seventeenth century the Muslim pirates or 'barbary corsairs' operated mostly from the north African coast, while Malta sheltered the most fearsome Christian predators, the Knights Hospitaller of St John, who harassed the rich Muslim convoys sailing between Egypt and Istanbul. Piracy had lucrative offshoots, such as the sale of safe-conduct passes to protect the buyer from corsairs. It also inaugurated another modern institution, the car-boot sale, or at any rate a city-sized forerunner of it, in the shape of Leghorn. This was a free port founded by the Medicis in the 1590s, specifically to dispose of stolen goods. The way the system worked was that Christian traders in North Africa would buy up plundered merchandise from the corsairs and send it to Leghorn, where it would be resold, quite possibly to the original owners. The Muslims operated a similar racket at Smyrna.

A pleasure of the book is its up-to-date historical evidence. Some of this comes from newly discovered wrecks. A Roman cargo ship, with its amphorae still neatly stacked in interlocking rows, can give a modern researcher the kind of practical experience that the clerk who supervised its loading would have had. Documents, too, are still coming to light. There was a luxury trade between Rome and India. A recently published papyrus from Vienna shows that wealthy Egyptian families maintained agents in the Red Sea ports to handle it, and at Muziris in southwest India quantities of Roman gold and silver coins have been found. Abulafia is good not only on history but on historical fashions. Scholars have always taken what they want from the past, called that 'history', and ignored the rest. Until recently Byzantium was thought not worth serious study, and archaeologists digging on Greek sites would throw away Byzantine pottery as trash. Then mid-twentieth century academic popularisers such as David Runciman aroused interest in the medieval Greek world, and the trash became treasure.

The twentieth-century globalisation of the Mediterranean, recorded in the final chapter, may seem a sorry decline, heralding as it does the advent of mass tourism. But set against the region's savage and murderous past it does not look so bad. If the beaches have to be drenched in something, then better suntan oil than blood. Once America had been discovered, it was, in any case, only a matter of time before the Mediterranean's central importance dwindled. It is most valuable, now, for the ruins of past civilisations. As you soak up the sun, you also imbibe a relaxing sense of human futility. The evidence confronts you everywhere – a crumbling Roman column, or the Lion of St Mark carved on some ruined Venetian fort in the Greek islands. If it is true that Americans are more hopeful than Europeans, and more dangerously trusting in human power, then it may be because their landscapes do not yet speak of disappointment and failure, while we choose to holiday in the graveyard of vanished cultures.

The Rise and Fall of Adam and Eve:
The Story that Created Us
Stephen Greenblatt, 2017

Stephen Greenblatt, now a senior professor at Harvard University, changed literary criticism. In the 1980s and 1990s he steered it away from the abstractions of continental theory and introduced an approach called new historicism. It was not essentially different from old historicism, in that it entailed putting literary works into their cultural and political contexts. However, as practised by Greenblatt it was challenging, imaginative and flamboyant in a way that outstripped all precedents. It soon became the dominant mode in Britain and America (though generally in stuffier versions than his), and still is.

His latest book applies new historicism to the Genesis story of Adam and Eve. It is, Greenblatt observes, a brilliantly successful tale, irrespective of its truth or falsehood, in that it is known to millions who have never even opened a Bible. His concern, though, is how it originated. It must have begun, he believes, as an oral folk tale. But it was shaped by historical events. In 597 BC Judah was conquered by the kingdom of Babylon, and its people taken into captivity, as Psalm 137 recalls: 'By the waters of Babylon, there we sat down, yea, we wept.'

The Babylonians worshipped a god called Marduk. But the captive Jews clung to their belief in Yahweh, and strove to keep their legends untainted by Babylonian myths. They did not quite succeed. The snake who robs mankind of immortality in Genesis is already present in the *Epic of Gilgamesh*, a Babylonian text far older than the Hebrew scriptures.

When the Jews returned to Judah in 539 BC and set about amalgamating their legends into a sacred book, the Torah, they included the Genesis story, snake and all. But the sacred book insists that Yahweh is the one true god, omnipotent and all-knowing, and quite different from false gods such as Marduk.

This emphasis on their god's supremacy was understandable. But it ruptured the story's inner logic. For if God was all-knowing, why did he forbid Adam and Eve to eat the fruit, knowing they would disobey? Why did he create them at all, since he intended to kill them? As Greenblatt shows, much of the huge body of rabbinical and Christian exegesis that mushroomed around the Genesis story devoted itself to trying to answer these unanswerable questions.

A way out of the impasse was to claim that the story was allegorical and that God never meant it to be taken literally. Jewish and Christian commentators clutched at this straw, until St Augustine appeared on the scene and insisted on the story's literal truth. As his *Confessions* make clear, he was troubled by sexual desire, and he believed that was what made him a fallen man. Contemplating this, he evolved the theory that in paradise Adam had been able to have erections voluntarily, just as (Augustine helpfully explains) some people are able, even now, to move unexpected parts of their bodies, such as their ears. But once Adam had fallen, he was powerless to control his body, as Augustine found he was to control his.

Convinced that fallen Adam was still alive in him, Augustine introduced the doctrine of original sin, which meant that evil is innate in all humans because Adam ate the forbidden fruit. The doctrine had fearsome consequences, such as the belief that unbaptised babies suffer in hell for all eternity. Also, Augustine's return to a literal reading of Genesis, which blamed Eve for the fall, stoked the pathological misogyny inherent in medieval Christianity.

In line with these woeful beliefs, early artistic portrayals of Adam and Eve show them, as Greenblatt illustrates, bowed down in guilt and shame. In Renaissance art, though, a transformation takes place. Adam and Eve are no longer cowed but splendid, their perfect bodies often modelled on classical statues. The technical development of engraving allowed this new, proud image of our first parents to spread across Europe, initially in Albrecht Dürer's 1504 masterpiece, *Adam and Eve*.

Greenblatt sees John Milton's *Paradise Lost*, with Adam and Eve majestic in their nakedness, as the literary counterpart of this artistic advance. He associates Eve with Milton's first wife, Mary Powell, which, given the unhappiness of the marriage, may raise eyebrows. But Greenblatt might reply that Mary was almost certainly the only woman Milton ever saw naked. By the time he married his second wife he was blind. So imagining naked Eve he would almost inevitably imagine Mary.

Paradise Lost, published in 1667, was the story's last gasp. The Enlightenment had no time for talking snakes or magic trees, and Voltaire mercilessly ridiculed the whole Genesis account. Darwin's 1871 *The Descent of Man* finished it off as a credible explanation of how we got here.

This is a learned book, but Greenblatt's passion for story-telling makes it read like a series of fascinating anecdotes. Some are about his Jewish upbringing and his travels in Bible lands. Others focus on individuals who changed history, such as the self-taught, working-class Victorian Londoner George Smith, who cracked cuneiform script and discovered the *Epic of Gilgamesh*, or the Egyptian peasant who, in 1945, unearthed an urn full of books, some of which his mother used to light the bread oven. Rescued, the remainder were identified as fourth-century Coptic texts denouncing God's vicious conduct in the fall story.

In the last chapter, Greenblatt visits the Kibale National Park in Uganda, to observe a group of chimpanzees. Since they do not know good from evil, and copulate publicly without shame, he believes they might reveal what life in Eden was really like. Alas, it turns out that they are perpetually at war with other chimp groups, and that the males frequently beat up the females – just like humans, in fact. They seem to know about guilt, too. One furtive couple slinks away for illicit sex while the alpha male is preoccupied. So the chimps are a grotesque letdown. But in every other respect *The Rise and Fall of Adam and Eve* is exhilarating to read and a feast for the mind.

Madness in Civilization: A Cultural History of Insanity
Andrew Scull, 2015

The title of Andrew Scull's powerful and disturbing book alludes to one of the sacred texts of the 1960s counter-culture, Michel Foucault's *Madness and Civilization*. Foucault and his disciples held that madness was a social construct: a pretext that allowed the state to lock up those who did not abide by its norms. For Scull, a professor of sociology and science studies at the University of California, such theories are 'emotional nonsense'. Madness, he insists, is real, and its symptoms (delusion, hallucination, self-harm) have been recorded in all human societies.

But his book, a panoramic survey of the treatment of madness in western and eastern medicine from the earliest times, has a more serious aim than faulting Foucault. The causes of madness, he contends, are still as mysterious to us as they were to the ancients. We are as incapable as they were of reaching a satisfactory scientific diagnosis of any mental illness, let alone curing it. The response of the sane to the mad throughout history is, in his account, largely an amalgam of ignorance and cruelty.

For the friends and loved ones of patients, a distressing feature of mental illness is that it seems to turn them into different people. Perhaps this accounts for the common early belief that the mad were possessed by demons who might, if commanded, depart. A more persistent idea, though, seems to be that the mad are just pretending and will stop if they are punished severely enough.

Unless something like this was believed, it is hard to explain the brutalities inflicted by evidently well-meaning doctors and carers. Recommended cures that Scull collects range from chains, manacles, beating and starvation to more imaginative expedients such as a small iron cage called the Chinese Temple, which could be lowered into water with the patient inside. Its inventor, an eighteenth-century

Dutch physician, expressed the hope that the sensation of near drowning might shock patients back to reality.

A modern shock treatment, electroconvulsive therapy (ECT), was developed by two Italian doctors who were visiting a slaughterhouse and observed how pigs were stunned by passing a current through their heads prior to having their throats cut. It occurred to them that the technique might be used on the mentally ill, and the first human trial took place in 1938. Critics of ECT have protested that it is not based on any scientific understanding of its effects and causes irreparable brain damage. However, it still has adherents.

Another 1930s innovation, lobotomy, entailed boring a hole in the skull and destroying brain tissue in the frontal lobes. It proved popular – with doctors – and an American surgeon developed a speeded-up version that dispensed with the need to bore through the skull. His method was to introduce an ice-pick under the patient's eyelid and employ a mallet to break through the eye socket and penetrate the frontal lobes. A sweeping motion was then used to sever brain tissues. Scull notes that, in its heyday, lobotomy was a source of great pride to the psychiatric profession, though all it did was inflict random damage on patients' brains. It is no longer in use.

The U-turns that Scull identifies in the treatment of the insane indicate, for him, its lack of any dependable medical basis. The most drastic revolution he records relates to asylums. There had been private asylums in earlier periods, but in the nineteenth century publicly funded asylums spread through Europe and North America.

Possessing an insane asylum, staffed by medical professionals, became a symbol of civilisation. The plan was that, after a brief sojourn, patients would return to their families cured. What happened, however, was that they became institutionalised and stayed put.

Overcrowding and squalor resulted. One of Scull's many illustrations, a photo of the male incontinent ward in the Pennsylvania state asylum, taken surreptitiously in 1944, resembles a scene from Dante's *Inferno*.

Such horrors could not be allowed to continue. Besides, money ran out. So it was decided that the mentally ill would be better off in the community. Beginning in the 1950s, asylums closed. There has been no systematic study in Britain of what became of their former residents, but Scull suspects that many ended up in prison or on the streets.

Although destructive of life and happiness, madness has been a great boon to the arts. Scull, in a fascinating chapter, detects a surge during the Renaissance with Ariosto's *Orlando Furioso*, Cervantes's *Don Quixote* and Shakespeare's *Hamlet* and *King Lear*. Maybe the relatively new experience of city-living in the sixteenth century upped the incidence of art and insanity, or perhaps the obvious affinities between madness and the imagination were enough to attract writers and artists. The new genre of opera, Scull suggests, might be seen as the natural medium for madness, with its absurd plots, melodramatic passions and performers singing arias while in agony or dying.

He rounds off his book with a blistering attack on current beliefs. The late-twentieth-century orthodoxy that mental illness can be traced to faulty brain chemistry (defects of dopamine or a shortage of serotonin) is, he declares, so much 'biobabble'. The causes of madness remain mysterious. MRI, though much vaunted, is merely a crude way of measuring blood flow to the brain, and affords no insight into how the brain works. Psychoactive drugs such as tranquillisers and antidepressants are not cures but palliatives – if that – and risk profound and disabling side effects.

The beneficiaries are the pharmaceutical companies. They reward medical professionals with research grants for discovering mental illnesses (such as 'binge-eating disorder') that provide new markets for drugs, though the illnesses do not exist. He quotes, approvingly, the director of the National Institute of Mental Health as saying, in a private conversation, that schizophrenia and depression do not really exist either, but are just constructs. The more Scull goes on like this the more he sounds like Foucault. But that is a sign of the complexity his engrossing book encompasses.

Eat Me: A Natural and Unnatural
History of Cannibalism
Bill Schutt, 2017

Cannibalism is our last taboo. Incest, to which Freud also awarded taboo status, is still a recurrent social problem, but it is not a visceral horror that repels and fascinates us, as cannibalism does. Instinct tells us that cannibalism is unnatural, but instinct lies. In fact, cannibalism is common throughout the natural world, as Bill Schutt explains in this gripping and often disturbing book.

Schutt is a biology professor with a rare gift for making biology dramatic. His accounts of family life among invertebrates are hair-raising. When black lace-weaver spiders, for example, grow too big for their mother to care for them, she drums on the web to summon them and allows them to swarm over her and eat her alive. Male spiders can be equally self-sacrificing. While Australian redbacks are copulating, the female eats the male's abdomen. When the sex act is complete he crawls off, half-eaten, but then comes back for a second go, during which his mate completes her meal. This has terminal disadvantages for the male but, Schutt points out, it makes good evolutionary sense. By feeding his mate he improves her chances of surviving and perpetuating his genes.

Invertebrates are the star performers at this kind of showy exit, but cannibalism also occurs in every class of vertebrates from fish to mammals, including chimpanzees, our closest relatives. It can begin horrifyingly early in the life cycle. The oviducts of the female sand tiger shark, for example, contain embryos at different stages of development. The largest of the embryos start by gobbling up the eggs around them, and then consume their smaller siblings until only two foetal sharks are left, one in each oviduct. Shark experts believe that this prenatal killing practice gives the young sand tigers an advantage later when competing with other predatory species.

That humans will resort to cannibalism to avoid starvation has been known since biblical times, and Schutt revisits some famous examples, including the blockade of Leningrad by German and Finnish armies in the Second World War. The most lethal siege in world history, it lasted more than two years, during which 1.5 million died. Official Soviet accounts omitted any mention of cannibalism, but NKVD records, published in 2004, revealed that approximately 2,000 cannibals were arrested during the siege, mostly for eating flesh from dead bodies rather than killing for food. That the number was so low testifies to the heroism of the Leningraders and the revulsion cannibalism inspired even when it meant survival.

Whether humans have ever resorted to 'cultural' as opposed to survival cannibalism has been disputed. The stories of cannibal rites that the conquistadors brought from the Caribbean were quite likely invented as a pretext for killing or enslaving defenceless natives. However, Schutt is satisfied that there is more recent dependable evidence from Fiji, Papua New Guinea and elsewhere that eating enemies killed in battle and honouring deceased relatives by eating their body parts are modes of cannibalism that have been widely practised. This raises the question of whether revulsion from cannibalism is really hard-wired in our brains, or whether it is just a western prejudice, as Montaigne suggested in his essay 'Of Cannibals'.

Schutt approaches the question scientifically, asking if there is any record of a human culture that has not condemned cannibalism. The answer he comes up with is China. Chinese classics and dynastic chronicles reveal a long history of cultural cannibalism activated by motives ranging from revenge to an epicurean taste for human flesh. Could this spread to the West? Schutt thinks so, and instances the present fad for cooking placenta. At a friend's house he is served placenta osso buco (the placenta being, until shortly before, a part of his hostess's daughter), and pronounces it highly palatable, resembling fried chicken gizzards.

More seriously, he notes that, more than a century ago, H.G. Wells had already foreseen that the human race would be driven to survival cannibalism. In his futurist novella *The Time Machine*, humans have morphed into two distinct species, the Morlocks, ape-like descendants of the working class, and the effete, helpless Eloi, whose ancestors were the old privileged classes, and whom the Morlocks devour to survive.

Perhaps overinfluenced by his years of work among spiders, Schutt shares Wells's pessimism. Across wide expanses of China, Syria and central Africa, he observes, once-fertile land is already turning to desert, and in a world ravaged by climate change, overpopulation and pollution, humans will 'almost certainly', he asserts, resort to survival cannibalism. However, he urges us not to be dismayed. Far from being 'the nightmarish aberration we tell ourselves it is', cannibalism, he reminds us, has added much to the varied tapestry of our lives, enriching myth and folktale, and providing a fascinating pastime for biologists.

Somehow I do not think readers will be as cheered by these reflections as he supposes, and the final phase of his book might cause alarm. Turning from morality to a medical reason for not eating people, he points out that, among the Fore of Papua New Guinea, cannibalism has been found to spread a deadly disease called kuru. It resembles, in some respects, CJD (a form of mad cow disease), caused, we now know, by feeding livestock meat and bonemeal, so forcing them to become cannibals. Schutt retells the shameful story of how CJD was hushed up to protect the British beef industry. A government inspector called on the grandmother of the first British victim, a schoolgirl, warning her not to discuss the child's condition lest it should adversely affect the Common Market. A working party, led by a distinguished Oxford professor, reported that the risk of the disease spreading to humans was 'remote'. Since then there have been 177 deaths, but that, some believe, might be only the start. Thousands of the Fore have died as adults, sometimes fifty years after being exposed to kuru via ritual cannibalism.

So, if kuru and CJD are truly akin, people who ate contaminated British beef in the 1970s and 1980s might yet start to show symptoms.

Stonehenge
Rosemary Hill, 2008

What is it about Stonehenge that makes people take leave of their senses? Why should a harmless-looking group of megaliths induce softening of the brain? These are questions that Rosemary Hill's witty, erudite book persistently prompts. Oddly, she points out, nobody in the Roman period or the early Middle Ages seems to have noticed that Stonehenge existed. Or maybe they had other things on their minds than antiquarian research. At all events, they left no written record. But from the twelfth century on, theories and explanations about the monument proliferate. It was made by giants in Ireland and transported to Salisbury Plain by the wizard Merlin. Or it had something to do with King Arthur. Or with Joseph of Arimathea, in whose tomb Christ was buried, and who came to Britain after the resurrection with the disciples. Or it was built by Hebrew-speaking Phoenicians, worshippers of Hercules, who very probably helped to carry the stones. Or it was a Roman temple (this was Inigo Jones's idea, who had been to Rome and ought to have known better). Or it was the tomb of Boadicea. Or a post-Roman Buddhist temple (this was the historian James Fergusson, writing in the *Quarterly Review* in 1860).

Then there were the druids. In reality, there is not a shred of evidence that a druid ever set foot in Stonehenge. Caesar and Tacitus both describe druids, but do not site them there. Tacitus connects them with Anglesey where, he says, a fanatical band of druids, shrieking curses, waylaid a detachment of legionaries, but was chased off. It was the magpie-minded antiquary John Aubrey who in the 1660s first connected Stonehenge with druids, and it soon became an established fact that they built it as their headquarters. It was there that they did solemn things with mistletoe and performed human sacrifice. Caesar had written that druids built wicker effigies, placed living men inside, and set them on fire. It is just the kind of atrocity story that conquerors have always invented about the conquered, but it has been eagerly believed since the seventeenth century, and inspired Robin Hardy's classic 1973 horror film *The Wicker Man*. An alternative version of the druids made them gentle proto-Christians who had intuitive knowledge of the Virgin Birth and the Crucifixion centuries before they happened. William Stukeley, the friend and biographer of Sir Isaac Newton, favoured this view, and provided an illustration of a druid – an ascetic-looking sage in primitive hiking gear and sandals.

The Romantics preferred the human-sacrifice version. Wordsworth and Blake both relished the thought of Stonehenge as a 'cruel druid temple' full of 'horrid shrieks'. J.M.W. Turner completed the descent into melodrama with a painting that showed the monument illuminated by a violent electric storm. In the foreground a shepherd lies dead, struck by lightning. His dog howls beside him, and there are evidently several casualties among the sheep. In 1781, the Ancient Order of Druids was founded in the Kings Arms public house in Poland Street, and eleven years later Edward Williams, a laudanum addict and forger of ancient Welsh poetry, who called himself Iolo Morganwg, 'revived' the Gorsedd (or community) of Bards and celebrated the autumn equinox in an improvised stone circle on Primrose Hill. After that there was no stopping druids. They have multiplied and spawned endless splinter groups – half a dozen new orders a year, Hill reckons, since 1990. Meanwhile, throughout the 1980s, druids were joined for their midsummer ceremonies by representatives of many other persuasions (countercultural philosophers, UFO-spotters, ley-line tracers, rock musicians, mystics) all exercising their immemorial right to watch sunrise over Stonehenge and fight the police.

A great strength of Hill's method is that she is by no means inclined just to laugh at what seem ludicrous beliefs. She carefully unpicks them, showing what made them attractive in their cultures, and how scholarly their adherents often were, apart from their brief descent into Stonehenge madness. John Wood, for example, who published a book on Stonehenge in 1747, believed that it should rightly be called 'Choir gaur', a name he derived from Hebrew via Welsh, and that the druid priesthood had locked up astronomical secrets emblematically in the design of their temples. Even fellow druid-fanciers mocked these 'whimseys' of a 'crackt imagination'. But astro-archaeology has shown that Stonehenge is, in effect, an observatory, and that the outer ring of Aubrey holes (called after John Aubrey, who discovered them) were designed to predict lunar eclipses on a fifty-six-year cycle. Besides, Wood was also the architect who, with his son, created Georgian Bath, and when he designed the Circus he based it on Stonehenge. It is sixty Hebrew cubits wide (the measure Wood believed druids used), its thirty houses equal in number to the outer row of sarsen stones, and it is crowned with large acorns, dear to the druids as 'priests of the hollow oak'. Wood also believed that the stone circle at Stanton Drew, near Bristol, was a temple to the moon and a druid university, and his son built the Royal Crescent at Bath as a lunar symbol. Wood's Circus was imitated by other architects. Without it we should not have Oxford Circus or Piccadilly Circus, or, Hill argues, the modern traffic island, which is a town planner's adaptation of Wood's idea.

Archaeologists, if not quite the villains of Hill's story, are taken to task by her for their overweening confidence in scientific method and their impatience with druids old and new. All the same the archaeologists' discoveries about Stonehenge are the most wonderful things in her book, and her survey of them is lucid and enthralling. Near the future site of Stonehenge, wooden posts were raised, perhaps for a ritual purpose, some time between 8500 and 6700 BC. By way of comparison, the pyramid of Cheops, the oldest of the Giza pyramids, dates from 2560 BC. That is also approximately the date when Stonehenge's ring of sarsen stones was raised. The lintels on top are held in place by mortice and tenon joints, and linked by tongue-and-groove joints. These are woodworking techniques: Stonehenge is a wooden building imitated in stone. Nobody knows why. Nor does anyone know who the builders were, what their purpose was, or why or how they transported bluestones from the Mynydd Preseli area of south Wales to form a matching circle inside the locally quarried sarsens.

Long before any stones arrived, a ditch was dug and a bank built, forming an almost perfect circle round the whole site, and faced with gleaming chalk. Nearby were seventeen long barrows, earth mounds raised above communal graves, some of which had been there 1,000 years when Stonehenge was begun. The team currently digging at Stonehenge announced last month that they think the site was used as a royal cemetery, a theory already noted in Hill's book. Perhaps the transition from communal to single graves marked the emergence of a social élite – the beginning of traditional British class distinction. Like most thinking about Stonehenge, that is speculation. But it is the kind of idea that Hill stimulates, because she values imagination as much as scientific certainty. Her book is a treasure: stylish, thoughtful, miraculously condensed, and as full of knowledge as a megalith is full of megalith.

Universe of Stone: Chartres Cathedral and the Triumph of the Medieval Mind
Philip Ball, 2008

Chartres cathedral is a marvel but also a mystery. Nobody knows who designed it or what they were trying to express. Begun in 1200 and finished in 1226, it was the crowning example of the Gothic style and marked, Philip Ball suggests in this lucid and resplendent book, a shift in the way the Western world thought about God, the universe and man's place in it. Romanesque churches with their vast walls and narrow windows had been dark and inward-looking, and signified, he argues, monastic seclusion. Chartres changed all that. Its walls were diaphanous membranes of glass set in cobwebs of stone. On the outside, flying buttresses propped them up to prevent them collapsing under the soaring vaults of the roof. It was 'transparent logic', a celebration of the light of reason, banishing the old gloom, and progressing from an age when God was feared to one where his works could be understood.

That, at any rate, is the theory. Ball makes no pretence to have thought it up himself. It had been aired in the nineteenth century and was elaborated in the twentieth by the great German art historian Erwin Panofsky. What makes it plausible is that the school of Chartres, in the decades before work on the cathedral began, had become one of the great centres of European learning, a principal conduit for Arabic science and mathematics, and a pioneer in the rediscovery of Plato, Aristotle and Euclid. It was progressive and humanist, encouraging a rational understanding of the physical world, advancing geometry, and promoting the belief that the universe was a system of eternal order based on numerical proportions.

Is this what Chartres cathedral was trying to say, and if so how were these ideas imparted to the people who actually built it? Ball finds Panofsky's vision inspiring, but sees difficulties fitting it to the facts. Nine successive teams of contractors seem to have worked on the building, so continuity of design must have been imposed by someone, but there is no evidence it was anyone connected with the school of Chartres. The idea of an architect in the modern sense had not yet developed, and decisions may have been taken piecemeal by clerics or patrons or by the master builders, whoever they were. No plans survive, and quite likely none were made, as there was no tradition of architectural drawing. The builders may have carried the design in their heads like mental arithmetic.

There is evidence that bishops were spurred on in their building projects by pride and envy, and it seems possible that the brilliantly ostentatious architecture of Chartres was conceived to satisfy these passions rather than to convey universal rationality. Ball's idea that the building of Chartres began 'the age of reason' is the shakiest part of his case. As he points out, the cathedral's most precious relic was the tunic that the Virgin Mary wore when giving birth to Jesus. A later acquisition was the head of Mary's mother, Anne. These rarities attracted pilgrims and wealth, but it is hard to see them as congruent with rational thought in any other respect. More persuasive is Ball's scepticism about the romantic notion that medieval cathedrals were produced by the pious efforts of the whole community. At Chartres, on the contrary, relations between town and clergy were hostile. The church fattened on taxes and tithes (the bishop's income was the equivalent of $1.5 million annually) and the building of the cathedral merely served to remind the citizenry of the hierarchy of wealth and power they were at the bottom of. In 1210, they rioted, and a mob attacked the dean's house. In retaliation, the canons excommunicated the whole town. A curious feature of the cathedral is a number of little doorways high up in the walls, and it seems that these led onto wooden walkways, mounted on scaffolding, that allowed the canons to get from one part of the concourse to another without having to encounter their obstreperous flock.

Another popular belief that Ball demolishes is that the workers who built cathedrals were pious folk devoted to the glory of God and elevated above mercenary considerations. No such beings appear in the historical record. The cathedrals were built by wage earners who would go on strike if their interests were threatened, fight rival teams who tried to undercut them, and steal building materials when the opportunity arose. They would also scamp their work unless closely supervised, which may be why their cathedrals sometimes fell down. Beauvais collapsed three times, Troyes four. It even appears, though it seems heretical even to whisper it, that they were not uniformly skilful. Many monastic buildings were brought down in the early thirteenth century merely by a high wind. Part of the trouble was that accurate calculation of the stresses within a building was beyond the competence even of master builders.

No reader of Ball's book will have any excuse for similar ignorance. His section on how to build your own medieval cathedral, backed up by stylish diagrams, is a model of explanatory writing. It makes clear, even to the least mathematical, how the vast tonnage of masonry in a barrel vault can actually strengthen the building under it, and why a pointed Gothic arch is less likely to fall down than a round one. Pointed arches were common in Islamic architecture from the eighth century, and they may have been brought to the West by Muslim workers. The superior masonry skills of Muslims have been detected in the twelfth-century stonework of Winchester Cathedral. This is typical of the fascinating data that Ball unearths. His most engrossing section is on the famous blue glass of Chartres. It appears that this was scavenged from Roman and Byzantine sites, shipped to France in the shape of shards, melted down and reused. A treatise by a twelfth-century Benedictine describes the practice, and a sunken ship, laden with blue glass, has been found off Turkey. Analysis shows it to contain sodium, from the ash of coastal and desert plants of the Mediterranean, whereas northern European medieval glass, made from beechwood ash, is rich in potassium. The limestone for the cathedral was dug from local quarries, but the blue glass, as a foreign import, was far more expensive. Chartres contains about an acre of it, and it accounted for 10 per cent of the building cost.

The impulse, after finishing Ball's book, to catch the next Eurostar and head out to Chartres from Paris, is strong. He says that if you sit in the cathedral late in the day, when the tourists have gone, you can believe that the place embodies the last moment when a reconciliation of faith and reason seemed possible. It seems likelier that it embodies a time when no reconciliation of faith and reason seemed needed, because it was assumed that reason, like faith, would lead the mind to God. The famous labyrinth on the floor of the nave has never been explained. But a thing you notice at once is that it is not a labyrinth. There are no possible wrong turnings. The path looks complicated but leads inevitably to the centre. Perhaps whoever designed it meant that life, for the faithful, was like that.

Vauxhall Gardens: A History
David Coke and Alan Borg, 2011

At the centre of English cultural life in the eighteenth century was a man almost nobody has heard of. He was called Jonathan Tyers and he was born in Bermondsey in 1702 into a family that had made money in leather. He did well in leather himself, and in 1729 acquired an eleven-acre woodland site south of the Thames known as the New Spring Gardens. It had been celebrated since the seventeeth century for its nightingales, grassy walks and prostitutes. Samuel Pepys was a regular visitor. But Tyers had other aims. He planned to make it a showplace of art and civilisation, and under his management it became the most famous pleasure garden in Europe – Vauxhall.

David Coke and Alan Borg's magnificent book is as sumptuous and surprising as its subject, packed with new research, and glowing with contemporary prints and paintings that invite you to wander in imagination along the tree-lined avenues and mingle with the excited crowds. Pleasure gardens on the continent usually belonged, Coke and Borg note, to royal courts and noble houses. But Tyers's Vauxhall was democratic, open to anyone who could pay the shilling entrance fee, and once inside there were no private enclosures. Tradesmen and apprentices rubbed shoulders with dukes and princes.

The gardens opened each evening from May to September and music, listened to in the open air while strolling through leafy groves, was the prime attraction. The first building you saw, on entering, was an octagonal rococo 'temple', in effect Britain's first bandstand. Its upper floor was big enough to house a full orchestra and there was a balcony for singers. Tyers aimed to bring contemporary music to a mass public, and poets, among them Christopher Smart, wrote many hundreds of songs especially for Vauxhall. Thomas Arne and William Boyce were favoured composers, but in Tyers's time it was Handel's music that dominated the repertory, and a marble statue of Handel by Roubiliac, now in the Victoria and Albert Museum, presided over the gardens. In April 1749 the Music for the Royal Fireworks had its grand rehearsal at Vauxhall, prior to its damp exposure on the Thames, and 12,000 fans flocked to hear it, causing a three-hour traffic jam on London Bridge. The 100,000 visitors per season that Vauxhall averaged were, Coke and Borg estimate, the largest audience for serious music that had ever been gathered.

Vauxhall also provided England with a public art gallery long before the Royal Academy and the National Gallery were thought of. Tyers's artistic adviser was his friend William Hogarth, who employed tutors and students from his St Martin's Lane Academy to produce a series of big genre paintings for the gardens, many of them by Francis Hayman who is now almost as forgotten as Tyers. Championing English naturalism against French artificiality, they depicted slices of everyday life – children dancing or playing leapfrog or on a seesaw, a gipsy fortune-teller, a game of cricket. Hogarth's deliberate promotion of home-grown artists was an entirely new idea, and Tyers was so pleased with the result that he presented him with a solid gold perpetual season ticket to the gardens.

Many of the genre paintings were mounted on rollers so that they could be lowered to form partitions between the 'supper-boxes', or small open-fronted dining rooms that lined the gardens' colonnades and piazzas. Catering was another artistic field in which Tyers proved brilliantly inventive. Restaurants as we now know them did not exist in the mid-eighteenth century, and the English middle classes found eating in public embarrassing at first.

But, encouraged by Tyers, they soon took to it. He preferred plain English food to Frenchified flummery, and his staples were cold roast chickens and Vauxhall's famous paper-thin slices of ham, which outraged newcomers and were part of the fun for regulars. In the 1780s lobsters, anchovies and potted pigeon joined the menu. Sweets included custards, pastries and cheesecakes, and drinks ranged from ale and table wines to arrack punch, a fiery concoction based on a Middle Eastern spirit distilled from dates, which was notorious for flooring unwary revellers. Eating and drinking could go on till dawn, and on a busy night Tyers's highly trained waiters might serve 5,000 meals. A novelty was that waiters paid for the food as they collected it from the kitchens and had to recoup the cost from customers, which meant they kept a sharp lookout for non-payers.

Hung among the trees and encrusting the buildings were thousands of lamps, and the most spectacular moment each evening came when they were lit, generally about nine o'clock. The operators used an intricate system of fuses to light several lamps at once so that, at a given signal, the whole site was suddenly illuminated. Artificial lighting on such a scale had never been seen before, and spectators were astonished. The 'wilderness of lamps' dimmed the stars, reported eighteen-year-old William Wordsworth, and Samuel Morse, inventor of the Morse code, remembered being 'almost struck blind' by the blaze.

Under Tyers, the Gardens had their own special police force, blue-coated constables who discouraged rowdiness and tried to exclude the cheaper type of prostitute. At the same time he was keen to advertise Vauxhall as a place of romantic adventure, to entice the young. Letters appeared in the newspapers from lovesick beaux who had lost their hearts in the gardens to a paragon of female beauty, once glimpsed but never to be forgotten, and begged her to get in touch. Many of these were written by Vauxhall's publicity department, but they allured because there was always a chance they were genuine. Keats's sonnet 'To a Lady Seen for a Few Moments at Vauxhall' tells an unknown beauty how he was 'snared by the ungloving of thine hand' and has never got over it.

By the time Keats wrote that in 1818, Vauxhall had changed. Tyers died in 1767, and his son inaugurated improvements. The walks were covered by rainproof awnings, derided by the old guard, and Haydn, who declared that Vauxhall had 'no equal in the world' when he visited it in 1792, replaced Handel as the leading composer. But the great transformation came in the nineteenth century, to satisfy the new taste for spectacle and sensationalism. Instead of lamenting this development, as accounts of Vauxhall customarily do, Coke and Borg clearly relish the new thrills. Fireworks, first seen at Vauxhall in 1783, became a regular feature, with great set-piece fire-dramas representing the eruption of Vesuvius or the Battle of Waterloo. Rope-dancers, led by the famed Madame Saqui from Paris, first appeared in 1816, and hot-air balloon rides were an enormous draw throughout the 1820s. Charles Green, the resident balloonist, was prolific with new stunts. He dropped a cat by parachute – it landed safely in Millbank – made an ascent on horseback, with the horse's hooves nailed to a wooden platform, and wanted to go up with a Bengal tiger, but was forbidden by the magistrates.

When the Gardens finally closed in 1859 it was not for lack of inventiveness. Rather it was because the suburbs had spread to Vauxhall, and the noise and crowds were intolerable for the new residents. Also, rail travel had put alternative amusements, notably the seaside, within reach. So history overtook them and they had to go. But Coke and Borg's gorgeous book makes you wish they hadn't.

A Thing in Disguise: The Visionary Life of Joseph Paxton
Kate Colquhoun, 2003

In nearly every sphere – art, literature, business enterprise, global clout – the Victorians were giants compared to us, and none was more gigantic than Joseph Paxton, the subject of Kate Colquhoun's superb biography. His start in life was unpromising. A farm labourer's son, one of nine children, he had little if any education. Hunger was habitual. 'You never know how much nourishment there is in a turnip until you have to live on it,' he recalled. At the age of fifteen he got work as a gardener's boy, and his first break came five years later when he was taken on as a labourer at the Horticultural Society's gardens in Chiswick. These were boom times in gardening. Since the eighteenth-century voyages of exploration, hundreds of plant species had been pouring into Britain. The aspidistra, the fuchsia and the petunia all arrived in the year Paxton began his new job. The Chiswick gardens were on land owned by the fabulously wealthy George Spencer Cavendish, 6th Duke of Devonshire, who was also a pillar of the Horticultural Society. He spotted quality in the young Paxton, and two years later he appointed him head gardener at Chatsworth, one of the grandest estates in the realm.

Paxton's journal entry for 9 May, 1826, his first day in the post, is a classic. He left London by the Comet Coach and reached Chatsworth at 4.30am. Nobody was about, so he climbed the wall and inspected the grounds. At 6am he went down to the twelve-acre kitchen gardens and allocated the men jobs as they arrived for their day's work. Then he checked out the ornamental fountains and had them turned on. That done, he breakfasted with the housekeeper and her niece Sarah, with whom he fell in love, and she with him. By 9am he was fixed up with a partner for life. They were married within the year.

His improvements at Chatsworth, funded by the open-handed duke, were not half-hearted. He planted the largest arboretum in

Europe. His rockery covered six acres, with a 45ft central crag down which a waterfall plummeted. When he installed a new fountain, gangs of men worked round the clock to remove 100,000 cubic yards of soil, creating a nine-acre reservoir on nearby high ground. Two hundred tons of iron pipes were laid, and Paxton designed a special valve that would withstand the enormous pressure. The result was the highest gravity-fed fountain in the world – a 260ft jet that burst from a sheet of water in front of the house. His most ambitious project was the Great Stove, a colossal greenhouse, extending over an acre, with a drive down the middle that could take a carriage and four, and a basement housing eight boilers that maintained tropical temperatures. An underground road was dug for the wagons that fed the boilers' enormous appetite for coal. At the time of its completion it was the world's biggest glass structure, and Paxton filled it with orange trees, date palms, bananas and rare jungle climbers. Tropical birds fluttered through the foliage.

Contrary to our stereotypes of Victorian class division, Paxton and his employer became close friends. Sensitive, extravagant and lonely, especially after the break-up with his mistress, Eliza Warwick, the duke was a noted patron of the arts. He took Paxton on continental tours – France, Switzerland, Italy, Greece, Turkey – taught him about painting, sculpture and cigar-smoking, introduced him to aristocratic friends, and had him sit for his portrait. An apt pupil, Paxton learnt Italian and boned up on ancient history. A stream of vivid letters went back to Sarah at Chatsworth, who tended their growing family while supervising the estate's entire workforce in her husband's absence.

Winning medals for Chatsworth's melons, figs and peaches was child's play for Paxton, but he and the duke were insatiable innovators. In the 1830s they decided to go in for orchids. An expedition was sent to India, returning after a year with thousands of tender exotics, including 100 previously undiscovered orchid varieties. An entire genus was named Cavendishia in the duke's honour. It was the richest collection of living plants ever brought to England, and passed into Paxton's care. In 1849, seeking a new challenge, he obtained a seedling of the Amazonian water lily *Victoria regia*, which had never flowered in Britain. Surrounded by heating pipes, liquid sewage and every kind of Paxtonian ingenuity, it thrived. Leaves 5ft in diameter gradually crept across its huge custom-built tank. Then, one still November evening, a bud rose above the surface, opening to reveal a white flower, 1ft across, smelling of pineapple. Enthusiasts crossed the world to see it. Paxton sent one bloom to Queen Victoria, and *The Illustrated London News* carried a picture of his daughter Annie standing on a leaf in the middle of the tank.

It was the rib structure of these leaves that gave Paxton the idea for his masterpiece the Crystal Palace, erected in Hyde Park in 1851 to house the Great Exhibition. The first building in the world to be made from mass-produced, standardised parts, it opened a new architectural era. Le Corbusier acknowledged it as an inspiration. Its proportions were breathtaking. Nine hundred thousand sq ft of glass covered 1 million sq ft of floor space and ten miles of exhibition frontage. Built in twenty-two weeks, it was six times the size of St Paul's cathedral, which had taken thirty-five years. When it was re-erected, after the exhibition, in parkland near Sydenham, it became not just a pleasure dome but an experiment in popular education – an art gallery, a science museum and a concert hall rolled into one. There were massed choirs and Handel festivals. The grounds had life-size model dinosaurs, and Paxton designed cascades and fountains to rival Versailles. Its destruction by fire in 1936 was like the passing of a socialist dream.

The palace earned Paxton a knighthood but it was only a fraction of his achievement. He was a director of railway companies, laying lines in Spain and India as well as all over England. A self-taught architect, he built mansions for the Rothschilds at Mentmore and Ferrières in France. He planned public parks, one at Birkenhead becoming the model for Central Park in New York. During the Crimean War he designed frost-proof huts for the troops, and organised the Army Works Corps to build roads and entrenchments. He founded horticultural magazines, published the first gardening weekly, and marketed glasshouses for the masses. He wanted to encircle London with a glassed-in arcade, ten miles long, incorporating road, rail and pedestrian walkways. A parliamentary commission approved his plans, but in the end the Great Victorian Way proved too daunting even for the Victorians.

His most remarkable accomplishment, given his dynamism and his success, was that he made no enemies. Modest, confident, passionate about his enthusiasms, he could get on with anyone. Writers and politicians, including Dickens and Gladstone, were among his friends, and the young satirists who founded *Punch* welcomed him at their dinners. Colquhoun's elegantly illustrated, admirably succinct biography is written with true Paxtonian verve. Praise comes no higher.

Singled Out: How Two Million Women Survived Without Men after the First World War
Virginia Nicholson, 2007

The slaughter of a generation of young men in the First World War left a generation of young women without their normal chance of marriage and motherhood. Their fate was already apparent before the war ended. In 1917, the senior mistress of Bournemouth High School for Girls stood up before the assembled sixth form and broke the news: 'I have come to tell you a terrible fact. Only one out of ten of you girls can ever hope to marry.' Her estimate, a former pupil later recorded, proved exactly right. What this generation of women made of their diminished lives, and how the rest of the population regarded them, are the questions that Virginia Nicholson's pioneering book confronts.

The answer to the second question is – with astonishing spite, resentment and lack of sympathy. When the 1921 census revealed that women outnumbered men by almost 2 million, it unleashed a frenzy of vituperation. 'The superfluous women,' proclaimed the *Daily Mail*, 'are a disaster to the human race.' They were labelled 'limpets' and 'bread-snatchers' for taking jobs from demobbed soldiers. They were reviled for forming 'unwholesome female friendships' and mocked for lavishing their stifled affection on cats and lapdogs. Sexual psychologists pronounced them unnatural, and Oswald Mosley found them 'distressing'. A popular solution was that they should be exported to the colonies. Canada, it was pointed out, had an excess of male trappers and lumberjacks, and even Australia offered many 'simple pleasures'.

When, desperate to fill the gap in their lives, they wrote for advice to women's magazines, they met with heartless optimism ('Cheer up, dears') or insulting tips on man-catching ('If you use a henna shampoo, don't overdo it'). Self-help books, with titles such as *The Sex Philosophy of a Bachelor Girl* (1920) and *Live Alone and Like It* (1936), prattled on about taking up folk dancing, astrology or amateur dramatics. But for women whose men had died, the need was to find some way of appeasing their desire for love and their guilt at surviving. An advertisement in the *Matrimonial Times* read 'Lady, fiancé killed, will gladly marry officer totally blinded or otherwise incapacitated by the war.'

Nicholson's book centres, however, on women who refused to be overwhelmed by grief and struck out in new directions. One of her heroines is Gertrude Caton-Thompson, the distinguished archaeologist. The love of her life, a hussar officer, had been killed, and, like many of the bereaved, she felt at first that it was a treachery to him even to breathe and eat. But after the war she enrolled for classes at University College London, learnt Arabic and studied African prehistory. She braved leopards, fleas, fevers, swamps and crocodiles to excavate Neolithic sites in Malta, South Africa, Arabia and Egypt – where she camped out in a tomb with a family of cobras. Other 'superfluous women' whose stories Nicholson tells achieved eminence as explorers, entomologists, marine engineers, doctors, mountaineers and fashion models. Some devoted themselves to slum improvement or famine relief, or broke into what had been male preserves – as the first woman solicitor, the first woman director of a firm of stockbrokers, the first woman privy councillor and cabinet member, the first women vets, civil servants and architects. Meanwhile, women novelists shattered the old spinster stereotypes. Muriel Spark's Miss Jean Brodie transformed the schoolmarm into a sexy élitist; Sylvia Townsend Warner's Lolly Willowes blossomed into a happy practising witch.

Most of these enterprising single women, Nicholson acknowledges, were from affluent middle-class families. But there were exceptions. Florence White, a Bradford millhand, became a leading political activist and the founder of the National Spinsters' Pension Association. Gladys Aylward, a London parlour maid, saved up her wages and travelled on the Trans-Siberian railway to China, where, for twenty years, she worked as a missionary, tending lepers and caring for sick children. Less outstanding, but as heroic in their way, were the women who remained satisfied with little. By 1921, there were half a million female clerks (typists, lowly civil servants, secretaries) who lived in bedsits and spent their days clattering away at Remingtons. They earned thirty shillings a week, and lunched off a penny bun or a Marmite sandwich. Social historians have tended to pity them, but Nicholson, interviewing survivors, found them upbeat. They were all girls together and stayed friends for life. They enjoyed dancing at the Locarno or the Palais, walking in Kensington Gardens, and consuming wonderful bacon-and-eggs teas at Lyons Corner House. It was a brave new world – much better than slaving for a husband.

Other single women, with no particular talents beyond the ability to make children happy, found fulfilment as nannies, wheeling perambulators in London's parks. Often the bonds they formed were closer than those the children formed with their parents, and lasted a lifetime. In 1921, a maiden aunt called Gertie Maclean, much in demand for taking nephews and nieces back and forth to school, decided to make aunthood professional and set up Universal Aunts in the back room of a bootmaker's in Sloane Street. Soon her 'Ladies of Irreproachable Background' were escorting children around London, organising trips abroad and doing other people's shopping for everything 'from a hairpin to a Moth aeroplane'.

Gertie, like the trailblazers in male professions, freed single women from dependence and contempt. Another liberator was Radclyffe Hall, the author of the lesbian novel *The Well of Loneliness*. Many single women had found happiness with members of their own sex, but the subject was deemed unmentionable until Hall came along.

Even Marie Stopes, renowned as a birth-control campaigner, proved hostile. The letters of women who wrote to her about their sexual feelings provide an extraordinary archive of ignorance, fear and unhappiness. Asked about lesbianism, Stopes replied firmly that it was a 'disease'. Hall, by contrast, made it fashionable. When *The Well* was prosecuted as an obscene libel she appeared in court in a Spanish riding hat and long leather coat, and though her novel was condemned to be burnt, it became a clandestine bestseller. The centre of a galaxy of artistic and theatrical types, including Tallulah Bankhead and the cellist Gwen Farrar, Hall made it her mission that lesbians should never again be 'driven back to their holes and corners'.

The women Nicholson celebrates changed our culture. They turned the Victorian spinster into the modern career woman. But, she believes, they were also different from modern women. Like anyone who has lived through a war, they had lower expectations of happiness and a stoicism and dignity that were all their own. Her book applauds the celebrities but does not forget the obscure. Beside Caton-Thompson she sets May Jones, who wrote her autobiography, in Biro, on scraps of coloured paper, when she was eighty-five. She was a Welsh carpenter's daughter and fell in love with Philip, a young Quaker intellectual, who went to France with an ambulance unit and was killed. 'I knew then,' May wrote, 'that I should die an old maid.' Then she added, in pencil, 'I was only twenty years old.' The rest of the page is blank. It is moments such as this that make *Singled Out* so powerful and so inspiring.

Private Words: Letters and Diaries from the Second World War
edited by Ronald Blythe, 1991

Written on troopships or from battlefields or in prison camps, these letters and diaries are surprisingly gentle. You would scarcely guess there was a war on. They describe the scenery, or homesickness, or the books the writers are reading. When violence occurs, it seems impolitely intrusive, as if someone had let off a fire-cracker in the library: 'A man has just been shot and killed. He was reaching through the fence to pick some wild strawberries when a German soldier drew his pistol and killed him.'

Ronald Blythe includes a highish proportion of artists and poets in his mix, and that partly accounts for the studious tone. But the Second World War was, as he reminds us, an unprecedentedly literate conflict. The vast outburst of letter-writing that it promoted testified to the high standards of pre-war elementary schooling, and reflected the efforts of a teaching profession that still considered misspelling and bad grammar disgraceful.

Another contrast with the present day is the innocence of the writers. Before the war, travel had meant for most people a week's holiday at a local seaside resort each year. War broadened horizons, eliciting views of foreigners that would now be judged indiscreet. A young sailor, landing in Sicily, reports that the inhabitants are 'a queer lot, and filthy beyond words'. From Russia he sends the news that vodka 'looks like clear water and tastes something horrible'. Gunner Fred Hawkridge finds weather in the Mediterranean unexpectedly cool: 'how the Wogs stick it out in their flimsy nighties I'm sure I don't know'. Though four centuries have passed, these reactions to Abroad are still essentially those of the Elizabethan seamen.

About half Blythe's material is drawn from the Imperial War Museum archives, but the rest is made up of the wartime writing of his friends. This means he can tell us the circumstances and sequels, whereas the archival excerpts tend to leave you wondering what happened next. The more fully documented letters, like those between David and Diana Hopkinson, cousins of *Picture Post*'s editor Tom, read like instalments of a novel. Intelligent, cultured young-marrieds, the Hopkinsons struggle to preserve normality. She tells him about cycle rides in deepest Wiltshire, and about an *Iris stylosa* that has just flowered in the garden 'like a dragonfly growing close to the ground'. He writes from the Western Desert, watching a platoon of cigarette ends glow beneath the stars.

Equally but differently typical of wartime romance are the letters of a young GI, fighting in Germany, to the English girl whom he recently and hastily married when she found she was pregnant. Seemingly intimidated by her disapproving family, she does not answer his letters, which pass from entreaty, to anger, to goodbye as, having won the war, he flies back to the States.

A discerning anthologist, Blythe persistently chooses pieces that tease the imagination. A journal, entrusted to an Italian farmer by two escaped POWs, tells how one of them, a working-class school-master in pre-war life, had fallen in love, while in prison camp, with the other, an ex-public schoolboy. After handing over the journal, neither man was ever heard of again. A set of letters between the members of a family records the disappearance of an elder son after capture by the Japanese. His schoolboy brother writes to the Air Ministry, and to villagers in the Malayan jungle, and eventually locates his brother's grave, identified by his aircraftsman's cap.

Several writers represent fringe groups that a less thoughtful collector would have overlooked. The wife of a Mosleyite, interned on the Isle of Man, reflects on the business failure that drove her husband to fascism, and recalls jolly weekend parties before the war at the seaside bungalow of William Joyce (Lord Haw-Haw) – a 'funny little man' with a scar on his face (from duelling, he said). A conscientious objector, forcibly conscripted and incarcerated in a training barracks, describes the brutality and starvation that have broken his will. A Japanese prisoncamp guard, who later survived Hiroshima, recounts the fall of Singapore.

Blythe's most guileless contributor is a mentally retarded baronet, Sir James Stephen. Certified insane after the war, he escaped notice during it, perhaps because there were so many other lunatics around. His journal registers utter bewilderment at army life. Among other mysteries, he cannot fathom why his barrack-room comrades pin above their beds photographs of women 'none of them having the slightest vestiges of clothing'.

Though Sir James is an extreme case, his predicament is typical of all these writers in that he is forced to take a fresh look at the ordinary. War and distance give it a new value. Letters from home concentrate on small things – such as the sayings of children. A little boy asks his mother: 'Do walruses love us?' and, told they do not, bursts into tears. Diana Hopkinson's son, lifted out of the bath, touches her collar bone and says: 'Bones are like the stalks of flowers'. You could guess from these letters that English writing after the war would renounce the ivory tower of modernism and return, in the work of the Movement poets, to the everyday.

Political change is incubating too. In the spring of 1943 the Beveridge Report, germ of the Welfare State, arrives in Army Education centres, and the war zones become discussion groups. At a slightly lower level the robustly democratic Gunner Fred Hawkridge takes note of a recent royal catastrophe: 'Fancy the poor old Duke of Kent getting bumped off. Still, why not?'

Blythe's perceptive introductions greatly add to the collection's value, drawing attention to such factors as the widespread survival of old-style copperplate script in servicemen's letters, and the wartime significance of the Polyfoto machine, which gave even the plain forty-eight chances of looking beautiful to distant loved-ones. Heartening and tragic by turns, this is one of the most engrossing anthologies I have ever read.

In the Fifties
Peter Vansittart, 1995

In 1950 Peter Vansittart got a temporary job showing some German students round London. They grunted with approval at the huge craters and ruined buildings, and gave an appreciative run-down of the types of bomb employed. That St Paul's had survived unscathed upset them. The anecdote is typical Vansittart: sharp, amused, immune to wishful thinking. He does not waste time reprimanding his Luftwaffe buffs, noting, rather, that in Oxford Street crowds are queueing to see a film of German war criminals being publicly hanged.

Vansittart is a writer, and there are a good many non-literary aspects of the Fifties, ranging from 'sartorial fashion' to the Korean War, that do not much interest him. But his style and eye for oddity make him an addictive guide. A vilified decade ('the disgusting, posturing Fifties', Hannah Arendt; 'the miserable Fifties', Sir Peter Hall) emerges from his scrutiny as a time of surprisingly widespread idealism and cultural promise, before the Sixties blew it all away.

There were plentiful jobs, equable labour relations, acceptable prices, respectable Royals. Adult education thrived; public libraries lent 400 million books a year; seventeen new universities were planned. Few decades could muster so many books and plays that would come to be seen as literary landmarks – *Waiting for Godot*, *Lucky Jim*, *Lord of the Flies*, *Under the Net*, *Look Back in Anger*, Larkin's early poems.

The list of giants surviving when the decade began may surprise even those who lived through it. T.S. Eliot, I.A. Richards and the Leavises debated at the (newly founded) Institute of Contemporary Arts. Wyndham Lewis held court in Notting Hill. George Bernard Shaw still emitted Shavianisms. George Orwell gave the struggling Vansittart books to review for *Tribune*. Robert Graves's Clark Lectures trounced the 'charlatan' Ezra Pound (alive and well in a hospital for the Criminally Insane). The earth still held two secular St Alberts – Einstein, teaching in America; Schweitzer, running his African clinic.

Vansittart does not pretend to have known any of these closely. His encounters with the famous were shaky. He once advised a fat, loquacious man that he should try writing a book, only to discover it was J.B. Priestley. Graham Greene (tipped in the Fifties for a Nobel Prize for Literature) would shrug wryly at him across restaurants. He consorted with other young Bohemians, not always attractively. His art-critic friend David Sylvester pranced and swaggered, and, in Vansittart's company, informed a bewildered stranger on a bus that he looked like Dostoyevsky's Idiot. Nowadays an aspirant aesthete would probably get his teeth kicked in for effrontery of this kind, so some things have improved. But Vansittart's collusion in the incident is a temporary lapse. Mostly he sees through intellectuals and their pretensions.

He memorialises Fifties idol Bertold Brecht as 'a Communist millionaire in worker's uniform', reminding Brecht's admirers (should any remain) that he praised Stalin as a 'justified murderer of the people'. Of W.H. Auden, who decamped for America before the start of the Second World War, he predicates: 'Many whom Auden derided – colonels, retarded public schoolboys, suburban golfers, trite-tongued mediocrities, romantic but goofy stuffed shirts – saved Western civilization'.

Alert to the dislike of England common among English intellectuals, he devises a test of their objectivity, which consists of reading aloud to them from Captain Scott's last journal: 'We are showing that Englishmen can still die with a bold spirit, fighting it out to the end ...'. His hearers assume he is being ironic and respond with appreciative titters. Later he emends it slightly, as if it had come from the Warsaw Ghetto in 1944, or from Moa or Che Guevara. It invariably earns respectful applause.

As the decade went on, advanced thinkers began to dismantle the English educational system. Labour savant Anthony Crosland vowed to eliminate every effing grammar school in the country. The philosopher A.J. Ayer enthusiastically agreed, while sending his own son to Eton. London's first comprehensive, Kidbrooke, opened. Vansittart found himself teaching at an experimental school for the children of 'rich, nervy' Hampsteadites, dedicated to freedom and self-expression. In the interest of rooting out 'bourgeois' tendencies, it was laid down that no pupil should be encouraged to read or count. Grammar, spelling and decimal points were treated as matters for democratic discussion, not despotic facts. By the time he left, he had seen enough of wealthy Socialists to deter him from joining his wife on the first CND march to Aldermaston in 1958.

As admirers of his *Voices* anthologies will know, he has a Chief Inquisitor's genius for spotting the quotable. No recording angel could more damningly gather gaffes, and the Fifties provide a rich haul. Sir Winston Churchill advises Anthony Eden that Egyptians are 'lower than the most degraded savages now known'. A Scotland Yard spokesman explains that murderers are 'not all serious; some are just husbands killing their wives'. Of Derek Bentley, controversially hanged in 1952, the poet Walter de la Mare observes: 'He had to die sometime. He was of no conceivable value to the world' – criteria which, if generally applied, might considerably thin the population.

For someone whose normal beat is bounded by Hampstead and Soho, he runs into a remarkable number of crises and contretemps, sometimes tense, sometimes marvellously funny. He watches T.S. Eliot, hunched in the audience at the ICA, while Emanuel Litvinoff reads a poem blisteringly indicting Eliot for anti-Semitism. An uproar ensues, led by the chairman Herbert Read. But Eliot, head bowed, is heard to murmur that the poem is very good, very good.

In 1956 he attends a Shaw Centenary Dinner, where guests include Clement Atlee and Sybil Thorndike, Shaw's original St Joan, then aged about seventy. At speech time, an American academic, very loud and drunk, gets to his feet and, mistaking the occasion for the centenary of Sybil Thorndike, delivers a tribute: 'A hundred years ago a little lady came amongst us ... does not look a day over eighty-five ... I cherish this day'. Frantic hands drag the speaker down, while Atlee goggles 'like an astonished hare'.

It might seem that amalgamating autobiography and social survey as Vansittart does would result in skimping both. In fact it gives him an anthologist's freedom to switch perspective and miss out the boring bits. His book is enormously readable. Like the best conversation, it keeps you longing for the next story. The style is beautifully judged, scoring its hits with a fencing-master's grace. Of the French politician René Bousquet, responsible for rounding up 10,000 Jewish children for extermination during the war, we are told: 'Mysteriously, though not untypically, he was released in 1951, and could thenceforward be seen, if not encountered, in Paris, living luxuriously as a banker until, very properly, he was murdered.'

To cap it all, Vansittart commands an armoury of curious facts, which he wields spellbindingly. What, for example, have the following in common: Laxness, Sienkiewiez, Gjellerup, Sillanpää, Echegaray, Pontoppidan? Answer: they all won the Nobel Prize for Literature. It makes Greene's failure seem rather distinguished.

The Greatest Shows on Earth:
A History of the Circus
Linda Simon, 2014

In 1942, the Ringling Brothers and Barnum & Bailey circus staged a ballet in New York's Madison Square Garden. Igor Stravinsky wrote the music, George Balanchine did the choreography and it was danced by fifty ballerinas and fifty elephants, all wearing pink tutus. This striking innovation attracted some criticism, but it was true to the infinitely adaptable nature of circus that, as Linda Simon's engrossing book bears out, was the most comprehensive popular art form ever invented.

When it began is a bit foggy. Simon thinks contortionists were the first circus performers, and they go back to prehistory. A 1200 BC Egyptian wall painting shows a dancing girl arching backwards to form a hoop. In ancient Rome, acrobats and jugglers provided light entertainment in between the chariot races and wild-beast shows, and were popular, it seems, with the young. Circus scenes appear on children's tombs. The annual fairs in medieval Europe had tightrope walkers and performing dogs and monkeys, but the modern circus did not really emerge until the late eighteenth century, at first in London and Paris, reaching America in 1793.

Initially the only acts were feats of daring horsemanship, and the tone was rather upper-class. But the circus's genius for diversification soon prevailed. Clowns and rope-dancers were added. So were women riders, who proved as daring as the men, balancing on tiptoe on horseback as they sped round the ring, and turning somersaults. Close-fitting pink silk body suits, giving the appearance of nakedness, added to their appeal.

The circus mirrored the dynamic growth and ruthless competition that epitomised the nineteenth century. Barnum & Bailey's circus, the creation of the American impresario Phineas Barnum, accommodated 11,000 spectators and his big top had not just one ring but two, then three, each with different acts going on simultaneously. It travelled from city to city by special trains, like a small town on the move, and the pre-show parade through the streets had twelve golden chariots, a hundred animal cages and a revolving Temple of Juno. It stretched for three miles. 'The greatest show on earth' was educational as well as awesome, with an orchestra, a polytechnic institute, a museum and a hall of classical statuary. When it came to London in 1889, it dazzled audiences, and climaxed with a historical extravaganza, Nero and the Destruction of Rome, which depicted Christianity emerging triumphant from the ruins of paganism.

Like the circus itself, each individual act rapidly grew more competitive and more avid for originality. The trapeze was invented in 1859 by Jules Léotard, flying through the air between high bars dangling from the roof of the Cirque Napoléon in Paris. It seemed superhuman at the time, but more death-defying refinements were soon introduced. A second aerialist, hanging upside down, would catch the first, who would turn a double or triple somersault on the way across. Women aerialists drew gasps by their risk-taking – such as the wondrous Lillian Leitzel, who performed without a safety net and fell to her death in Copenhagen in 1931. Juggling acts reached levels of almost unbelievable complexity. In the 1920s Enrico Rastelli could juggle seven balls, spin another ball on a stick held in his mouth and twirl three rings on one leg while with the other leg he balanced on a board mounted on a rolling cylinder.

The modern wild animal act, created by the American Isaac A. Van Amburgh, showed the same rage for innovation. He had become famous for prising open a lion's jaws and putting his head in its mouth, and London audiences in 1831 were astonished to see him striding fearlessly among leopards, tigers and lions as they snarled and grovelled. The Duke of Wellington was a fan and commissioned Edwin Landseer to paint Van Amburgh, clad in a toga and gesturing imperiously at two lions and a tiger, to illustrate man's biblical dominion over the beasts of the field. But these simple pleasures soon waned. Within a few decades the lions at Forepaugh's Circus were riding bicycles and firing pistols.

In this sphere, as in other circus acts, women were men's equals. Mabel Stark from Tennessee claimed she had a mystical, erotic bond with tigers; in her act she appeared alone surrounded by twenty-one of them, getting them to embrace her. She raised the cubs at home, sharing her bed with them and taking them for drives in the car.

In the circus's enterprise culture, physical abnormality could be turned to account. Sufferers from hypertrichosis (excessive hairiness) were exhibited as the Missing Link or, in one case, the Human Skye Terrier. Conjoined twins known as Millie-Christine, daughters of a North Carolina farmer, travelled the world in various freak shows and met Queen Victoria, who 'talked tenderly' to them. Proud to be a 'living curiosity', they earned enough to buy their father's farm and donate to charity.

The circus inspired modernist painters by its daring, and by contesting the distinction between high and low art. Picasso and Braque spent evenings drinking with clowns at the Medrano circus in Montmartre, Roualt portrayed clowns as Christ figures, Degas painted Miss La La, the 'Black Venus', suspended from the rafters of the Cirque Fernando by a leather bit clamped between her teeth. Cézanne, Renoir, Bonnard, Seurat and Toulouse-Lautrec were all drawn to the idea of the circus as a community of free spirits. Alexander Calder, the originator of the mobile, made his own miniature circus out of wire figures and gave performances for friends, including Miró, Mondrian and Cocteau.

Now, suddenly, our sensibilities have changed. We regard training wild animals to perform as cruel and unnatural. The idea of displaying humans as freaks sickens us. Even clowns seem to us sinister or grotesque rather than funny. So the traditional circus has vanished, leaving us to our chill rectitude. It takes a book such as Simon's, vividly written and richly illustrated, to give us some inkling of what Emily Dickinson felt when she wrote: 'Friday I tasted life. It was a vast morsel. A Circus passed the house – still I feel the red in my mind.'

A Great Feast of Light: Growing Up Irish in the Television Age
John Doyle, 2006

One day in the late summer of 1961, an electrical engineer in Limerick adjusted his rooftop aerial, came down into the house, and turned on his set. A test card glimmered into view and a fly flittered across it. This was the first live-action broadcast on Irish television. Regular transmissions began the following New Year's Eve with the broadcast of a grand party from Dublin's Gresham Hotel. The band of the Dublin reformatory for poverty-stricken and wayward boys played, and a huge crowd gathered outside to glimpse the celebrations on a tiny set elevated on a pedestal. President Eamon de Valera and leading cleric Cardinal D'Alton both came on-camera, and warned of the evil influence television could have.

In this gentle, funny book, John Doyle makes the case that it was wholly a force for good, an agent of enlightenment that helped to free Ireland from the Catholic Church and from obsession with its own cruel past. He writes the best kind of cultural history, based not on statistics and generalisations but on first-hand experience. At the time of the Gresham Hotel merrymaking he was five, living with his parents in Nenagh, Tipperary. There was a cattle market on Mondays and a pig market on Fridays. If it rained, as it often did, you could watch the sugar-beet factory workers cycling home with sugar bags on their heads to keep dry. Otherwise there were few entertainments. Catholicism was all-powerful. What seemed like an army of priests stalked the streets, glaring at you in silent contempt if you ventured a greeting. A body of pious parishioners called the Legion of Mary aided them in their ministry, spying on errant neighbours and reporting them, if need be, to their spiritual overlords. Ignorance of the outside world was virtually total.

In its early days Raidió Teilifís Éireann (RTÉ) was culturally conservative. It came on air at 5.30 each afternoon with a children's programme in Gaelic, to remind the mostly mystified viewers that this was their official language. Everything stopped for the angelus at six o'clock, when a religious image appeared on the screen and a bell rang. Programmes ended at about 11pm, with a priest saying prayers. At Easter, there were just the Stations of the Cross on Good Friday, then shutdown until Easter Sunday morning.

For little Doyle, the attraction of television lay in its difference from all this. Westerns, notably *Bat Masterson*, enchanted him, not for their violence, but because Bat's elegance and courteous way with the ladies seemed so outlandish and so civilised compared with anything that happened in Nenagh. The same went for comedy series about American family life such as *The Donna Reed Show* and *I Love Lucy*, where women and mothers were the stars. To the Doyles, these people with their cars and barbecues and laughter and glittering kitchen gadgets were a new species. There were no priests, and no arguments about contraception and abortion. You could not even tell who was Catholic and who was not. It was unnatural. Layers of habit and conformity peeled away as they watched, and the smallness of their old world stood revealed. Doyle remembers Lucille Ball in *I Love Lucy* as the funniest and happiest woman he had ever seen. Thinking of her in dark, rainy Nenagh, was like carrying sunshine around in his head.

The new medium encouraged debate and open-mindedness. A bright, cool young Dubliner called Gay Byrne hosted *The Late, Late Show* on Saturday nights, where arguments about sex and religion were allowed, and even the priesthood came in for criticism. Diehards fumed. 'There was no sex in Ireland before television,' spluttered one rural conservative MP. Mission priests arrived in Nenagh to rail against the new abomination. Television, they declared, was an English influence. It was responsible for the spread of dancing, lewdness and two-children families. Young Doyle watched the spittle fly from their mouths as they promised that anyone who listened to foreign music would go to hell. Television, they insisted, should be used only for the news and important announcements by bishops and cardinals.

In 1967, the Doyles moved to Carrick-on-Shannon near the Northern Irish border, and two years later to Dublin. This greatly improved their access to television. In Carrick you could get the BBC Northern Ireland service and commercial Ulster TV as well as RTÉ. In Dublin everyone watched the new BBC Two. Brought up on songs and ballads about the dark centuries of English rule and the Irish fight for freedom, Doyle instinctively hated the English, and his occasional contact with snobbish Anglo-Irish families reinforced his prejudice. English television made him think again. Watching Cilla Black on Saturday nights shattered his image of the English as uniformly posh and stuck-up. So did *The Liver Birds*, about two girls sharing a flat in Liverpool, which being just over the water, and full of Irish Catholics, seemed like home, only more fun. *Monty Python's Flying Circus* was a revelation. Its mockery of army officers and upper-class twits gave Doyle a view of England as 'foreign, new and funny', not just a land of bigots and oppressors.

But it was football that worked the strongest magic. At school the Christian Brothers had denounced soccer as an English invention, a 'garrison' sport that no decent Irishman would sully his feet with. Hurling was the true patriotic game. Doyle knew he would never be any good at it because he was too small and disliked crashing into people. Football, though, depended on pure skill. There was something 'liberating and unfettered' about running with a ball. Dublin was football mad. Everyone watched *Match of the Day*, and nearly everyone supported Manchester United, because it was known that they had scoured Ireland for promising youngsters, not caring if they were Irish or Catholic, and because their star, George Best, was Irish. Watching English football on television drew people together. It was bigger than anti-English prejudice.

In 1979, while Doyle was an undergraduate at University College, Dublin, the Pope visited Ireland, and the frenzied crowds that welcomed him hardly suggested that Catholic power was on the wane. For all that, people's values had changed. In the same year as the Pope's visit, *Dallas* began weekly on RTÉ, and the Irish were instantly besotted. Even university students watched it avidly. Its luxury seemed a world away from pinched and gloomy Ireland, and its casual affairs and divorces pointed up the difference in social restriction. Doyle sees its popularity as an index to the future. By 1993, his afterword notes, Ireland had the strongest economy in Europe.

If you talk to older Dubliners today you find many who regret the new materialism, and Saturday night in Temple Bar is scarcely a scene of enlightenment. Doyle emigrated to Canada in 1980, where he is television critic of *The Globe and Mail* in Toronto, and his failure to assess current developments back home may seem evasive. But his book crackles with unexpected angles and is written with a kind of naive delight.

It is the ideal present for anyone given to pontificating about the brain-deadening effects of television.

Consuming Passions: Leisure and Pleasure in Victorian Britain
Judith Flanders, 2006

It's easy to condemn consumerism, until you consider what life was like before consumerism happened. At the start of the eighteenth century only one in ten people in Britain possessed a knife and fork; five out of six did not own a cup. Judith Flanders's bulging bran tub of a book is packed with statistics of this attention-grabbing calibre. She traces how, in the course of 200 years, things that had been luxuries, such as tea and sugar, became available to everyone, and how the masses found time for fun and frivolity where before there had been want. Her range is vast, covering virtually everything people spent money and leisure on – holidays, shopping, music, fairs, theatres, peep shows, circuses, art, books, newspapers, racing, football and, at the period's end, the perilous thrills of cycling. Language changed to accommodate the new happiness. In 1700 'comfort' had meant spiritual succour. By the mid-nineteenth century it meant material well-being.

There were plenty of people, Flanders shows, who wanted to stop it happening. Leisure, they insisted, should remain the prerogative of the rich. A working man at rest was idle, not leisured. The organisers of the 1851 Great Exhibition deliberately fixed entrance fees to exclude the poorer classes, on the grounds that, if they were admitted, they would become a revolutionary mob and assault the showcases. One of those who campaigned successfully for lower ticket prices was Henry (later Sir Henry) Cole, who would be the hero of

Flanders's book if a volume so various could have one hero. Starting as a humble clerk, Cole single-handedly changed Victorian life. He wrote children's books and invented numerous toys, including building blocks and the first children's paintbox. He founded *The Journal of Design and Manufactures* and devised the first Christmas card. Exasperated by the exclusiveness of the British Museum, which demanded a written application and character references before admitting anyone, he founded the South Kensington Museum (now the Victoria and Albert Museum) as a place for families to spend the day, with the first ever museum refreshment room.

But even pioneers such as Cole could have done little without technology. Railways were the real reformers, and Flanders shows how they altered every aspect of life. Clocks across Britain, which had previously displayed local times according to longitude, were (after stubborn resistance) synchronised to 'railway time'. The Duke of Wellington had warned that trains would encourage 'the lower orders to go uselessly wandering about the country', and he was absolutely right. Rail travel spawned excursions, day-trippers and Thomas Cook, who offered an 800-mile tour of Scotland for one guinea in 1846, and was taking tourists to Egypt by the 1860s.

Killjoys were aghast. John Ruskin had horrified visions of the lower classes sliding down the Alps with 'shrieks of delight'. The new popularity of seaside holidays created a huge demand for entertainment at the resorts, fostering, along with piers and Punch and Judy shows, Britain's first permanent municipal orchestra, the Bournemouth Symphony. Theatre was transformed, too. Trains made touring practicable, and D'Oyly Carte alone ran seven touring companies by the 1880s. In London the almost infinitely renewable audience that trains brought to the capital introduced the phenomenon of the West End run, with the same play lasting for hundreds of performances.

Before the railways, football teams across the country had played to local rules with no agreement even about the number of players. Rail travel enforced standardisation, monitored by the Football

Association, which started up in 1863. In pre-railway racing, horses had to walk from one race to another, which sometimes took weeks. Trains changed all that. Meetings became more frequent, a nation-wide betting-industry developed, and two-year-olds, which did not have the stamina for long-distance walking, could now be raced. But the railways' greatest and most unexpected impact was on books and reading. For most people in the early nineteenth century, books were prohibitively expensive, and bodies such as the Society for the Suppression of Vice strove to keep it that way, arguing that cheap reading matter would 'pervert the public mind'. The breakthrough came in 1848 with Routledge's hugely successful 'Railway Library' editions. W.H. Smith's station bookstalls began in the same year, the one at Paddington stocking 1,000 titles. Suddenly, cheap books were everywhere. A complete Shakespeare could be bought for a shilling.

Technology revolutionised other realms apart from travel. Sewing machines brought mass-produced shoes in standard sizes and ready-to-wear clothes within universal reach. Fashion was now something anyone could afford. In Petticoat Lane, delighted crowds decked them-selves in 'pea-green, orange, and rose-pink', while, a rung up the social ladder, shoppers in the dazzling new department stores bought into a complete lifestyle, where even the string tying your parcels was part of a distinctive vision and colour scheme. Improved print technology sparked off a galaxy of new magazines. At one end of the scale, penny dreadfuls carried police court news of murder, rape and violent crime, which must have brightened many a dull life. At the other, organs of self-improvement such as the *Penny Magazine* recommended great works of art as guides to conduct. Leonardo's *The Last Supper* was used to exemplify 'seemly behaviour in trying circumstances'.

It seems quite possible that the same readers bought both penny-worths. For the remarkable thing about Flanders's wonderfully rich chapters on theatres and popular spectacles is how little distinction there was between what we now think of as high and low art. This went back a long way. In the 1820s, a foreign visitor saw Kemble play

Falstaff on the same playbill as a melodrama in which a Newfoundland dog fought gallantly against overwhelming odds, expiring at length 'in the most masterly manner, with a last wag of the tail that was really full of genius'. A performance of *Macbeth*, attended by Queen Victoria, was part of the same evening's entertainment as a 'lion drama' in which wild beasts roamed the stage, apparently at large, but actually confined behind wire netting concealed in the scenery. Byron's poem *Mazeppa* was rejigged as a sensationally popular equestrian spectacle incorporating a wild stallion and a cavalry charge, while at the Surrey Zoological Gardens you could listen to Mozart, Mendelssohn or the Beethoven symphonies in between watching the animals' feeding-time and a firework display. The music halls inherited this eclecticism. At the Empire Leicester Square, for example, you might see, on the same evening, a ballet, a juggler, silent films and a performance of *Faust*. Such a mix of high and low culture under one roof was not, Flanders observes, to disappear until the twentieth century.

Her own book with its kaleidoscope of subjects and its blend of the erudite and the ephemeral belongs to the same palace-of-varieties tradition, and is hugely enjoyable as a consequence. There is something dizzily acrobatic about the mountains of evidence she constructs, and she produces her punchlines with a conjuror's panache. You would scarcely be surprised to see a lion slipping out of sight as you turned the page.

IQ: The Brilliant Idea that Failed
Stephen Murdoch, 2007

The reason why the subject of intelligence tests arouses such fury (try discussing the eleven-plus at a dinner party) is that the pros and cons are evenly balanced. One side argues that human beings are infinitely various, so any standard test is bound to be unjust. The other side replies that a test that selects on grounds of ability, however imperfect, is fairer than the alternatives universally favoured before intelligence tests were thought of, namely, selection on grounds of family, money, social class, race or colour. Both sides are right, which means that each is driven to devise passionate and contorted arguments to prove the other wrong.

Stephen Murdoch's well-informed and violently prejudiced book illustrates this. He hates intelligence tests and abominates psychologists for inventing them. In his opinion, they are a ruthless set of parvenus, avid for funding and respect, neither of which they deserve, and unable even to define the 'intelligence' they are supposed to be testing. The worldwide ascendancy they now enjoy came about, he contends, through historical accident. The advent of universal education in several countries at the end of the nineteenth century meant that retarded children had to be identified, so as to receive special provision, and a French psychologist, Alfred Binet, came up with a test for this, from which all modern IQ tests derive. The idea caught on in America, which was facing a population boom. Immigration officers on Ellis Island were empowered to turn back the feeble-minded, as well as beggars, anarchists, epileptics and other undesirables, and in 1910 tests were introduced to sort out the confusion in America's overcrowded public schools.

In the First World War, a group of psychologists administered Binet type tests to 1.7 million recruits to the American army and, taking this as a cross-section, they concluded that about half the American population were morons (a technical term, indicating a mental age of eight to twelve, whereas imbeciles have a mental age of three to seven, and idiots of two or less). Opinions will differ as to the probable reliability of these results, but Americans seem to have taken them in their stride. A mental age of eight was considered adequate for military service, so recruitment was not hindered, and word quickly spread through the American advertising industry that they should aim at an audience with the mentality of twelve-year-olds. Meanwhile, schools and colleges eagerly adopted intelligence testing, including time-saving novelties such as multiple-choice questions. Attacked by diehards as 'assembly-line' education, these efficiencies helped America send more of its young people to college than any other nation.

Murdoch insists that IQ tests have an 'appalling' history, and he is partly right. Even before Binet, Francis Galton, the founder of eugenics, had suggested that tests could be used to identify imbeciles, who might then be sterilised to prevent them breeding more imbeciles. Although well meant, these plans were based on an inadequate understanding of genetics, and had no regard for the rights of imbeciles. The same objections apply to the utopian proposals of H.G. Wells, who advocated restricting parenthood to people who had passed tests of physical as well as mental fitness. But the eugenics movement cannot, despite Murdoch's efforts, be represented as a sinister precursor of the eleven-plus. Its aim was to preserve the existing class system. 'The brains of our nation', Galton proclaimed, 'lie in the higher of our classes' – precisely the assumption the eleven-plus was designed to challenge.

While it remained just an idea in Britain, eugenics proved popular in America. Virginia passed a law authorising sterilisation of the feeble-minded in 1927, and in the next five years twenty-six other states followed suit. At least 60,000 Americans were sterilised as a result. However, as Murdoch's research indicates, it would be over-simple to blame intelligence tests for these developments. The victims were usually poor whites, resented by their communities, and their alleged low intelligence was no more than a pretext for neutering them and shutting them away. In the hands of the Nazis, too, the tests were a smokescreen for barbarity. Hitler studied the American legislation with interest and modelled his Law for the Prevention of Offspring with Hereditary Diseases on it. Those targeted were often prostitutes, political activists and other 'asocial' elements. By the end of the Second World War, 400,000 people had been sterilised throughout the Third Reich, while in Nazi institutions for the handicapped a further 200,000 were put to death, some diagnosed as feeble-minded as a result of tests concocted for the occasion, but often for bedwetting, being a 'burdensome life' or 'useless eater'. What this proves is that IQ tests can be fashioned into an instrument for evil, but to blame them for Nazi atrocities would be like blaming Zyklon B for Auschwitz.

Murdoch is an American, and his understanding of British education is patchy. The eleven-plus, he claims, was the result of the nation's determination 'to ignore a vast majority of its people in the belief that only a slim minority, the very brightest, must be cultivated and cared for'. That scarcely reads like an objective assessment, and his assertion that the grammar schools 'had institutional links to the colleges and universities of the nation' is untrue. He is aware that Britain has things called public schools, but that grammar schools were an attempt to counter the social injustices enshrined in these does not engage his attention. On American education, though, he is consistently interesting. Black students in America, he observes, have always scored, on average, fifteen points lower than whites in intelligence tests, a result that racists happily advertise. However, recent research suggests that this is because tests are set in standard English, whereas young Black people speak and hear black English. When nonlinguistic tests are used, Black and white students from similar backgrounds score close together.

What this shows is that IQ tests must be intelligently adapted. This was recognised way back in the history of American intelligence testing, with the development of picture-based tests for illiterates and non-English speakers.

A puzzle of Murdoch's book is its title. What can have led him to suppose that the idea of IQ tests has failed when he clearly shows it to be rampant worldwide, and the basis, as he sourly reports, of a lucrative industry? Tests have triumphed at every level. Businesses use them to decide who to hire and promote; social-security mental-health benefits are fixed by reference to applicants' test scores.

American colleges require all candidates to take a SAT, a standard test first adopted at Harvard in the 1930s to ensure equal access to higher education.

Of course intelligence tests are not infallible. They would be intolerable if they were, for then those who failed them would have no recourse but to accept their own inferiority. But for all their imperfections they reflect a belief in inner worth, which is possibly a hangover from religious faith, and a hope that natural gifts can be rescued despite disadvantages of birth. These ideas may be naive, but they do not seem to deserve the relentless animosity that Murdoch's undoubtedly powerful book directs at them.

The Spirit Level: Why More Equal Societies Almost Always Do Better
Richard Wilkinson and Kate Pickett, 2009

This is a book with a big idea, big enough to change political thinking, and bigger than its authors at first intended. The problem they originally set out to solve was why health within a population gets progressively worse further down the social scale; they estimate that together they have clocked up more than fifty-person-years gathering information from research teams across the globe. Their eureka moment came when they thought of putting the medical data alongside figures showing the extent of economic inequality within each country. They say modestly that since dependable statistics both on health and on income distribution are internationally available, it was only a matter of time before someone put the two together. All the same, they are the first to have done so.

Their book charts the level of health and social problems – as many as they could find reliable figures for – against the level of income inequality in twenty of the world's richest nations, and in each of the fifty United States. They allocate a brief chapter to each problem, supplying graphs that display the evidence starkly and unarguably. What they find is that, in states and countries where there is a big gap between the incomes of rich and poor, mental illness, drug and alcohol abuse, obesity and teenage pregnancy are more common, the homicide rate is higher, life expectancy is shorter, and children's educational performance and literacy scores are worse. The Scandinavian countries and Japan consistently come at the positive end of this spectrum. They have the smallest differences between higher and lower incomes, and the best record of psychosocial health. The countries with the widest gulf between rich and poor, and the highest incidence of most health and social problems, are Britain, America and Portugal.

Richard Wilkinson, a professor of medical epidemiology at Nottingham University, and Kate Pickett, a lecturer in epidemiology at York University, emphasise that it is not only the poor who suffer from the effects of inequality, but the majority of the population. For example, rates of mental illness are five times higher across the whole population in the most unequal than in the least unequal societies in their survey. One explanation, they suggest, is that inequality increases stress right across society, not just among the least advantaged. Much research has been done on the stress hormone cortisol, which can be measured in saliva or blood, and it emerges that chronic stress affects the neural system and in turn the immune system. When stressed, we are more prone to depression and anxiety, and more likely to develop a host of bodily ills including heart disease, obesity, drug addiction, liability to infection and rapid ageing.

Societies where incomes are relatively equal have low levels of stress and high levels of trust, so that people feel secure and see others as co-operative. In unequal societies, by contrast, the rich suffer from fear of the poor, while those lower down the social order experience status anxiety, looking upon those who are more successful with bitterness and upon themselves with shame. In the 1980s and 1990s, when inequality was rapidly rising in Britain and America, the rich bought home-security systems, and started to drive 4x4s with names such as Defender and Crossfire, reflecting a need to intimidate attackers. Meanwhile the poor grew obese on comfort foods and took more legal and illegal drugs. In 2005, doctors in England alone wrote 29 million prescriptions for antidepressants, costing the NHS £400 million.

Status anxiety and how we respond to it are basic, it seems, to our animal natures. In an experiment with macaque monkeys, the animals were housed in groups, and the social hierarchies that developed among them were observed. Then the monkeys were taught to administer cocaine to themselves by pressing a lever. The dominant monkeys in each group were relatively abstemious, but the subordinate monkeys took a lot of cocaine to medicate themselves against the pain of low social status. In a similar experiment, high-status monkeys from different groups were housed together, so that some of them became low status. The downwardly mobile monkeys accumulated abdominal fat and developed a rapid build-up of atherosclerosis in their arteries, just like humans.

The different social problems that stem from income inequality often, Wilkinson and Pickett show, form circuits or spirals. Babies born to teenage mothers are at greater risk, as they grow up, of educational failure, juvenile crime, and becoming teenage parents themselves. In societies with greater income inequality, more people are sent to prison, and less is spent on education and welfare. In Britain the prison population has doubled since 1990; in America it has quadrupled since the late 1970s. American states with a wide gap between rich and poor are likelier to retain the death penalty, and to hand out long sentences for minor crimes. In California in 2004, there were 360 people serving life sentences for shoplifting. California has built only one new college since 1984, but twenty-one new prisons. Whereas societies with high income differentials are exceptionally punitive, in Japan imprisonment rates are low and offenders who confess their crimes and express a desire to reform are generally trusted to do so by the judiciary and the public.

The authors' method is objective and scientific, so that the human distress behind their statistics mostly remains hidden. But when they quote from interviews conducted by social researchers, passion and resentment flood into their book. A working-class man in Rotherham tells of the shame he felt having to sit next to a middle-class woman ('this stuck-up cow, you know, slim, attractive'); how he felt over-weight and started sweating; how he imagined her thinking, 'listen, low-life, don't even come near me. We pay to get away from scum like you.' In half a page it tells you more about the pain of inequality than any play or novel could.

It might be said that *The Spirit Level* merely formulates what everyone has always felt. Western European utopias have almost all been egalitarian. Polls in Britain over the past twenty years show that the proportion of the population who think income differences too big is on average 80 per cent. But what is new about their book, the authors insist, is that it turns personal intuitions into publicly demon-strable facts. With the evidence they have supplied, politicians now have a chance to 'do genuine good'. By reducing income inequality, they can improve the health and well-being of the whole population. How this should be effected, Wilkinson and Pickett do not think it is their job to say, but increasing top tax rates or legislating to limit maximum pay are possibilities they suggest. They warn, though, that short-term remedies like this could be reversed by a change of government, and that we need to find ways of rooting greater equality more deeply in our society. This is their book's mission, and they have set up a not-for-profit trust (equalitytrust.org) to make the evidence they set out better known. One illusion that, cheeringly, they hope to dispel is that the super-rich are some kind of asset we should all cherish, rather than, from the viewpoint of social health, the equiva-lent of the seven plagues of Egypt.

Leadville: A Biography of the A40
Edward Platt, 2000

Western Avenue – for those lucky enough not to know it – is the après-motorway bottleneck, flanked by suburban villas, many of them boarded up, that you get to just after the Hoover Building on the A40 into London. It is also the site of one of the most embarrassing planning fiascoes of recent years. A scheme to widen the road was hatched in the mid-1960s. A public inquiry in 1989 gave the go-ahead, despite local protests, and 210 houses were scheduled for demolition. Homeowners were served with compulsory purchase orders, and evictions began in January 1995. Towards the end of the year the bulldozers moved in. Then in July 1997, when half the neighbourhood had been flattened, the scheme was axed. It was unacceptable, the transport minister announced, because it would have increased car commuting where public transport alternatives were available – just as the protesters had said all along.

Local residents were philosophical about the cock-up on the whole. One observed ironically to Edward Platt that the scheme did, after all, have its beneficiaries. Though Western Avenue suffered, the many millions of pounds expended had helped to line the pockets of the lawyers and consultants engaged in the various inquiries and disputes. So it made a modest contribution towards widening the gap between the top ten per cent of the country's earners and the rest.

Platt, a freelance journalist, became intrigued by Western Avenue in 1995, a few months before the demolitions began. He was puzzled that anyone should choose to live there, and started knocking at front doors and asking questions. Only one resident, a woman, told him to 'eff off'. Most were glad to talk. He also researched the road's history. It originated, he found, as a key component of the post-First World War suburban boom. Lloyd George had promised 'Homes for Heroes', with gardens, hedges and other 'middle-class amenities'.

Providing these was seen as a bulwark against Bolshevism, 'visible proof of the irrelevance of revolution'. To connect the city with the suburbs, arterial roads were needed, and Western Avenue led the way. Construction began in 1921. But until the railway bridges were built seven years later the isolated lengths of dual carriageway were of little use. Stretching across the fields of west Middlesex, Western Avenue was, the *Acton Gazette* reported, 'probably the finest bit of road in the world ever dedicated to lonely moonlight walks for lovers'. Once the bridges were in place, however, the car began to take over. By 1938 traffic volume and accidents had increased so alarmingly that torchlit processions, accompanied by a dog with a red light on its collar, and four bearers carrying a coffin, blocked the road every night for a week.

Platt found elderly couples who still cherished their vision of Western Avenue as a tree-lined suburban street. To working-class kids, reared in nearby Wormwood Scrubs, it had seemed a nirvana. They nicknamed it Toffville. The owners of its gleaming new mock-Tudor houses sent their children to school, it was whispered, by taxi. To scrape and save for a home in this leafy sanctuary had still seemed a worthwhile ambition in the years after the Second World War. The neat front gardens bespoke civic pride. The back gardens were alive with birds and squirrels. You could sit outside on summer evenings and think you were in the country.

These memories are entrusted to Platt in dark parlours, double-glazed against the tumult outside. The din and stench of the urban motorway are now the only reality. Trees and shrubs in the gardens wither. When it rains, everything goes brown. Fumes rot curtains and fabrics. The walls shake as lorries pass. The noise is so loud you can't hear the TV. The homeless people given temporary accommodation in some of the condemned properties by the council are another problem. They don't look after their houses. Their gardens are waste-tips. The rat population of Western Avenue has multiplied enormously. One couple found they had devoured almost the entire contents of their garden shed, including two sunloungers that had been wedding presents. Then there are the Gypsies. They deliberately park their lorries in front of driveways and threaten you if you ask them to move. They are 'nature's thieves'. One couple have been burgled eight times.

Platt does not risk visiting the Gypsies, but he makes friends with several of the council tenants, and finds them a surprisingly cheerful bunch of failures and wastrels, mostly living alone. Schooled by adversity, they are sometimes more thoughtful than the homeowners about how social attitudes develop. One, an out-of-work photographer, is persecuted by his neighbour, a vociferous feminist, and explains that it took him a long time to work out why he could never say 'no' to a woman like her. In the end he realised that when you have grown up on social welfare you learn to say 'yes' and 'please' automatically, but 'no' always seems too presumptuous to utter. Among the man's possessions Platt notices a copy of Joyce's *Ulysses*.

By comparison the squatters are a disappointment. Young, idealistic, dirty and not very bright, they welcome Platt to their commune. Inside, the walls have been sprayed with day-glo murals. Outside, gardens have been knocked into one to form a rubbish-heaped wilderness. In an atmosphere thick with the scent of dope, they mull over their contempt for 'the bloody media and society'. But they have no alternatives to offer beyond feeble, welfare-dependent anarchism. One of them has just expressed his disapproval of the status quo by smashing a telephone kiosk. To the homeowners, barricaded behind their padlocked garden gates, they must seem a race of barbarians. Yet Platt finds them generally tolerant of the squatters, deploring instead the senseless vandalism of council bailiffs, who rip up floorboards and pulverise bathroom fittings in empty properties, to make them squat-proof.

Western Avenue emerges from the book not just as an isolated disaster-area but as a microcosm of modern England, congested, polluted, mismanaged, and fixated on the past. It is also a story about the end of the automobile age. Interspersed among the oral history are sections on discredited twentieth-century utopians – Le Corbusier, who wanted to rebuild the world's cities to accommodate the car, Robert Moses who designed New York's parkways, only to see them become clogged with traffic. The lesson is that the car, a beautiful, irresistible, man-made parasite, has proved more destructive of human habitats than any plague in history. Its increase has been epidemic, as Platt notes: 50 million cars in the world in 1950, 350 million by 1980, 500 million now. By keeping his work on a human scale, Platt brings home the true meaning of these unimaginable statistics. Lively, trenchant, fair-minded, sad, funny, his book should be bought by every thinking motorist. The traffic jams of the future will provide plenty of leisure for reading it.

SCIENCE

The Jewel House: Elizabethan London and the Scientific Revolution
Deborah E. Harkness, 2007

As a prelude to writing this book, Deborah Harkness, who is a professor of history at the University of Southern California, compiled a database of 1,800 Elizabethan Londoners, all of whom had an interest, however unofficial, in some aspect of science or technology. They were midwives, gardeners, clockmakers, barber-surgeons, alchemists, apothecaries, engineers and naturalists, and Harkness tracks them through the city's back alleys, workshops and taverns. Some of them remain shadowy figures, such as the Smithfield alewife who administered pregnancy tests, or the mountebank known as Dutch Hans who used to astonish the clientele in a crowded pub near the Globe playhouse by stirring a pot of molten lead with his finger. But, wherever possible, Harkness finds out where they lived and who they associated with, and in this way she constructs a map of the swarming, fractious, competitive, largely unregulated and almost wholly unexplored underworld of Elizabethan science.

Many of her most fascinating discoveries were immigrants. In 1573, a German called Valentine Russwurin set up a stall outside the Royal Exchange. He said he had a degree from the university of Frankfurt, and displayed a banner showing the bladder stones that he had extracted from satisfied patients. He soon gained a reputation for the skilful surgical removal of cataracts, and the Queen's minister William Cecil was among his clients. But he attracted the jealous attention of the London barber-surgeons because he used the newfangled chemical medicines of Paracelsus, such as mercury for curing syphilis, as opposed to the traditional botanical remedies, and they seem to have hounded him out of town. Anyway, he disappeared. Equally unfortunate was the Polish alchemist Cornelius de Lannoy whom Elizabeth employed to turn base metals into gold, and who was subsequently confined to the Tower for taking advantage of Her Majesty's gullibility.

People of similar interests tended, Harkness finds, to group. In Lime Street, near the present Lloyd's building, there lived a thriving community of botanists, entomologists and plant-hunters with widespread European connections. One resident, the silk merchant James Cole, was the nephew of the great Antwerp map-maker Abraham Ortelius, and the son-in-law of the Flemish naturalist Mathias L'Obel who gave his name to the lobelia. A neighbour was the naturalist Thomas Moffett whose interest in spiders is commemorated in the nursery rhyme about his stepdaughter Little Miss Muffet. The Flemish apothecary and tulip fanatic James Garrett was another member of this coterie, and his shop seems to have served as a post office for fellow enthusiasts. Specimens poured in from all over the globe – a Neapolitan tarantula, a grasshopper from Guinea, African marigold seeds and plants from the East and West Indies that Garrett cultivated in his garden plot along the city's crumbling wall in Aldgate. The barber-surgeon John Gerard, the author of the most famous English botanical treatise, *The Herbal*, was, it turns out, a hanger-on of the Lime Street fraternity, but aroused their resentment by filching their ideas and making such a mess of it that the printers had to call in L'Obel to correct Gerard's blunders while the book was going through the press.

A scientific researcher of extraordinary pathos whose work Harkness unearths is Clement Draper, a member of the Ironmongers' Company and of good Leicestershire family, who was imprisoned for debt in the King's Bench from the early 1580s to 1593. Although deprived of freedom, he kept his mind active by reading and talking to other prisoners and filling his notebooks with the practical information about medicine, mining and chemistry that he learnt from them. Some of his informants sound even more interesting than Draper himself. Joachim Gans, who taught him chemistry, was a Jewish metallurgist from Prague, who sailed with Raleigh as a mineral expert on his 1585 Roanoke voyage, and was arrested in a Bristol tavern in 1589 while engaging in a heated debate with a local cleric about the divinity of Christ.

But Harkness's prize exhibit is Hugh Plat, the Cambridge-educated son of a wealthy London brewer. Almost nothing has been written about Plat, but he was a figure of boundless intellectual vitality, with a wide network of consultants in London and the provinces. Soap-boilers, tallow-chandlers, midwives, carpenters and wine-coopers told him their trade secrets. The great William Gilbert showed him how to magnetise needles and float them in a bowl of water so that they pointed north, an Irish salt-maker taught him to grow thin-shelled walnuts, a celebrated London preacher instructed him in the manufacture of green ink from iris flowers. His notebooks are a treasury of practical tips on everything from food preservation to making artificial coral. Besides his city house, he had a country property in Bethnal Green where he carried out horticultural experiments. He published a popular cookbook, *Delights for Ladies*, and his macaroni recipe for feeding sailors on long voyages was adopted by Sir Francis Drake. His famous plague cakes were widely believed to cure bubonic plague. Concocted from chemicals, herbs and the gallstones of Peruvian goats, they won the approval of the highest in the land. Elizabeth's privy council ordered sixty-six of them. He was knighted by James I in 1605.

Harkness's enthusiasm for her subject sometimes outruns her evidence. She believes that Elizabethan London had a keen interest in mathematics and witnessed rising rates of 'mathematical literacy'. This seems doubtful. The standard Elizabethan grammar-school curriculum did not include even simple arithmetic, and superstitious citizens, as she notes, opposed their sons learning maths because it was associated with sorcery and the black arts. The fact that a Londoner called Humfrey Baker published an introduction to mathematics in 1590, in which he undertakes to teach his adult readers how to make elementary calculations, is not, as Harkness seems to imply, evidence of widespread numeracy, but of the contrary. Also questionable is her judgment that 'London's medical market functioned well'. She means by this that practitioners with sufficient persistence and guile could make a living. But that is a curious criterion for a healthcare system, and it omits to note that Elizabethan medical knowledge was largely an amalgam of ignorance and superstition. Physicians were powerless to cure even the commonest diseases or mitigate suffering, and young Englishmen wishing for a medical training in touch with modern advances had to travel to universities abroad such as Padua, Montpellier or Leyden.

Harkness winds up with an ill-advised attack on the reputation of Sir Francis Bacon. Because he was upper class he has, she suggests, received the credit for inaugurating the Scientific Revolution that should by rights go to humbler folk such as Plat. Everything that Bacon describes in his futurist science-fiction novel *The New Atlantis* was, she claims, already taking place in Elizabethan London. This is not true. *The New Atlantis* has, for example, submarines, telephones and flying machines, and Harkness cites no instances of these among her Elizabethans. Besides, Bacon was a profound thinker, and Plat was not. Still, sticking up for one's own side of an argument is no crime, and Harkness has written a truly wonderful book, deeply researched, full of original material, and exhilarating to read. Its grown-up realism puts to shame the glamorised pap currently spooned out on film and television as a depiction of sixteenth-century England.

Darwin's Island: The Galapagos in the Garden of England
Steve Jones, 2009

Darwin's Sacred Cause: Race Slavery and the Quest for Human Origins
Adrian Desmond and James Moore, 2009

Darwin's theory of evolution is often imagined to be the result of his voyage to the Galápagos Islands aboard HMS *Beagle*. But as Steve Jones points out at the start of his enthralling book, he spent only five weeks in the Galápagos, whereas for forty years following the *Beagle*'s return he explored the biology and geology of Britain, crisscrossing the land in search of specimens that he took back to his experimental station and family home at Down House in Kent. During this time he wrote nineteen books and hundreds of scientific papers, totalling 6 million words. Their subjects ranged from barnacles, orchids, insect-eating plants and earthworms to the expression of emotions in dogs, apes and people. But they all contributed to his great evolutionary idea, which was perhaps the most world-changing thought anyone has ever had.

Darwin's Island takes us through the projects and experiments of those forty years. What constantly astonishes is the homeliness of Darwin's methods. He had none of the expensive equipment modern science requires, just the simple aids available to any Victorian gentleman botanist. But his strengths were indefatigable curiosity and imaginative sympathy with the natural world. Jones's chapter on climbing plants, for example, is both a masterpiece of science writing and a revelation of Darwin's almost poetic sensitivity. Why, he wondered, did plants grow towards the light? What made them reach their tendrils towards supports and twine round them? He found that if he buried a plant in sand the tip would still grow. Clearly the tip was sensitive to light, and it seemed to act, he wrote, like the brain in an animal collecting information about the world and directing the plant's movements accordingly. But if that were so, the tip must have some way of communicating with the rest of the plant, telling its buried roots about the change of seasons, or instructing the leaves to fall in autumn. There must, he deduced, be a chemical messenger that passes down through the plant carrying the tip's instructions. He was right, and what he had discovered was the first known hormone, though the chemical that carried the messages was not extracted and identified until forty years after his death.

Besides disclosing the beautiful ingenuities of Darwin's thought, Jones updates Darwin's science. With dazzling versatility he traverses the field of modern genetics to show how evolutionary theory has become fact, and how DNA evidence, together with the fossil record, has allowed Darwin's speculations about past biological events to be confirmed, extended and given approximate dates. We now know that humans are related not just to chimpanzees and gorillas but to plants and bacteria. Humans and chimps separated into distinct species 5 million to 7 million years ago, and their common ancestor broke away from the gorilla line about 1 million years before that. Genetic evidence sheds light on more recent developments in human history. Louse DNA shows that the body louse and the head louse separated some 50,000 years back, and this, Jones suggests, may mark the moment when humans first wore clothes, giving the louse a new place to live.

Crossovers between what seem different parts of creation were crucial to Darwin's theory. Insect-eating plants fascinated him because they developed the equivalent of teeth, gullets and stomachs, like animals. Jones shows how enormously, and how surprisingly, modern genetics has added to this kind of knowledge. Touch genes have been identified in plants, which are activated by a drop of rain or a gust of wind. More than 500 parts of DNA respond when a leaf is prodded. The touch genes in plants are related to genes in young rats that are activated when they are caressed by their mothers. If they are not caressed, their physical and emotional growth is stunted. Some of the signal proteins that plants use to detect touch resemble the molecules that control our heartbeats and switch on the hormones that determine our growth. As Jones accumulates his evidence, the vision of the relatedness of all life becomes more and more breathtaking. I have never read a book that made me gasp with amazement so often.

Darwin was worried about the dangers of inbreeding, since he had married his cousin, Emma Wedgwood, and feared this might have caused the death of their young daughter Annie. Pollinating cowslips in his greenhouse, he found that female flowers of one strain were readier to accept pollen from males of another, rather than their own. Could this mean nature abhorred inbreeding? Again, he was right, and modern genetics have shown why. Inbreeding, Jones explains, carries perils because damaged genes may become harmful when inherited in double copy. Plants accept or reject pollen on genetic grounds. The female parts judge male cells by comparing their genes with their own, and reject any pollen grain if it is too alike. Animals have similar safeguards. The smell of a male mouse's urine conveys important genetic information to female mice, who avoid males with the same odour and the same family history as themselves. Our noses have grown dull, so we can no longer smell our close relatives. But rats can still sniff out human kinship, distinguishing between sweat-soaked shirts that have been worn by brothers and those belonging to cousins.

It is unlucky for Adrian Desmond and James Moore that their book should have come out at the same time as *Darwin's Island*, since the case they make out is bound to look narrow and reductive when compared with Jones's world of wonders. For all that, *Darwin's Sacred Cause* is prodigiously researched and propelled by its own excitements, though they are political as much as scientific. Their argument is that Darwin was driven not simply by a zeal for scientific knowledge but by a moral passion. His motive was hatred of black slavery and the cruelties it sanctioned. On the *Beagle* voyage he had witnessed the treatment of slaves in South America and been revolted by it. He was haunted by the scream of a tortured slave he had overheard in Brazil. The Darwins and Wedgwoods were all ardent abolitionists, and he joined the family crusade. In the run-up to the American Civil War, scientists who sided with the slave-owning South argued that the black and white races were separate species, and Darwin's conviction, confirmed by modern genetics, that they share a common ancestor was abhorrent to them.

The Desmond–Moore case would be damaging to Darwin if they were suggesting that he had allowed political considerations to influence his scientific findings. But it seems clear they are not. In *On the Origin of Species* he proposed that the different breeds of dogs did not have a common ancestor, but were descended from various wild stocks. A friend pointed out that this played into the slave-owners' hands, since they believed the same of humans. Desmond and Moore quote Darwin's reply, which was that he would 'infinitely prefer the theory of single origin in all cases' if the facts allowed it, but they did not. *Darwin's Sacred Cause* does not question Darwin's scientific integrity but illustrates his hatred of cruelty. In that respect it examines a particular aspect of the sympathy with other organisms – human, animal and plant – that Jones's book explores with such bravura.

The Age of Wonder: How the Romantic Generation Discovered the Beauty and Terror of Science
Richard Holmes, 2008

'Bliss was it in that dawn to be alive,' Wordsworth recalled, thinking of the fall of the Bastille in 1789. But Richard Holmes's exuberant group biography celebrates the scientific revolution that preceded and outsoared the political one, changing life, the universe and everything in the last decades of the eighteenth century. The guiding light was Sir Joseph Banks, who was fortunate in having both an original mind and a great deal of money. At the age of twenty-six he joined Captain James Cook's round-the-world expedition aboard the *Endeavour* as a naturalist, to collect plant and animal specimens. But when they made landfall in Tahiti he pioneered a new kind of science, later called anthropology. Unlike other Europeans, he strove to understand the Tahitians, learnt their language, ate their food (he declared roast dog 'delicious') and danced naked with a witch doctor after ceremonially smearing his body with charcoal and wood ash. Tahitian women were renowned for their sexual freedoms, but they seem to have found this gentle, courteous old Etonian especially winning, and his hut in the woods was the venue for happy, indiscriminate love-making. His journal records every aspect of the Tahitians' lives – how they tattooed themselves, wrestled, played a kind of flute through their noses, and rode the huge Pacific rollers on bits of wood (the first European account of surfing).

Banks's insatiable curiosity and his superiority to the prejudices of his class made him a perfect talent spotter, and he was soon in a position to change the course of science. Back home he found himself a celebrity. Naturalists from all over Europe flocked to see his collections. He was painted by Reynolds, elected to Dr Johnson's exclusive 'club', and appointed keeper of Kew Gardens by George III. He planted new, exotic species, including magnolias, fuchsias and the monkey puzzle tree, and received a knighthood in return. At the age of thirty-five he became president of the Royal Society. Among his protégés was a man as far as possible from himself in origins and fortune, William Herschel. The son of a military bandsman in Hanover, Herschel had joined the band himself at the age of fourteen but fled to England when the French invaded Germany. A penniless refugee, he scraped a living as a music teacher and freelance composer (three of his compositions, including an oboe concerto, are available, Holmes notes, on CD). But he developed a passion for astronomy, and began constructing his own reflector telescopes. The labour of grinding and polishing the mirrors was immense, but he had a devoted assistant in his sister Caroline, who had joined him in England. On one occasion he polished for sixteen hours nonstop while she put bits of food into his mouth. His plan was to observe every visible star – between eight and 10,000 – and when he had done it once he began again. They stayed up every night until dawn, swaddled and anointed with onion juice against the cold, with Caroline taking notes as he shouted out observations. On 13 March 1781 he saw what he took to be a comet in the constellation of Gemini. Further observation confirmed that it was not a comet but the first new planet to be discovered for more than 1,000 years – Uranus.

Banks introduced Herschel to George III, who adopted him as his personal astronomer, and with the funds made available he built the most powerful telescope in the world on a site near Slough. It was 40ft long, with 4ft mirrors weighing half a ton each, and was mounted on a wooden gantry as high as a house. Herschel perched on the viewing platform while Caroline, connected by speaking-tube, was shut in a special booth below, to avoid light pollution, with her lamp, journals and coffee flask. It was Herschel's work on nebulae that had the most far-reaching implications, and showed science replacing philosophy as the generator of modern thought. When he began observing, nebulae were believed to be loose clouds of gas, and about a hundred had been spotted. He located more than 2,000, and identified them as galaxies beyond our own, existing in inconceivably remote gulfs of space. He called them the 'laboratories of the universe', because they were continually forming new stars. The cosmos, he revealed, far from being fixed by divine edict, was unfolding like some enormous flower, and our galaxy, the Milky Way, was just one among millions, and would inevitably wither and die like the rest.

The other genius Banks promoted did not shatter presuppositions quite as spectacularly as Herschel, but had more practical impact. He was Humphry Davy, a self-taught chemist from Cornwall who nearly killed himself at an early age by inhaling carbon monoxide to see if it was poisonous. He used electricity to isolate new elements, potassium and sodium, and he lectured to vast audiences eager for scientific truth. Albemarle Street was designated London's first one-way street to avoid the traffic jam of carriages on his lecture days. His miners' safety lamp, which made him a household name, was brilliantly simple. The lamp's flame was enclosed in iron gauze, so that methane could pass through and burn, but not re-emerge at a high enough temperature to ignite the atmosphere. He refused to patent his invention, allowing it to be imitated worldwide and save countless lives.

Holmes shows how richly science and Romanticism overlapped Davy was a poet himself, and mystically inclined, believing in a universal life force called 'animal electricity'. Developing this idea, some argued that human corpses could be reanimated by attaching voltaic batteries to them, a theory explored in Mary Shelley's *Frankenstein*. Coleridge and Southey both befriended Davy and visited him to inhale gases. Herschel too had Romantic leanings. He believed in extraterrestrial life, and thought the craters on the moon were cities. Keats put him into his sonnet 'On First Looking into Chapman's Homer' as the 'watcher of the skies' who discovers a new planet, and Byron went to Slough to look through his telescope.

Shelley was highly excited by science, especially hot-air ballooning, which enjoyed a tremendous vogue in the 1780s. When a young Parisian doctor, Pilâtre de Rozier, made the first manned flight in 1783, he was mobbed on landing by an enthusiastic crowd who tore his green topcoat to pieces as souvenirs. A year later a Neapolitan, Vincent Lunardi, accompanied by his pet cat and dog, made the first flight from English soil, and won public favour by landing temporarily to hand the cat, which was suffering from cold, to a woman farm worker. Shelley suggested that reformers might use balloons to distribute atheistical pamphlets, or to float across Africa and emancipate slaves.

Holmes suffuses his book with the joy, hope and wonder of the revolutionary era. Reading it is like a holiday in a sunny landscape, full of fascinating bypaths that lead to unexpected vistas. He believes that we must engage the minds of young people with science by writing about it in a new way, entering imaginatively into the biographies of individual scientists and showing what makes them just as creative as poets, painters and musicians. *The Age of Wonder* is offered, with due modesty, as a model, and it succeeds inspiringly.

You're Looking Very Well: The Surprising Nature of Getting Old
Lewis Wolpert, 2011

The biggest surprise in Lewis Wolpert's often surprising book is that human beings may one day have a lifespan of 600 years. It used to be thought that we age because ageing is programmed into our genes, like growing from birth to adulthood, and most people (including, Wolpert says, scientists) still believe this. However, genetic research indicates otherwise. No normal genes promote ageing, and nobody dies just of old age (in America 'old age' is no longer permitted as the cause of death on death certificates). We age because random molecular damage accumulates in our cells over our lifetime, and our cells' ability to repair the damage decreases as we grow older. As Wolpert points out, this is in line with Darwinian natural selection. From an evolutionary point of view, once we are past the age of reproduction and caring for our young we are useless, so our cells' repair mechanisms become unnecessary.

It might not seem to make much difference whether we age because we are programmed to, or because our cell-repair system packs up. Either way we get old. But the difference could be crucial. In some laboratory animals, such as worms and fruit flies, it has been found that the cell-repair system can be kept going, increasing healthy lifespan as much as fivefold. In humans an equivalent effect, Wolpert estimates, would have us living an average of 400 years and a maximum of 600.

Not that he thinks 600-year-old humans are likely soon – or, maybe, ever. In genetics, he emphasises, our ignorance vastly exceeds our knowledge, and investigating cell life is mind-crushingly complex. Besides, even if an infinitely extended lifespan became technically possible, who would want it? Who would have, as George Bernard Shaw put it, the 'insane self-conceit' to believe that 'an eternity of himself would be tolerable even to himself?' Actually, when you take a look at dictators and other powerful maniacs across the globe, Shaw's rhetorical question does not seem as rhetorical as he evidently intended. All the same, Wolpert is inclined to agree with him, and this book is mostly concerned with how to keep the worst effects of ageing at bay within the limits of current life expectancy.

He quickly disposes of most of the touted remedies. Supplements and anti-ageing tonics are useless, if not positively harmful. The herbal treatment ginkgo, used by the Chinese for thousands of years to combat memory loss in the old, has been shown to be totally ineffective. The miraculous tonic discovered by the ancient Indian sage Maharishi Chyavana, and prized in Ayurvedic medicine, turns out to be composed mainly of gooseberries. 'Monkey gland' transplants and hormone-replacement therapy for tired males are equally futile. In the 1930s, Wolpert relates, a Swiss clinic set up in business injecting organs from sheep embryos into patients' buttocks for a large fee. Churchill, Eisenhower and Pope Pius XII all, apparently, underwent this treatment, without any recorded benefit.

So how can we improve our chances of healthy old age? It helps to be rich, well-educated and intelligent. People in the poorest fifth of the population are more likely to be unhealthy and die younger than those in the richest fifth. Those with low education levels suffer more disabilities and experience a lesser quality of life when old than the better educated, and lack of education can be a contributory cause of dementia. There is a strong correlation between high IQ when young and good health in old age.

None of these factors can be changed if you happen to be on the wrong side of the equation, but plenty of other things can. Eating less and avoiding obesity come first. Restricting calorie intake is the most consistent factor that slows ageing in all animals, from simple organisms to primates. A diet rich in fruits, vegetables, cereal and fish (especially fish), but low in meat and poultry, is best, and reduces the risk of dementia by 40 per cent. A small amount of alcohol can also help, but 10 per cent of dementia cases involve too much drink. Caffeine is good. Mice with the rodent equivalent of Alzheimer's improve markedly when their drinking water is laced with caffeine.

Keeping physically and mentally active also matters greatly, and this is an argument, Wolpert urges, for raising the retirement age or even, in some professions, abolishing it. Research shows that every extra year worked delays the onset of dementia by just over a month. Stress, especially short-term stress, is also, surprisingly, beneficial. So is a positive outlook. Those who think of themselves as younger than their age enjoy better health than those who think of themselves as older. It seems, too, that having a religious faith, keeping a pet, and living in the country can all be better promoters of healthy old age than their opposites.

We live longer than at any time in human history, and the statistics Wolpert gathers suggest that most of the elderly are grateful for it. In Britain, 60 per cent of those over eighty describe their health as good to excellent. The belief that the old are more prone to depression than younger people is false. The most common age for depression is around forty-five. The association of happiness with youth is another illusion. A Europe-wide survey of 21,000 people, who were asked how happy they were on a graduated scale, found that happiness peaks at seventy-four. A statistic that will bring a smile to many an ageing face is that young people who endorse negative stereotypes about the old, labelling them feeble and helpless, are at a higher risk of suffering heart disease or a stroke when they grow older themselves.

Population ageing is a worldwide phenomenon, and in five years or so, for the first time ever, there will be more people over the age of sixty-five than children under five. This is viewed with alarm by some, but for the elderly it may have advantages. By 2050 one third of the British electorate will be over sixty-five, and their numbers may force governments to concede to their demands on issues that particularly affect them. For Wolpert, the legalisation of voluntary euthanasia and assisted suicide for the terminally ill would come high on the list.

Not that he has that in mind just now. At eighty-one he still cycles, plays tennis twice a week and jogs once a week (slowly, he says). Friends are equally, or more, resilient. One neighbour aged 106 plays the piano several hours each day, and insists there are 'no bad things' about growing old. 'When I am faced with a bad situation,' she explains, 'I immediately find something good in it.' Wolpert admits to occasional depression (and has written a book on it), but he cheers himself by compiling a list of late achievers. Sophocles was over eighty when he wrote *Oedipus at Colonus*, and he produced it in court as evidence against his sons who had accused him of imbecility. Verdi composed *Falstaff* as an octogenarian, and the great Japanese artist Hokusai, still busily creating masterpieces in his eighties, said that everything he had done before seventy was worthless. Wolpert would not put himself in that company, but the acumen and drive exhibited in this book are mightily encouraging for all that.

The Science of Love and Betrayal
Robin Dunbar, 2012

Can science explain why we fall in love? Robin Dunbar is not afraid of big questions and he tackles this one with relish. He quickly disposes of the idea that romantic love is a modern Western invention. There is strong evidence it is a human universal, crossing historical and cultural boundaries. The earliest surviving love poem is in cuneiform script on a Sumerian clay tablet dating from 2025 BC.

Accounting for romantic love in terms of the body's chemistry is more a problem, and Dunbar is critical of the current state of knowledge – or, to be more exact, ignorance. There was great excitement in the 1990s over the neurohormone oxytocin, which was linked (wrongly, it turned out) with monogamy in prairie voles, and dubbed 'the monogamy hormone'. It is released during human cuddling and orgasm, and a whiff of oxytocin up the nose has been shown to make people more generous. However, oxytocin does not seem helpful in explaining why we prefer a particular person to all others, which is the essence of romantic love.

Personal smell, Dunbar thinks, may be a richer territory to explore. When Eskimos 'rub noses' they are really breathing in each other's smell. Maoris do the same. Your scent is determined by the same set of genes (MHC) as your immune system, and it could make sense to choose a mate with different MHC genes from your own, as this might provide a wider set of immune responses in your offspring. So having a good sniff at first meeting may be important. Women can identify their children and their lovers by smell alone, but men, it seems, prefer visual clues.

On the other hand, men can tell when women are ovulating simply from their smell, and ovulating women (as filmed by a research unit in Viennese nightclubs and dance halls) give off other signals. They sway their hips more when walking and choose clothes that expose more bare flesh than at other times in the menstrual cycle. It is because men seem to be attracted to ovulating women that, Dunbar suggests, women wear dark eye make-up – a practice traceable, he points out, to at least 1400 BC, when three ladies at the court of the pharaoh Thutmose III were buried with jars of a cosmetic made from kohl. Eye shadow mimics the darkening of the lids around the time of ovulation, and so seems to promise higher fertility.

Was Juliet perhaps ovulating when Romeo fell for her on that unfortunate night in Verona? Even if she was, it seems unlikely that she would be the only ovulating female at the Capulet ball, so the mystery of Romeo's attraction remains. An alternative is that Juliet was more symmetrical than the other ladies at the ball (and Romeo more symmetrical than the other men). To readers who are not evolutionary anthropologists the claims made for symmetry in Dunbar's book will be surprising. Symmetry (of ears, arms, legs, each side of the face, and other bilateral body parts) is taken to be a virtually infallible indicator of gene quality. Symmetrical humans, we are told, are more intelligent, more able to resist disease, and more fertile and attractive to the opposite sex than their asymmetrical counterparts. Further, it is claimed, we can spot tiny, almost imperceptible asymmetries in other humans – a difference in the length of ear lobes, say, or of the index fingers. These findings, Dunbar assures us, are based on three decades of experimental studies of symmetry and mate choice in humans and other animals, so it seems pointless to question them. All the same, there must be quite a few of us who couldn't say whether our spouses' (or our own) earlobes and index fingers are precisely symmetrical, and the chances of picking out any small discrepancy on some enchanted evening when you see a stranger across a crowded room are obviously pretty low.

Perhaps because of difficulties of this kind, Dunbar's book tends to drift away from the currently unanswerable question of falling in love to the more general issue of why human beings became monogamous in the first place. A surprising finding is that monogamous species have bigger brains, indicating that fidelity is more psychologically demanding than promiscuity. This may help to account for its unpopularity in the natural world. Only 5 per cent of mammals and 15 per cent of primates are monogamous. The old explanation for human monogamy was that both parents were needed to rear the young – mother nursed them, father hunted and brought back food. Research among surviving hunter-gatherers does not bear this out. Hunting is an excuse for male showing-off and seldom produces food. The helper provided by nature is not the father but the grandmother, who conveniently undergoes menopause (unique to humans) at about the age when her daughters start to reproduce, leaving her free to gather food and take turn at child care. The father is needed, in Dunbar's thesis, only as a 'hired gun' to protect the family from a new male who would kill the children and take the mother, as happens in some animal species and in humans when civilisation breaks down.

The modern equivalent of the hired gun's strength is wealth and status. These come high among women's priorities when they advertise for boyfriends, whereas men's lonely hearts ads seek women who are young, attractive and have no children from previous relationships (a gesture towards the infanticide the hired gun guards against). Women's ads often also require a good sense of humour (GSOH); Dunbar thinks that laughter, which releases endorphins ('the brain's painkillers'), is ancient, older than language, and was originally a kind of chorus that reinforced the soothing effect of social grooming, as used by monkeys and apes.

That is typical of his book's speculative fascination. When we fall in love, he emphasises, it is with a fiction we have ourselves invented. Brain scans indicate that women, because of their need for wealth and status in a partner, are particularly prone to make-believe love with charismatic figures – political and religious leaders, sports stars, musicians – and with God who is, for Dunbar, simply a charismatic fictional figure writ large. Lonely, single women, desperate to find love, are easy prey to internet fraudsters who (in cases that Dunbar cites) fleece them of their savings by masquerading as lovestruck swains – a fiction in which the women eagerly co-operate.

Social networking sites such as Facebook, offering the prospect of thousands of new 'friends' across the world, might seem to question Dunbar's most famous theory, which is that we are not capable of more than about 150 friendships – the average size of ancient hunter-gatherer communities. Research shows, however, that Facebook users do not have larger social networks than most people, and their friend-ships may be less satisfying. Time spent on the internet is, Dunbar warns, time taken away from interacting with friends and family face to face. It prevents the young from acquiring social skills and can leave them callow and gullible. What's more, investigation suggests that face-to-face meetings rate higher as bringers of happiness than emails, texting and all other instant messaging. It is a fittingly human note for this brilliantly stimulating book to end on.

Laughter: A Scientific Investigation
Robert R. Provine, 2000

Crying: The Natural and Cultural History of Tears
Tom Lutz, 2000

The arts can tell us more about human emotions than the sciences, or so non-scientists like to think. A comparison of these two books suggests the opposite. Tom Lutz's study of crying comes from the arts side – he teaches English at Iowa University. A huge miscellany of pronouncements on and descriptions of tears, drawn from art, literature, religion, anthropology, and every other shelf in the library, it makes absolutely no headway in answering the questions – Why do we cry? Why are there tears of joy as well as sorrow? – that Lutz periodically ponders. Robert Provine's investigation of laughter, by contrast, is a model of constructive scientific thinking, and can be recommended as a shampoo and conditioner for the brains of arts aficionados everywhere.

Instead of relying on received opinion about why we laugh, Provine, who was trained in behavioural neuroscience and is a Professor of Psychology at Maryland, decided to observe people actually laughing and analyse the results. Over a period of several years he and his team of researchers eavesdropped on conversations in shopping malls and city streets, building up a database of thousands of laugh-incidents. His findings were revolutionary. Whereas previous writers on laughter (Freud, for example) had associated laughter with jokes, he discovered that most laughter is not prompted by jokes or other formal attempts at humour, but is a response to quite innocent comments like 'It was nice seeing you' or 'We can handle this'. Laughter, Provine deduced, is a mode of pre-linguistic social bonding, and writers who have related it to our higher critical faculties (Plato thought we laughed at evil; Aristotle, at ugliness) were on the wrong track.

Also new is Provine's discovery that speakers, on average, laugh more than their audiences. Previous studies had assumed the opposite. The only exception, he found, was when the speaker was male and the audience female, in which case it was the females who laughed. This pattern emerges early. Already by the age of six females are the leading laughers, males the best laugh-getters. Provine sees this as an expression of power relations between the sexes, and cites instances of laughter-as-subservience from other cultures. Lower caste Tamil villagers (Harijan), for example, giggle, mumble and appear deliberately dim-witted when addressing those of higher caste. From a survey of thousands of personal ads from a wide range of newspapers, Provine finds that women are far likelier than men to seek a sense of humour in their prospective partners, and this demand for men who will make them laugh may, he suggests, be a veiled request for dominant males.

The question of whether human beings are the only creatures who laugh prompts Provine's most fascinating speculations. It has often been claimed that chimpanzees and other primates laugh when engaged in rough-and-tumble tickling play. In fact the ritualised panting sound they make is very unlike a human laugh. Humans laugh by chopping an exhaled breath into sections (ha-ha-ha). But a chimp breathes in and out when making its laugh noise (ha-ah-ha-ah). Chopping an exhaled breath into sections also allows human beings to speak – it is how we make words – and Provine thinks that we gained the ability to do this and to laugh when we started to walk upright. A four-footed animal has to tense its abdomen every time its front feet hit the ground, rather like a human being doing press-ups, and this means it cannot have the control over its breathing necessary for speech or human laughter.

Provine's argument that we learned to speak only because we started to walk upright has become known in America, where his book was first published, as the Walkie-Talkie theory. It allows him to recognise a chimp's excited panting as a genuine ancestor of a human laugh, and conversely to relate our laughter to older and deeper levels of brain activity than speech or rationality. Other observations, he finds, back this up. Laughter bypasses our intellect and our conscious control. Even trained actors find it hard to laugh to order, while group-laughter is irrationally and inexplicably contagious – witness the successful use of canned laughter on TV and radio, and laughter epidemics such as that which enforced the closure of fourteen schools in Tanzania, and spread to surrounding villages, in 1964.

With chimps, laughter and tickling are closely related. Both, Provine points out, are social activities, as they still are with us. We cannot tickle ourselves, oddly enough, and solitary laughter (except over a book, say, where another person is notionally present) is abnormal. This too squares with Provine's model of laughter's genealogy. When we laugh we should think of ourselves not as ironical lords of the universe, but as juvenile chimps panting in delighted anticipation of a parent-chimp's or playmate-chimp's prying fingers. The world's first joke, Provine hazards, was a chimp's feigned tickle.

The freshness and challenge of his book are precisely what Lutz's lacks. His cultural bric-a-brac must have taken years to assemble, but seems random and potentially infinite. It suggests the stamina of a camel and the sense of relevance of an unusually scatter-brained jackdaw. Lutz appears to accept from the start that nothing can be discovered about crying or why we do it. He persistently sets the suggestions of physiologists and psychologists against the diametrically opposed views of rival theorists. The belief, for example, that tears are good for you because they are antibacterial, or because they rid the body of manganese, which might otherwise cause depression, or of lysozyme, which might otherwise cause stomach ulcers, all run up against counter-arguments drawn from Lutz's inexhaustible pack. In a sense this is commendable since it signals a desire for truth, but it also prevents anything dependable from emerging. We know nothing, it seems, about why tears happen, how they affect us, or what they mean.

Lutz is at his best when he turns this ignorance to account. A reigning popular myth at the end of the twentieth century, he points out, is that men do not cry enough. Because they are crippled by their social training, they identify crying with weakness, and this is what makes them destructively aggressive – or so modern folk wisdom has it. At the same time it is believed that women cry too much, and that their weeping is a sign of weakness and complicit with their oppression. As Lutz notes, these suppositions are based on contradictory assumptions, and there is no hard evidence to support either of them – though male politicians, eager to exhibit the new manliness, now readily shed tears in public, while female politicians recognise that to do so would be a serious error of judgment. Nor are only politicians affected. For decades therapists have taught that crying, screaming and casting off your inhibitions are good for you, though from a scientific angle their arguments are little more than superstition. If Lutz had stuck to this punchy mode, and stayed out of the cultural lumber-room, his book would have been better and shorter.

Mauve: How One Man Invented a Colour that Changed the World
Simon Garfield, 2000

In the summer of 1856, an eighteen-year-old student at the Royal College of Chemistry was working in a makeshift laboratory near his parents' home in London's East End. Following up one of his professor's ideas, he was trying to synthesise quinine from an alkali called aniline found in coal tar. The result was a disappointing black residue, and he was about to throw it away when it occurred to him to make a solution of it, whereupon, as he recalled, a 'strangely beautiful' colour introduced itself to human eyes. This was mauve, and the student was William, later Sir William, Perkin.

Although Perkin's discovery was a stroke of luck, he was, as Simon Garfield's appreciative biography shows, the kind of exemplary juvenile who was almost bound to make his mark sooner or later. He came from the upwardly mobile lower middle class, which so often proves the most useful element in the social stack. Though the family lived in the slums of Shadwell, his father was a successful carpenter, employing his own workforce, and he sent his son to the City of London School. The boy was artistic and musical, playing the violin and double bass, but he was also crazy about science. His father paid for extra chemistry lessons, and at fourteen William wrote to the great Michael Faraday asking to attend his Royal

Institution lectures. Faraday wrote giving permission in his own hand.

Once Perkin had found that his new colour would stain cloth, he acted quickly, taking out a patent and contacting a Scottish dyeworks. Within months he had built a factory near Harrow (his father's life savings went into the venture) and started production. Coal tar, the waste product from the coal used in London's street lighting, was available in huge quantities for next to nothing, and Perkin had a second bit of luck when Napoleon III's Empress Eugénie decided that the new colour matched her eyes. Fashionable Paris turned mauve overnight. Not to be outdone, Queen Victoria wore mauve for her daughter's wedding in January 1858. After that every woman wanted it – mauve mania swept London and Perkin's fortune was made.

But that was only the beginning. Once Perkin had shown the way hundreds more aniline dyes – reds, blues, greens, violets – burst upon the world. They were far cheaper and more brilliant than the old animal and vegetable dyes. Women who had never aspired to colour before could now revel in it. Satirists sneered, and the fastidious French historian Hippolyte Taine, walking in Hyde Park, complained that the glare was insufferable. What really alarmed these conservative males, Garfield shrewdly notes, was an early instance of the female as independent consumer. Perkin also changed the way women smelt. Producing coumarin from coal tar he simulated the perfumes of roses, jasmine, violets and musk.

His breakthrough had repercussions in many other fields. Coal-tar preparations led to the development of photographic plates and colour film, of aspirin and saccharin, and of more powerful explosives. The German bacteriologist Paul Ehrlich used coal-tar derivatives to pioneer immunology and chemotherapy, and Robert Koch acknowledged his debt to Perkin in discovering the tuberculosis and cholera bacilli. More than any artist, writer or musician, Perkin could claim to have created our modern world.

Of course he claimed no such thing. An exceptionally modest and self-effacing man, he shunned publicity and seems never to have made a clever or witty remark. He retired aged thirty-six, built a pleasant house with large gardens, devoted himself to good works in the local community and taught his sons to be useful citizens. All became scientists, and one invented non-inflammable underclothes, saving many young lives. An evangelical Christian, Perkin died quietly, having first sung a verse of the hymn 'When I survey the wondrous cross'. His last words were, 'Proud? Who could be proud?'

Uncle Tungsten: Memories of a Chemical Boyhood
Oliver Sacks, 2001

Would you give your eleven-year-old son dead babies to dissect? This was one of Oliver Sachs's mother's educational brainwaves. A gynaecologist, she acquired the corpses professionally. Some were stillborn; others were malformed foetuses that she and the midwife quietly drowned at birth. Cutting them up would, she reckoned, be a useful preparation for the medical career she had already decided Oliver would pursue. Three years later, she arranged for him to extend his knowledge in the dissecting room at London's Royal Free Hospital. Here the mere sight of the anatomy manual used by the students, its pages yellow with human fat, filled him with nausea. Almost fainting from the stench, he was thoughtfully presented with the body of a girl his own age to dissect. His mother never realised his distress. She was not, it seems, a monster – just blinded by the impenetrable stupidity that intellectuals with advanced educational ideas are prone to.

Young Sacks feared, after these ghoulish ordeals, that he might never manage to love 'the warm, quick bodies of the living', and we do not find out from this memoir whether he ever did. The only close bond he mentions, outside his immediate family, is with an octopus that he kept for a time in the bath. Human relations had been ruined for him even before his mother's anatomy lessons. At the outbreak of the Second World War, when he was six, his parents had sent him and his brother Michael to a boarding school in the Midlands. Here they were fed, he alleges, on swedes and mangelwur-zels and beaten by a sadistic headmaster. His behaviour on his rare home visits deteriorated. He cowered in the Morrison shelter, shaved his scalp, and locked the family dog in a coal bin. Apparently nobody saw cause for alarm. Soon after, Michael became psychotic, striding round the house hallucinating and declaring himself the Messiah. Whether this persuaded his parents that something was amiss, Sacks does not say, and by this time it was immaterial, for he had discov-ered how to rise above human concerns.

His redemption lay through chemistry and physics, and his fairy godfathers were two of his uncles, Dan and Abe. They both lived near the Sacks family home in Cricklewood. Dan was an industrial chemist and had his own factory that made electric light bulbs with tungsten filaments. A born teacher, he roused his nephew's interest not just in tungsten, which he loved best, but in the whole range of metals. He made him see them as sensuous and almost alive, capable of astonishing yet predictable reactions, and sometimes suicidally unstable. Sacks remembers how he and Dan watched a sample of calcium turn to lime before their eyes when it was exposed to air.

Uncle Abe had been a pioneer in the development of luminous paints. His house was a magical cave of phosphorescence, stacked with X-ray tubes, Geiger counters and every kind of electrical machine. There was an observatory on the roof. He taught Oliver about radioactivity with a gadget called a spinthariscope containing an infinitesimal speck of radium. When you peered through the eyepiece you could see tiny sparks caused by the disintegration of the individual radium atoms. He also had a spectroscope and charts showing the spectra of different elements. When he hitched it up to a telescope in his observatory, and pointed it at stars and planets, Sacks saw that the same spectra appeared, proving that our earthly elements are not just ours but extend through the whole universe.

Soon young Sacks set up his own laboratory at home. He found a chemical supplier in Finchley who, in those unregulated days, had no qualms about selling a schoolboy toxins and explosives, and Abe gave him a chunk of radioactive pitchblende which he took home in his school satchel. At first he contented himself with producing stinks and bangs, turning his voice squeaky by breathing in hydrogen, or making his brothers' hair stand on end with the electric charge from a Wimshurst machine. But he was a passionately inquisitive child and quickly outgrew these amusements. Guided by the uncles, he began to retrace the history of chemistry, rediscovering the phases through which it has passed, and where possible repeating crucial experiments himself. He assembled a pantheon of heroes – Dalton who, way back at the start of the nineteenth century, realised that different elements were made of different kinds of atoms; Mendeleev, who saw that the elements arranged themselves in a natural order – the periodic table – according to their properties and atomic weights; Bohr who, thanks to quantum theory, came to understand how electrons behave, and concluded that the position of each element in the table reflects the number of electrons in its atoms.

For Sacks, introduction to these masterminds provided the three great 'ecstasies' of his boyhood. His immersion in science was rapturous, akin to what less gifted boys might find in sexual awakening. When he first set eyes on the model of the periodic table in the Science Museum in South Kensington, with its compartments holding samples of the elements, he thought it the most beautiful thing he had ever seen. He could hardly sleep for excitement afterwards. The vast chaotic universe of matter was here reduced to order.

Writing of his discoveries, he combines clarity with lyricism, allowing the reader to share both the awe and the understanding. He remembers, for example, the day he learnt that the shape of any crystal reflects the lattices in which its atoms are arranged, so that crystals are, in effect, giant microscopes, showing the configuration of the atoms inside them. Making crystals interesting is a test for any popular science writer. Sacks passes it resplendently.

The human story on which the scientific adventures are threaded is thinner than Sacks's admirers might like. But he affectionately touches on the tensions and sanctities of a big, cultured orthodox Jewish household in the late 1930s. As in his famous case histories, there is an undercurrent of impish wit. His father, a GP, found human contact difficult, but had a deep affection for food, tucking into the available victuals at each patient's house on his rounds. Aunt Lina lacked social poise, and would blow her nose on the tablecloth, but was a highly successful blackmailer who raised millions of pounds for the Hebrew University in Jerusalem by threatening to reveal the secrets of society figures – or so Sacks assures us. He looks back on his own younger self with humour, too, recalling how he tested the existence of God by sowing two rows of radishes and praying that the Almighty would bless one and curse the other. Since there was no appreciable difference in their growth, he drew the appropriate conclusion. But these are no more than interludes in what is essentially a brilliant account of a scientific education. For readers with some knowledge of science it will be a constant delight. For those without, it is essential.

American Prometheus: The Triumph and Tragedy of J. Robert Oppenheimer
Kai Bird and Martin J. Sherwin, 2008

Do not be put off by the vaunting title. J. Robert Oppenheimer, the director of the Manhattan Project laboratory that developed the first atomic bomb, was not a mythical hero but a damaged and limited human being, as Kai Bird and Martin J. Sherwin amply demonstrate. His main problem was his prodigious brainpower, as unmistakable as a withered limb, which made it hard for him to mix with other people, or even recognise them as the same species. At the Ethical Culture Society school in New York to which his high-minded parents sent him, he outshone fellow pupils so spectacularly that he was put in a separate room to study and then come back and explain to the others what he had learnt. It did not make him popular. Nor did his eagerness to display his knowledge. 'Ask me a question in Latin and I'll answer you in Greek,' he suggested, aged nine, to a girl cousin. His classmates avenged themselves with teasing and ridicule. When his parents sent him to summer camp, hoping to integrate him with the human race, the other boys dubbed him 'Cutie', stripped him naked, daubed his buttocks and genitals with green paint, and locked him in the icehouse all night.

His wealth was another isolating factor. The Oppenheimers were German-Jewish immigrants who had made a fortune in the garment business. Their spacious apartment overlooking the Hudson river housed a distinguished art collection – a Vuillard, a Derain, a Renoir, three Van Goghs. They took drives in the countryside in their chauffeur-driven Packard, and owned a summer home on Long Island, where their yacht was moored. Afflicted by social guilt, Oppenheimer, as a student and young academic, sought the company of communists and subscribed to party funds. But he was also ashamed of his Jewish background and craved acceptance by the Establishment. He assumed patrician airs, alluding to his brother Frank's working-class wife as 'the waitress my brother married', and to child-minding as a 'peasant task'. His culture extended far beyond mathematics and theoretical physics. He devoured Gibbon and Proust, wrote poetry that tried to sound like T.S. Eliot, and learnt Sanskrit so that he could read the *Bhagavad Gita*. Exposure to these humane influences seems, if anything, to have made him less human. He claimed that it raised him above 'the accident of incarnation'.

Others saw him as boastful, caustic, patronising, and subject to fits of rage. During a disastrous year at the Cavendish laboratory in

Cambridge, he gave his supervisor an apple poisoned with chemicals, which fortunately he refrained from tasting, and tried to strangle his roommate with a luggage strap. Transferring to Göttingen, and the supervision of the future Nobel prizewinner Max Born, he felt more at home, but infuriated other students by his arrogance. In seminars he would routinely interrupt whoever was speaking, including Born, and step up to the blackboard, explaining 'This can be done much better in the following manner.'

He admitted that he lacked 'sensitiveness to human beings', and valued physics more than friends. The bare desert scenery of New Mexico, where his father bought him a ranch, captivated him, and he revelled in lonely horseback treks across the wilderness. Marriage to Kitty Harrison, herself a disturbed spirit, and thrice married by the time he met her, did not soften him appreciably. She became an alcoholic, and when their daughter was born he tried to give the baby away to a friend, explaining that he was 'not an attached sort of person'. She grew up with grave feelings of inadequacy and, after her parents' deaths, hanged herself.

The choice of this 'long-haired intellectual' as director of the Los Alamos nuclear weapons laboratory upset conservatives, but proved inspired. His wide culture and ascetic appearance gave him an almost saintly authority, and his quick brain allowed him to humiliate opponents. Although he was not (in the opinion of his peers) an original scientist, he was exceptionally sharp at using other people's ideas. In the race to develop a bomb before Nazi Germany could, his inhuman dedication was another asset. His 'triumph' came in July 1945 with the successful testing of the first atomic bomb in the New Mexico desert. His 'tragedy' is generally reckoned to have come nine years later when, in the midst of the McCarthyite hysteria, a committee of the Atomic Energy Commission (AEC), raking up his early communist associations, judged him unfit to be entrusted with nuclear secrets. But this was a minor mishap compared with his truly tragic acquiescence in the bombing of Hiroshima in August 1945. By that date, Hitler was dead and the war with Germany over. For many Los Alamos scientists these events removed all justification for using the bomb, especially against Japan, which had never had an atom-bomb programme. A majority of them favoured a demonstration explosion before invited observers, and argued this would force Japan to capitulate. Dropping a bomb without warning on a civilian population seemed to them criminal. Yet Oppenheimer went along with it, advising the military on the exact height at which to detonate to inflict maximum damage. Why, when his fellow scientists overwhelmingly opposed it? Because, the Bird–Sherwin analysis tempts us to conclude, events such as the green-paint prank had made it easier for him to regard fellow humans as alien, and because he yearned to be accepted into the Establishment and enjoy the honours it distributed.

When it was too late, he recanted. After the dropping of the Nagasaki bomb he became (according to the FBI, who kept him under close surveillance) a 'nervous wreck'. He secured an audience with President Truman to protest that he had blood on his hands. But Truman dismissed him as a 'cry-baby scientist', and the American military were unimpressed by his anguished campaign for an international agency to monitor atomic research. The H-bomb horrified him, and he refused to take part in its development – a reluctance the AEC security committee attributed to his communist sympathies. As he saw it, the advent of a weapon thousands of times more powerful than the Hiroshima bomb raised the question (still chillingly relevant) of whether it would be right to accept defeat in war rather than destroy the world. Yet even on such issues he seems to have vacillated. Within a few years he succumbed to the lure of the Establishment, and went along with the boneheaded generals and horror-comic politicians in countenancing a preventive nuclear airstrike that would obliterate every main Soviet city. As ever, the contrast was with Einstein, who disliked politicians and generals, and could not understand why Oppenheimer mixed with such people. He urged him simply to walk out of the AEC inquiry, which was a private kangaroo court with no judicial status, and be a free intellectual. Instead, Oppenheimer sat through it and was publicly shamed.

The Bird–Sherwin biography incorporates twenty-five years of research, mountains of documentary evidence and scores of interviews. Despite that, it reads like a thriller, gripping and terrifying by turns. I had the rare experience of glancing up at the page numbers and continually finding I was further on than I had thought. No more absorbing biography will, I predict, come out this year – nor, given the dangers we face, a more important one.

Being Mortal: Illness, Medicine, and What Matters in the End
Atul Gawande, 2014

Atul Gawande's wise and courageous book raises the questions that none of us wants to think about. What will happen to our loved ones when they become too old or ill to care for themselves? What will the end of their lives, and ours, be like? Gawande practises surgery at a Boston hospital and is also professor in the department of surgery at Harvard Medical School. His parents, immigrants to America from India, were both doctors. With this background he might be expected to echo the opinions of the medical establishment. Instead, his book is a scathing indictment of the way modern medicine treats the old and the dying.

Essentially his complaint is that medicine puts medical considerations first, and the rest nowhere. Keeping patients alive for as long as possible is its sole priority, and it has no views at all about what makes life worth living. In our society it is still quite usual for the elderly to be taken from their familiar surroundings and placed among strangers in a nursing home, where their lives are regimented. They wake, dress and eat at prescribed times, as if in prison. They have no privacy or freedom. These measures are enforced for excellent medical reasons – to ensure that they survive, take their medication on schedule and do not damage themselves by falling over. But the result is that they shrink and dwindle and their lives are robbed of purpose.

Gawande celebrates the pioneers who have tried to break away from this dismal pattern. In the 1980s Keren Brown Wilson built her first 'assisted living' home in Portland, Oregon. Round-the-clock medical care was on call if needed, but residents were given freedom and privacy. They had their own belongings around them and their own front door, which they could lock. There were no routines – they could stay awake all night and sleep all day if they chose. Opponents accused Wilson of endangering the elderly, but it was found that the residents' physical and cognitive functioning actually improved, while their satisfaction with their lives increased.

Since then Wilson's idea has spread and has been adapted to include those who want assisted living in their own homes. But any general realisation that the elderly need everyday comforts and companionship is still, Gawande finds, 'devastatingly lacking' among doctors. The insight he brings is that making lives meaningful in old age requires more imagination than making them safe does, and more than the medical profession currently possesses.

His criticisms are harshest in relation to the treatment of the dying. As he sees it, advances in medical science have spurred oncologists, radiation therapists and surgeons to keep pushing back the limits, subjecting their patients to increasingly 'barbaric' procedures, even though they know that the sufferers cannot be cured. In the process, they deprive death of the human meanings that it once had, and convert it into a purely medical process to be managed by healthcare professionals.

Gawande does not exempt himself or his own hospital from his criticisms. He remembers how, swept along by a dying patient's optimism, he raised the possibility that an experimental therapy might help her, though he knew it was 'sheer fantasy'. Recollecting such misjudgments aroused his interest in palliative care, which he now advocates. Whereas surgery and therapy sacrifice the patient's present quality of life in the hope of postponing death, palliative care, he explains, encourages the patient to accept the inevitability of death, and focuses on freedom from pain and anxiety.

The evidence convinces Gawande that it works. A landmark 2010 study divided a number of patients suffering from incurable lung cancer into two groups. The first group received the usual oncology care. The second group received, in addition, sessions with a palliative care specialist. In the event, the second group chose to stop chemotherapy and enter a hospice earlier, experienced less suffering at the end of their lives, and lived 25 per cent longer.

The lesson 'seems almost Zen', Gawande concludes: you live longer only when you stop trying to live longer. Over recent decades the hospice movement has grown steadily in the United States. In 2010, 45 per cent of Americans died in hospice, more than half of them receiving hospice care at home.

Gawande is aware of the flaws in his position. Miracle cures, he concedes, do happen, and it is only human to cling to the chance of one. He sees, too, that for some readers a doctor encouraging the acceptance of decline and death will smack of a society wishing to rid itself of the sick and the old. Whatever else, though, this book should calm that fear. Gawande's concern and dedication shine from every page. Its central chapters were first published as articles in *The New Yorker*, and in keeping with the style of that magazine it makes its point through human stories. Gawande's patients become real for us. We get to know their families, share their unquenchable hope, go with them into the operating theatre, rejoice over their remissions, are shaken by their hideous setbacks, understand their final resignation.

His father's death is the subject of his last and most moving chapter. A hale, dynamic man in his early seventies, his father discovers, out of the blue, that he has an inoperable tumour on his spine. Gawande becomes his carer, and complies, as far as he can, with his father's wish to pass away peacefully in sleep, without suffering. As a devout Hindu, his father wanted his ashes spread on the Ganges, and the book's last scene sees Gawande, his mother and sister and a holy man drifting down the sacred river at sunrise in a small wooden boat. Although not a believer, Gawande was expected, as the oldest male in the family, to assist in the rituals, which included drinking three spoonfuls of water from the river. He complied, but checked out the Ganges' bacterial counts on a website, and premedicated himself with the appropriate antibiotics. That alliance of human feeling with medical knowledge aptly symbolises this remarkable book.

MEMOIRS

The Piano Shop on the Left Bank: The Hidden World of a Paris Atelier
T.E. Carhart, 2000

Walking his children to and from school in the Left Bank *quartier* where he has made his home, the American freelance writer Thad Carhart found his attention drawn to a sleepy little shop down a cobbled side street. Stencilled on its windows was *Desforges Pianos, outillage, fourniture,* and, peering through the glass, he could glimpse the arcane materials of piano repair – tuning pins, wire, swatches of felt. He went in several times, to inquire about purchasing a second-hand piano, but was met with impenetrable Gallic reserve. Unfortunately they had no pianos in stock, it was explained, and in any case you needed a recommendation from a previous client before you could even be considered as a customer.

However, he persisted, and gradually won the confidence of the younger Desforges partner, Luc, who took him one day through the mysterious door at the back of the shop and into the glass-roofed atelier that lay beyond. It was enormous, flooded with sunlight, and stacked with pianos – upright, spinets, grands – in every state of disrepair. A recess housed the oldest inhabitants, delicate little nineteenth-century square pianos teetering on slender legs, their fall boards announcing their provenance – Paris, Amsterdam, Vienna – in curly gold scripts. On workbenches, the intimate insides of pianos were exposed to view.

Over the succeeding months, Carhart became a regular visitor. Luc would phone him when a particular treasure was due to arrive – an extravagantly glorious Steinway model C in tiger-striped Brazilian rosewood, a shimmering golden Gaveau in rare lemon-wood, more than a century old – and they would meet to inspect its wonders. On Friday evenings a group of addicts would gather in the atelier for piano talk over a glass of wine – a professor of linguistics from the Sorbonne, comparing the packaging of champagne bottles with piano design as semiotic systems, a vagabond Dutch piano-tuner with a drink problem, describing how he spends his nights in carriages parked in various Paris terminals.

Through Luc, Carhart comes to think of pianos as living things with distinct personalities. He feels their sounding boards tremble like animals as the hammers dance over the strings. He reads the cryptic messages and inscriptions left inside them by makers and repairers long dead. His interest divides between voluptuous reverie and hard fact. A piano is both an intricate jewel box of gold, red felt and silver, and a machine of high-grade carbon-steel wires stretched across a cast-iron frame that can stand an aggregate pull of more than twenty tons. Luc fills him in on the piano's social history, from its invention around 1700 to its apogee just before the First World War when half a million pianos a year were being manufactured. It was the first mass-produced consumer item that was also complicated and expensive, and one of the first to be available on easy-credit terms. Showy English uprights, survivors of the late Victorian middle-class piano boom, still regularly pass through Luc's workshop.

Pianos live in symbiosis with humans and have adapted to their mechanical progress. With the Industrial Revolution, cast-iron frames were introduced. Before that, pianos were more fragile and more delicate in tone. Even the stronger nineteenth-century piano could still succumb to the power of genius. In 1818 the English maker Broadwood gave Beethoven a sturdy grand incorporating all the latest features, but a contemporary reported that 'the broken strings were jumbled up like a thorn-bush in a storm' after one thunderous recital. At concerts Liszt would keep several pianos in reserve, to be carried on by stagehands as their predecessors wilted beneath the maestro's attack.

Carhart's own musical history gradually emerges in the intervals of his talks with Luc. He learnt to play the piano as a boy in Fontainebleau where his father was on the staff of the Allied Forces. Back in Virginia at the age of eight he was taught by an intimidating lady who dragooned her pupils into giving regular public recitals to improve their confidence. In Carhart she succeeded in inducing life-long stage-fright together with a realisation that his love affair with the piano was deeply private. Luc chooses a piano for him – a baby grand made by Stingl in Vienna in the 1930s. An inscription shows that it once belonged to someone in Braila, a port on the Danube, which sets Carhart romancing about its adventures in the Black Sea and the Mediterranean. Its arrival in his first-floor apartment is dramatic. A puffing, barrel-chested Hercules labours up the steps with the piano's fearsome bulk strapped sideways to his back. A weedy assistant follows, carrying the piano's legs.

After that Carhart's life changes. His apartment has a new and demanding occupant. Luc calls regularly to tend and tune it during its period of acclimatisation until its various woods and fittings are, as he puts it, breathing together. Carhart's wife registers amused tolerance, but his son and daughter are quickly intrigued, so that music lessons for them become imperative. Tucked away in the Latin Quarter he finds a pleasantly dilapidated private academy on the site of an old Benedictine convent. While the children are having their weekly lessons here, he rambles through the gardens and buildings, and makes the acquaintance of the academy's two pianos, a superb Yamaha and a Steinway concert grand. For his own instruction he travels by metro to a modest suburban apartment, dominated by a black Bechstein grand where Anna, a Lebanese *émigrée*, starts to rebuild his knowledge of music from the ground level. After his first few lessons she presents him, rather enigmatically, with a paperback on Zen and archery.

Carhart has written a captivating book, as desultory as an evening stroll, yet full of knowledge. It is suffused with Parisian sensations, the smell of fresh bread from the local bakery, water washing down the gutters in the morning. Remarkably, he can choose words that make us feel and hear the instruments he plays, as well as transmitting the excitement of each new musical adventure. On holiday in Italy he visits the Fazioli factory, a super-modern all-steel construction in the alpine foothills north of Venice. Here, in 1978, a team of experts met to plan the perfect piano. The first prototype came two years later. Now Faziolis are the most expensive pianos in the world. Paolo, the head of the firm, shows him round, and seats him at the keyboard of a concert grand ready to leave the factory. It stretches before him vast and glittering like a yacht. When he plays a chord, the quantity of sound coming back hits him like a wave surprising him on the beach.

Despite these spectacular moments, the ultimate message is quieter. It has to do with personal inwardness and the ability to transcend the world. As soon as she starts to play, Anna tells him, 'I'm gone. It's like a train – it leaves the station and you're already somewhere else.' Carhart's book is like that. You can read it in an evening. But when you close it you feel you have been on holiday.

No Voice from the Hall: Early Memories
of a Country House Snooper
John Harris, 1998

John Harris became a country house snooper at the age of fifteen. It was his uncle Sid's fault really. Sid had been a soldier, and after that a shepherd. But then he turned his hand to upholstery, which gave him a professional interest in antiques and the buildings that contained them. In 1946, when his nephew came to live with him, the south of England was dotted with large country houses that had been requisitioned during the war, and were either wrecked or too expensive for their owners to keep up, or both. They stood forlorn and deserted, just waiting to be broken into. Sid's other passion was fishing, which was convenient, for many of these mouldering mansions had lakes or ornamental canals stuffed with roach, perch and tench that had fattened undisturbed for years. With fishing rods tied to their cycle cross bars, uncle and nephew descended on the stately homes. Soon young Harris caught the bug and was going solo, hitch-hiking and youth-hostelling around England, intent on trespass.

In all he visited some 200 houses, and here, in what bids fair to become a cult book, he recounts the surreal visions of decay that he came upon. Once past the bramble-patch hedge and the Keep Out notices, there was no telling what would unfold. Sometimes there were dilapidated classical temples propped on crutches, or spectral greenhouses, smashed and gaping, with trees pushing up through their roofs. On balustraded terraces, overgrown topiary figures wagged in the wind like carnival floats. In spring and early summer the ungrazed parklands were thick with wild flowers. Empty Nissen huts and pilastered stable blocks waited silently for the explorer.

The interiors of the houses were dreamscapes of ruin. Tapestries hung in rags. Veneers curled up from tabletops like broken springs. Rubbish heaps of leatherbound volumes had avalanched from the walls of libraries. In one, a colony of wasps had built a huge nest from the pages. Ancestral portraits stared through films of mildew at the havoc. Sometimes the upper floors were open aviaries. Birds rose out of the bedrooms, with a tornado of flapping, at the intruder's approach. Grotesque relics remained. A bathtub had become a make-shift sarcophagus for the dried-up corpse of an alsatian dog.

Some otherwise undamaged houses had been taken over for agricultural use. Pushing open the front door of a palatial pile in Lincolnshire, Harris was engulfed by a stampeding flock of sheep that had been living in the marble hall. Beyond, snowdrifts of grain loomed beside Palladian chimney-pieces. The carved and panelled drawing room held hundreds of sacks of potatoes. As usual, Harris had his box Brownie with him, and his snapshot shows them crammed shoulder to shoulder beneath the candelabra like an audi-ence of shrouded corpses. In another Lincolnshire house, the ball-room was stacked to its gilded ceiling with bales of hay. Broken Meissen and Sèvres porcelain littered the floor.

It was here, in a walnut cabinet, that Harris found tray upon tray of gold and silver Roman coins, all neatly labelled. Security, in those innocent days, was lax. When he visited Kenwood, the caretaker left him to his own devices, asking him to put the key under the dustbin when he had finished. In the roof space he found the Iveagh Bequest pictures, millions of pounds worth of old masters, stacked like domi-noes without even a sheet of cardboard between them – Vermeer's *Guitar Player*, Turner's *Lee Shore*, a Rembrandt self-portrait. Given the temptations placed in his way, he seems to have been remarkably restrained. He once filched half a marble chimney piece from a Buckinghamshire house, under the nose of the village bobby. Odds and ends of sculpture accumulated in Sid's Uxbridge back yard. But mostly the two of them were connoisseurs of dilapidation, not thieves.

The adult Harris, it must be confessed, seems less appealing than the youngster whose misdeeds he chronicles. On his way to becoming a respected architectural historian, he cultivated the acquaintance of wealthy antique dealers, interior decorators, and other arty types. Their company, he assures us, was 'bewitching'. But to the unbiased reader they come across as rather a ghastly crew. Sid, surely, would have had no truck with them. One of them drove a white Rolls with polar-bear fur seats over which, Harris bravely recalls, he once vomited copiously after a party. In this company he developed aristocratic sympathies, lamenting the demise of noble dynasties – which never seems to have bothered him when he was poking around uninvited among their possessions – and remarking, with no trace of irony, on his own 'extraordinary facial resemblance to the family of Harris, Earls of Malmesbury'. In retrospect he fancies himself ill-used during his snooping years, complaining of the 'paltry' dole money he drew each week – though since he was perfectly able-bodied, and simply chose not to get a job, it is not clear why he feels he was entitled to anything.

Most of the houses he records in this book have now been demolished. In 1974 he co-organised the *Destruction of the Country House* exhibition at the Victoria and Albert Museum, to draw attention to what he considered a national scandal. This led, in turn, to the SAVE Britain's Heritage campaign. Opinions will differ, but the photos reproduced here of huge stone and brick excrescences plonked down on the innocent landscape strongly suggest that destruction was the best thing. When other buildings replaced them, the gain was, of course, minimal. But when they gave place to light, air and open countryside, their disappearance should surely lift the heart. Harris's favourite tragic statistic – that in 1955 one large country house was destroyed every two and a half days – is from this angle positively exhilarating. His moral stance is sometimes hard to fathom. Of one doomed property he remarks 'greedy town planners had long coveted the estate for a recreational park'. But was it greedier to want it open for everyone, or to keep it as an aristocratic preserve?

Alexander Pope, who was writing while many of these houses were being built, characterised them, with some exceptions, as 'huge heaps of littleness', monuments to pomp and vanity. He looked forward to the day when they would fall into ruin, and revert to green nature. Sid and his nephew were privileged to see what Pope could only imagine. To be fair, Harris, as a youngster, seems sometimes to have agreed with the great eighteenth-century satirist, though he gives no sign of having read him. The snobbish Tennyson d'Eyncourts, in whose favour the family of the poet Tennyson was disinherited, built a vast pseudo-medieval castle, Bayons Manor, in the 1830s. By the time Harris saw it it had spectacularly collapsed, trees sprouted from the masonry, Pugin papers fluttered from the walls. 'Bayons,' he noted, 'is now in total decay and never looked better.' Pope would have been delighted. So would Tennyson.

Gypsies: An English History
David Cressy, 2018

David Cressy's great-grandmother was a Gypsy and grew up in a horse-drawn van among Victorian tinsmiths and basket-weavers. After her marriage to a builder's labourer she settled down, but her siblings continued to live the Gypsy life. Cressy's mother remembered how she had been taken, as a child in the 1920s, to see two great-aunts in a caravan on Epsom Downs, and shown a basketful of gold sovereigns. That magic moment was perhaps the seed of Cressy's new book. But he is a distinguished social historian, so *Gypsies* is a work of impersonal, objective scholarship. It is also a colossal achievement, gathering thousands of shreds of evidence from a vast span of sources to trace the fates of English Gypsies from their first arrival among us until now.

Where they came from has been disputed. 'Gypsy' is a corruption of 'Egyptian', and early theorists suggested that Gypsies were descended from Pharaoh's scattered soldiery after the Israelites' exodus. But in the late eighteenth century German philologists discovered that Romany, the Gypsy language, is related to Sanskrit and Hindu, and carries linguistic clues that record the Gypsies' emigration route from north-east India through central Asia to the Byzantine Greek world. More recently DNA analysis has validated their Asian origin.

They are first recorded in England in 1504 when a Cornish knight paid twenty pence 'to the Egyptians when they danced afore me'. Gypsy-chic was briefly in vogue at Henry VIII's court, with ladies wearing turbans and swirling gowns, and having their fortunes told by Gypsy women. But, as usual when Gypsies were around, people started to allege they had been robbed, and Gypsies were soon being denounced as thieves and sorcerers. In 1531 Henry banished 'outlandish people calling themselves Egyptians' from his realms, and fortune-tellers were condemned to be whipped or, for a second offence, have their ears cut off.

These severities had no effect. Evidence shows that Gypsies could travel round England, visiting a circuit of markets and fairs, with little risk of molestation. So under Elizabeth sterner measures were taken. A statute of 1563 decreed that 'vagabonds calling themselves Egyptians' were felons, and would be hanged if they stayed in the country longer than a month. As Cressy points out, this legislation was unusual in criminalising people for who they were, or said they were, rather than what they did. It also proved hard to administer. In 1596 Yorkshire magistrates imprisoned 196 Gypsies, hanged 9 of them and were preparing to hang the rest when such 'doleful' cries went up from the children among them that they were all sent back to prison and eventually pardoned. Cressy thinks only 'a few dozen' Gypsies went to the gallows in Elizabeth's reign, and by the mid-seventeenth century the 1563 statute was virtually defunct.

This relative mildness contrasted with fearsome anti-Gypsy measures on the Continent and in Scotland. In Spain Gypsy women were flogged and the men sent to the galleys – in effect a death sentence. In the Netherlands Gypsies were treated as wild game and 'Gypsy-hunts' were organised. In Scotland it was legal to kill Gypsies on sight. If captured, the women were drowned and the men hanged. Understandably, Scottish Gypsies tended to drift south. England's more lenient regime seems to have been the result of several familiar English traits, a tendency to compromise, a dislike of officialdom and a talent for passing the buck. A Nottinghamshire justice, asked by the Star Chamber why he had allowed a large band of Gypsies to escape, explained that once across the Trent they became the responsibility of another county, whereas keeping them in gaol was expensive and the gaols were already full.

A Gypsy trick, much reported, and called, in Romany, 'hori hokani', the great swindle, involved a Gypsy 'sorceress' persuading her victim to make a bundle of the household gold and silver, and promising that its quantity could be greatly increased by magic. Spells were then intoned, and the victim was warned not to disturb the bundle for several days. When opened, it was found to contain trash, the gold and silver having disappeared with the Gypsy. Given its apparent success and profitability, it seems unlikely Gypsies had a monopoly on this clever ruse. However, it was added to the catalogue of their sins.

It was Romanticism, with its passion for wildness, freedom and the natural world, that changed the image of Gypsies. Within half a century they became powerful forces for good, like the prophetess Meg Merrilles in Walter Scott's novel *Guy Mannering*, or sexy bombshells like Heathcliff, with his 'dark-skinned Gypsy aspect', in Emily Brontë's *Wuthering Heights*. Glamorous, flamenco-dancing Gypsies like Bizet's Carmen continued the tradition. In the later nineteenth-century evangelicals and philanthropists assembled a more realistic account of Gypsies, visiting their encampments and reporting that they all slept together in family groups and consumed snail soup and baked hedgehog. Turning them into anthropological specimens satisfied the Victorian zest for knowledge, and led to the foundation of the Gypsy Lore Society in 1888.

But Cressy emphasises how mysterious Gypsies were, and still are. 'What went on within their camps and huts remains unknown.' Constant harassment by the authorities has made them secretive and self-reliant. Damian Le Bas, whose richly poetic memoir of his Gypsy family, *The Stopping Places*, was published too recently for Cressy to mention, has told how some of his relatives strongly disapproved of his drawing attention to himself and them by publishing at all.

Gypsies emerge from Cressy's book as a persecuted and maligned minority. Half a million of them perished in the Holocaust, and now political correctness is erasing even their historical identity. The Council of Europe decreed in 2010 that the word 'Gypsy' must no longer be used, because of its 'negative paternalistic stereotypes'. Roma and Traveller are acceptable alternatives. Cressy, however, defiantly uses 'Gypsy' with a capital G throughout, and his scholarly masterpiece is a lifeline to the true past.

Fishing in Utopia: Sweden and the Future that Disappeared
Andrew Brown, 2008

Sweden, when Andrew Brown arrived there in the 1970s, was as near as any country has ever come to a socialist paradise. Its people were, he found, bonded by a firm sense of civic duty and shared values. Everyone knew what it was acceptable to think. Society, it was agreed, would benefit more from co-operation than from selfishness. Affluence was bad for people. Failure to want social equality was regarded as a handicap to be pitied and, if possible, cured. Armed conflict was seen as wasteful and to be avoided. Sweden had avoided it for 150 years, remaining neutral in the Second World War. Drunkenness was an obvious evil, so teetotalism was encouraged. Alcohol could be bought only at government stores, which were ringed with health warnings and made as unalluring as possible. It was assumed that, as time went on, the world would become more peaceful, more egalitarian and more like Sweden. That was what progress meant.

Many young people in Europe and America felt this kind of optimism in the 1960s, but somehow it translated into reality only in

Sweden. The explanation, Brown suggests, may lie in the country's history and class structure. Scarcely anyone in Sweden was more than three generations away from subsistence farming. The disciplines of poverty had taught them frugality and solidarity, so that when prosperity came they were determined to make it communal and not to squander it. Under the leadership of prime minister Olof Palme, Sweden became one of the world's richest nations. There was full employment and no housing shortage. In the early 1970s, Palme's Social Democrats had built 1 million new, affordable, modern homes for workers, more than satisfying demand. Selective schooling was abolished, and the last powers of the Swedish monarchy removed. Lack of ostentation was a Social Democratic tradition. Palme lived in an ordinary terrace house, and what he most desired, Brown thinks, was not money or power but the admiration of all decent people. It is hard to think of any recent British politician of whom that could be said.

Brown landed up in Sweden more or less by chance. His father, a diplomat and the director of a shipping line, had sent him to a 'rather grand' school, from which he was expelled for some undisclosed offence at the age of sixteen. After several years of 'hippie-ish wanderings', also undisclosed, he worked as a carer in a Cheshire Home, thinking that, even if he had failed his parents' expectations, he was being useful. Among the nurses was a young Swedish woman, Anita, and in 1977 they hitch-hiked to Sweden and set up house together. It was the start of a struggle to find some meaning in life and in himself. He got a job in a small factory making wooden pallets. The work was exhausting but gave him time to think. He read a lot of philosophy, learnt Swedish, and became seriously interested in fishing. He had fished for pike and perch in nearby lakes when they first arrived, simply to put food on the table. But it soon outgrew practical considerations and became, in effect, his religion. It was inseparable in his mind from the freedom he felt when he was alone in the wild, surrounded by silence and the smell of trees. He graduated to fly fishing and became expert at making his own flies, and at guessing which of the innumerable varieties of insect available in Sweden the fish he was pursuing would prefer.

Clearly there is something rather sad about someone who devotes himself to outwitting fish. But Brown writes with enough skill and ardour to keep that thought at bay. His sanity, we come to realise, was at stake. He tells how on one of his solitary fishing trips he woke in the night, shaking with terror and a feeling of revulsion from the world. He rushed to the car, grabbed his fishing waistcoat, weighed down with boxes of imitation flies, and found he could breathe normally again. Next morning he woke up 'quite sane'.

Meanwhile, he and Anita married and had a son, Felix, with whom he tried, in vain, to share his piscatory obsession. It was not fishing, though, that put an end to the marriage but Brown's ambition to become a writer. He wanted to be 'one at whom the whole world marvelled', and the likely way to achieve this, he thought, was writing for *The Spectator*. He started sending the magazine pieces about Sweden in the 1980s, and fairly soon he abandoned Anita and Felix and moved to London. They tried joining him for a while, but quickly went back home. He found another wife, of whom we learn only that she was a 'pretty, intelligent English woman' who liked fishing, and he moved from *The Spectator* to the *Independent*, becoming its religious affairs correspondent in 1986. He had undergone, he tells us, at least one mystical experience while communing with fish, but whether that is what stimulated his interest in religious affairs remains unclear.

Much later he went back to Sweden and found it had changed beyond recognition. When the Social Democrats lost power their ideals had been speedily abandoned and their welfare system dismantled, to be replaced by a dogmatic distrust of state control. The railways and postal service had been privatised and private schooling encouraged. By the end of the 1990s, Sweden was no longer the safe, prosperous, tolerant country he had known. Violent crime had increased by 40 per cent, rape by 80 per cent. Obesity and drunkenness were common. Heroin smuggling and organised crime had created a new breed of super-rich gangsters. A large immigrant population, with a crime rate at least double that among native Swedes, was fomenting resentment and racial hatred.

Fishing in Utopia is a lament for a lost Eden. But it is more than that. Essentially it is a story of modern rootlessness and the search for something to believe in. The fact that that something turns out, absurdly, to be fishing only makes it more tragic. I can see it becoming a cult book, and not just among anglers. You do not (I can personally guarantee) need to have the slightest interest in fishing to be caught up in his rapt descriptions of reels and lines and casting and flies and the enormous quiet of Sweden's uninhabited places. In the last section he drives up into the Swedish arctic to be alone and write. It is a journey into the past. At a lonely farm he comes upon an old couple, and finds that the wife not only believes in trolls but has seen one, a little grey man about 2ft high. Trolls are, he learns, benevolent spirits, quite likely to take milk from a cow at night, but happy to do humans favours in return. Further on, he joins in a traditional midsummer festival. A maypole is decorated with birch branches and flowers and hauled aloft. Girls and men dance round it through the white summer night. The music comes from an instrument, special to the locality, with eleven steel strings and three banks of keys, which sounds 'like an accordion on the verge of tears'. That is not a bad description of the tone of this book.

Family Secrets
Derek Malcolm, 2003

Things started to go wrong for Malcolm fifteen years before he was born. In August 1917, his father, Douglas Malcolm, a brave, boneheaded artillery officer, came home on leave from the Western Front to find that his wife, Dorothy, was having an affair with a Russian immigrant called Anton Baumberg. She was quite open about it, informing her husband that she and Baumberg were lovers, and requesting a divorce. Douglas either could not or would not take this in. He insisted that Baumberg was a 'devil incarnate', and Dorothy an innocent victim whose spotless honour he was divinely appointed to preserve. Early on the morning of 14 August 1917, he tracked Baumberg down to a seedy lodging house in Paddington and shot him dead. Immediately afterwards he gave himself up to the police.

The trial aroused avid public interest. Sir John Simon, for Douglas, argued that his client had acted in self-defence, an explanation that raised some practical difficulties. Baumberg had been unarmed (he was in bed, wearing only a pyjama jacket, when his killer burst in), there were no signs of a struggle, and Douglas had put four bullets into him, the last through his forehead at point-blank range. However, these technicalities were outweighed, in the public's view, by the contrasting characters of the two men. Douglas was a gallant British officer, whereas Baumberg was foreign, half-Jewish and, it was alleged, a white-slave trafficker and a spy, although neither charge was supported by any evidence. Simon, in his summing-up, described the dead man as 'one of those pieces of refuse carried along in the tide of great cities'. The jury returned a not-guilty verdict with patriotic alacrity, and the cheering in court and from the huge crowd outside lasted five minutes.

How the Malcolms could bear each other after this remains a mystery, but presumably Douglas was too proud and obstinate to countenance a formal separation. While Dorothy occupied their London flat, he spent his time at the Northamptonshire manor house, where he kept fourteen horses and six grooms and hunted several times a week. He did not need to work. The Malcolm money was in jute, and the First World War, with its insatiable appetite for sandbags, had brought rich pickings.

Young Derek Malcolm, born in 1932, soon became aware of his parents' unhappiness, but his relations with them were rather distant. His educational career began when he was packed off to boarding school aged four. Greetings from home arrived in the form of one-liner postcards ('Isn't this a nice picture? Much love, Mummy'). In due course, he progressed to a horrible prep school in Oxford, where the staff-recruitment policy seems to have been designed to provide employment for paedophiles and sadists. Then came Eton where, since he was weedy, asthmatic and academically dim, popularity eluded him. True, that is commonplace with literary figures (Malcolm was to become *The Guardian*'s film critic). Among twentieth-century English authors, to have been bullied at boarding school is practically a vocational qualification. All the same, Malcolm's expensive schooling seems to have thrown him together with some exceptionally nasty types. An older boy in his house, who later became a successful solicitor, made a habit of mixing his own excrement with cold cream and forcing younger boys to eat it.

Given Baumberg's fate, you might suppose that Dorothy Malcolm would have found it tricky attracting new wooers. But, in fact, men swarmed around her. She had been a singer and actress before her marriage, so they were often from the world of entertainment. George Robey, Toscanini, Augustus John and Nigel Playfair all competed for her favours. Luckily, her trigger-happy husband had transferred his affections entirely to horses by this time, otherwise he might have cut a fearful swathe through English cultural life. Dorothy, it seems, also entered diplomatic circles. After her death, Malcolm received a postcard from an aunt telling him that his mother had wished him to know that his father was not Douglas Malcolm, but Mussolini's ambassador to London.

The Warden of Merton College, Oxford, was another old flame, a circumstance that Dorothy did not hesitate to exploit when the time arrived for Derek's university entrance. She wrote asking for help, and got a letter back (beginning 'O Seraph') in which the

Warden explained that there were many better-qualified candidates, but promised to use his influence to secure her son a place, which he did. I am sure this kind of injustice does not happen in Oxford any more, but it is not surprising that people think it does given that it was prevalent so recently.

By this time the fortunes of the Malcolms were on the wane. They had moved to Bexhill-on-Sea in Sussex during the Second World War to avoid the bombing. Douglas gambled most of their fortune away. The servants decamped, taking the family silver with them. With no experience of looking after themselves, and no inclination to learn, the ill-matched couple rapidly deteriorated. Porridge and boiled eggs were the limit of their culinary skills. The house was filthy, the garden overgrown, and they lingered on, woebegone survivors of an England that had died. Dorothy would lie in bed until midday, and gradually lost her wits.

Their son sketches in his own post-Oxford doings lightly. But two incidents stand out. At Bexhill he had a friend called Stanley, a businessman, with whom he played tennis, and one day Stanley made a pass at him. 'Shocked and angry', Malcolm shouted at him to stop. Stanley obeyed and put his sexuality under wraps again. But they stayed friends and, years later, shortly before he died of lung cancer, Stanley wrote to Malcolm ('Old Chum') to announce that, at the age of sixty-seven, he had finally had his first sex – with a friendly milkman whom he persuaded in for a cup of tea. Whatever you think of today's England, at least Stanley's guilty and unfulfilled life would be an anachronism in it. The second incident also has its hopeful side. After the failure of his first marriage, Malcolm took up with a Soho club hostess who was married, he discovered, to an associate of the Kray brothers. One night he awoke with a start to find the wronged husband towering over him with a cosh. On the Baumberg pattern, this clearly should have been curtains for Malcolm. But after beating him about the head a little, his nocturnal visitor demanded a cup of coffee and then left. So perhaps the gradual moral improvement of mankind is not such an illusion after all.

Swimming with My Father: A Memoir
Tim Jeal, 2004

You do not hear much about saints' families, presumably because so many saints have remained celibate. Tim Jeal's memoir of his father is unusual, in that it gives some inkling of what it would be like to be a saint's wife or son. Not good, is the answer. Clifford, Jeal's father, belonged to a fellowship of Christian mystics called The Order of the Cross, who sought oneness with 'the all-pervading divine presence, the Father-Mother'. Clifford found that swimming in various ponds and rivers scattered across the home counties brought him closest to this pantheistic deity, and when he was a little boy Jeal was encouraged to accompany him. He remembers the soggy, torso-covering bathing suit Clifford wore to pursue the godhead, and the many mouthfuls of muddy water he himself swallowed in the course of their quest. Unworldly, as saints are supposed to be, and utterly oblivious of his effect on other people, Clifford was a liability in public. He would embrace trees, listening to the noises they made. Once he underwent a course of eye-rolling exercises to cure his short sight, and practised these ostentatiously while travelling on the District Line, with his small son burning with shame beside him.

For Jeal's mother Norah, things were much worse. She and Clifford were an unlikely pair. Her ancestry was aristocratic and full of firebrand militarists, whose exploits on historic battlefields gave little Tim nervous palpitations when she told him about them. Clifford, on the other hand, was the son of a haulier, and was serving in Heal's furniture shop in the Tottenham Court Road when Norah met him. The First World War had diminished the supply of young men, and evidently Norah decided he was the best she would get.

Her father, Sir Thomas Pasley, Bart, a veteran of the Boer War, accepted his unlikely son-in-law with a good grace, and accommodated the newlyweds in his enormous Kensington flat.

At the time of his marriage Clifford showed no signs of mysticism. His saintliness began to burgeon some three years later, when he joined The Order of the Cross. Perhaps, at a subliminal level, it was a way of annoying his wife and her patrician relatives. If so, it succeeded admirably. When the Second World War broke out, he announced that he could kill no living thing – apart from the vegetables that provided his diet – and must become a conscientious objector. In retaliation Norah broke off conjugal relations. When a tribunal ordered him to serve, or face prison, he compromised by becoming a lance corporal in the Royal Army Ordnance Corps, a military status calculated to enrage Sir Thomas almost as much as his pacifism. Once Clifford was in khaki, however, Norah relaxed her embargo, and that is how Tim Jeal came to be conceived.

The rapprochement did not last long. Norah later told her son that after she became pregnant with him she and Clifford never made love again. Clifford's saintliness seems to have stood in the way. He told a bewildered Norah that the union of man and woman should be 'a cryptogram of the union of the soul with the One Life'. Besides, among the devotees of The Order of the Cross he had found a friend called Joy, with whom he achieved both spiritual and physical ecstasy. Going through his father's journals after his death, Jeal found a full account of the affair. Oppressed by the weight of his sin, Clifford strove to sever his association with Joy. But, after communing with God, he decided that the Almighty wanted it to continue, provided it was strictly platonic in future – a solution that caused the maximum dissatisfaction both to Joy and to Norah, who, thanks to Clifford's saintly frankness, was fully apprised of her rival's existence.

Jeal loved both his parents, and his book is at its best when recounting, with gentle amusement, their turbulent union. The second half, which tells of his father's slow death from Parkinson's disease, and his mother's descent into cantankerous decrepitude, is, by comparison, repugnant and pointless. Few can be under any illusion about the effects of old age, and to recount its symptoms – the dribbling, the incoherent ramblings – with such beady-eyed precision seems an insult to his parents' helplessness. It reads almost like a belated revenge for their one unkind act, which was to send him away to a horrible prep school at the age of eight. This turning-of-the-tables aspect seems, indeed, to have occurred to Jeal. Picking his mother up from her old folk's home he notices that she waits for him in the hall, so as to get away from the hated place as quickly as possible, just as he did when waiting to be picked up from school.

Vindictive or not, he has a sharp gift for anecdote, and can hit off a character in a few words. As a boy he considered the Navy as a career, until he found that ships made him sick. He was interviewed by a gnarled seadog from his mother's side of the family, and can recall, from the blur of terror that engulfed the occasion, only one sentence: 'We never saw the *Scharnhorst*, just the flash of her guns in the blackness.' T.S. Eliot figures unexpectedly in another story. His future second wife, Valerie Fletcher, lived opposite the Jeals in Earl's Court Gardens. Eliot often visited, and Clifford, in the pushy way some saints have, struck up an acquaintance. Jeal was at Westminster School by this time, and Clifford badgered him to interview Eliot for the house magazine. Eliot complied with great courtesy and patience, but when finished copies arrived from the printer Jeal was aghast to find that *The Waste Land* appeared throughout as *The Washstand*. In trepidation he called on the great man to confess, but Eliot, quaking with silent, ascetic mirth, requested a supply of uncorrected copies to distribute to friends. Clifford was not so gifted a mystic as Jeal imagines. He cites a fine sentence from his father's journal: 'There is a piece of divinity in us – something that was before the elements and owes no homage to the sun.' This is not, however, Clifford's, but a quotation from one of the masterworks of English prose, Sir Thomas Browne's *Religio Medici*. Perhaps Clifford found it in his Great

Thoughts calendar, from which he garnered daily wisdom. He came closer to a mystical experience one afternoon when Norah phoned her son to tell him that her favourite cat Smudge had been run over and killed. Pitying her distress, Jeal collected the cat from the gutter outside his parents' house, dug a grave in the garden, and buried it. Later that day his father phoned in rapture. Smudge was sitting in the flowerbed on top of his own grave. 'It's like the Resurrection,' he cried. When the phone rang again it was his mother, helpless with laughter. Smudge had just walked into the kitchen demanding her supper. 'I'm afraid,' gasped Norah, 'you've buried a complete stranger.'

Unapologetic: Why, Despite Everything, Christianity Can Still Make Surprising Emotional Sense
Francis Spufford, 2012

First-hand accounts of mystical experiences are rare nowadays, and to offer one as a reason for attending Church of England services seems somehow anticlimactic – like joining the Boy Scouts because you have discovered you are Superman. That, though, is the rationale of Francis Spufford's remarkable book, which is passionate, challenging, tumultuously articulate, and armed with anger to a degree unusual in works of Christian piety. What angers him is that in today's secular culture Christians are regarded as freaks. His daughter has just turned six, and he is afraid she will be taunted at school because her parents go to church. So this is a pre-emptive strike at the taunters.

The events that led up to his first mystical experience back in 1997 remain rather vague. He'd had a row with his then girlfriend – his fault, he says – and was sitting alone in a café, feeling miserable, when someone put on the adagio of Mozart's Clarinet Concerto.

He'd heard it many times before, but this time it sounded new, somehow merciful as well as joyful. It is not clear whether he gave it a religious interpretation at the time – he'd been an atheist for many years – but he now sees it as a foretaste of his conversion experience, which happened some time later, when he was, again, feeling miserable and worthless. He went into a church, sat in silence and closed his eyes. He thought of the immensities beyond himself, from the grass growing in the churchyard to the infinite galaxies. He thought of time speeded up – the continents changing shape, the mountain ranges melting. Gradually he became aware of something else, a 'whisper of presence', the sense of being watched but absolutely safe, and it brought with it the conviction that the universe is sustained by 'a continual and infinitely patient act of love'.

Summarising it like this doesn't do justice to Spufford's struggle to express the inexpressible, or to his constant awareness of the irrationality of what he feels. He readily concedes that identical feelings could be caused by sensory deprivation or biochemical imbalances or drugs or electrical stimulation of his brain. He admits that they correspond closely to the sensations of transcendence reported by worshippers in many other religions – and, he might have added, to the 'oceanic feeling' for which Freud offered a psychoanalytic explanation. Despite all this he feels certain that what he felt was the presence of the Christian God. For him that emotional conviction is primary; ideas and dogmas are secondary. He repeats the Apostles' Creed in church every Sunday and tries, he says, to believe it. But he believes because of his feelings, not the other way round.

He is, however, ruthlessly logical in following up the consequences of his belief. The God of everything, he insists, must be manifest in everything (in necrotising bacteria and anthrax spores and cancer cells) and in all human acts – massacres, atrocities, torture – 'the God of everything smiles on all alike'. He tots up the various excuses theologians have invented to explain why a loving God allows suffering, and shows they are all hopelessly flawed. When he goes on like this you start to wonder whether he is for Christianity or against it. But the truth seems to be he is so secure in his faith he doesn't worry about the contradictions. Or the impossibilities. It is its impossibility as a rule of life that, he contends, distinguishes Christianity from other religions. The Muslim and Jewish laws of behaviour may be demanding, but at least they can be kept. But Christ's injunctions can't be. Love strangers as much as your family, give your possessions away, refuse to defend yourself when attacked – these are 'lunatic principles' and, inevitably, Christians constantly fail to obey them. Yet that, for Spufford, is paradoxically how Christianity succeeds, because it makes Christians acknowledge their guilt. They are 'the international league of the guilty', debarred from feeling righteous, needing to be forgiven, and so obliged to forgive others. Here, too, though, he seems to go out of his way to make Christianity sound impossible. Forgiving others means, he reminds us, forgiving people who fly airliners into skyscrapers or shoot children at Norwegian summer camps.

His attempt to reconstruct the life of the historical Jesus is the least impressive part of his book. He has powerful competitors in this field, from Milton in *Paradise Regained* to Mikhail Bulgakov in *The Master and Margarita*, and they make him look facile. He diverges from the gospel stories unaccountably – his Christ is tied to the cross, not nailed – and, though he accepts Jesus' miracles, other supernatural events (the Virgin Birth, the Ascension) are omitted. Also left out is the scene in Gethsemane when Jesus prays to his Father to be spared his ordeal. Presumably Spufford rejects this because his personal take on the hugely contested issue of Christ's two natures is that, even as a man, Jesus was convinced he was the creator of the universe. This has the disadvantage of making the human Jesus seem non-human – or mad – and Spufford's firm rejection of belief in heaven, hell and eternal life may also come as a disappointment to some Christians.

He is much better in attack. His caustic dismemberment of the happiness promised by consumerism is a delight, and he is wonderfully funny about the 'sweet drivel' of John and Yoko and

'Imagine'. He mocks the smug certainty of the new atheists and their crass assumption that 'awe' at subatomic particles is a perfectly satisfactory substitute for belief in a living God. A highlight of the book is his vision of the philosopher A.C. Grayling leading us on the great journey into the secular light 'tossing his miraculously bouffant locks'.

Spufford's language will put some readers off. It seems unlikely he uses expressions such as 'total bollocks', 'crap', 'my arse' and 'sod off', or refers to original sin as 'the human propensity to f*** things up', at the little gatherings over coffee and biscuits after church on Sundays, of which he writes so affectionately. So why here? It seems like posturing. Still, that's a small grumble. For me *Unapologetic* is Spufford's most fascinating book since his 2002 memoir *The Child That Books Built*, which is saying a great deal. I don't think it will convert anyone. I found my agnosticism undented after reading it, despite listening optimistically to the Mozart Clarinet Concerto that evening. But conversion isn't the point. He admits he doesn't know if there's a God or not. Nobody does: it's unknowable. What's on offer here is vehement thought, ardent expostulation, and the conviction that what Spufford writes about is for him the most important thing in the world, or out of it.

Publisher
Tom Maschler, 2005

Tom Maschler is not prone to false modesty. He states frankly that when he was chairman of Jonathan Cape it was the best literary publishing house in Britain. 'We had the best authors, the best promotions and our production was the best.' In one of the many photographs of himself that grace this memoir he wears a T-shirt identifying him as 'the world's greatest publisher'. Others show him posing with the rich and famous, but in one, taken on the eve of the 1995 Booker prize, he is holding up a 65-kilo tuna, caught while

Maschler was cruising in the Indonesian ocean. You cannot help feeling sorry for the fish. It probably had little interest in books, and it was sheer bad luck that it swam into the great publisher's orbit. All the same, it provides an apt emblem for Maschler's career, since landing big fish has mattered to him more than anything else, and his book is laid out as a series of labelled sections, each devoted to a single well-known author from the Cape list.

There is no denying that it is an impressive haul. Cape introduced Gabriel García Márquez, Thomas Pynchon, Joseph Heller, Tom Wolfe and Kurt Vonnegut to British readers. Doris Lessing, John Fowles, Arnold Wesker, Roald Dahl, Ian McEwan, Julian Barnes and Martin Amis also became Cape authors during Maschler's reign. So did Salman Rushdie, although he defected when Penguin outbid Cape for *The Satanic Verses* – a lucky break for Cape, given the whirlwind it stirred up. With a cast of this distinction, Maschler's book should have been the literary event of the decade, providing intimate insight into the shaping spirits of contemporary literature. Instead, it is an embarrassment. He keeps telling us what scintillating talkers his authors were, yet he records virtually nothing of what they said. Arthur Miller's 'conversation flowed', he remembers, but the only detail that sticks in his mind is that he had big feet. David Hockney, he assures us, was 'always ready to talk seriously about art', but not a single remark comes our way. Was Maschler, you start to wonder, deaf? He admits, fairly late in the book, to being hard of hearing. Maybe the handicap was long term.

Another problem is his style, which, for someone who has honed his wits on the foremost penmen of the era, is strangely ponderous. The Frankfurt Book Fair, he tells us, 'takes place in Frankfurt, so that if I wish to attend, I am obliged to go to Germany'. Quite so. It is as well to get these things straight before you start out. His comments about books are uniformly banal. Of Rushdie's *Midnight's Children* he reveals: 'the novel belongs firmly to the literature that has been called "magic realism"'. Barnes's *Flaubert's Parrot* 'is both highly original and extremely entertaining'. Apparently, when Barnes gave a dinner party for Maschler it was noticed, halfway through the meal, that the host had disappeared, and he was found fast asleep in bed. It is a reaction to Maschler's company that readers of this book will readily understand.

However, although he betrays no interest in ideas, his attention to the inner man is earnest and thoughtful. A surprising proportion of his book is about seeking refreshment. Staying with the publisher Bob Gottlieb in New York he wakes to find there are no eggs in the house, and has to make two trips to the deli to assemble the ingredients of a satisfactory breakfast. Dining with Heller, the sight of a single bottle of wine on the table alarms him, and he seeks Heller's permission to go out and buy a few more. A meal he fondly remembers is with Philippe de Rothschild: 'I have never before (or since) had the opportunity of consuming so much great wine, and totally regardless of cost.' With Fowles, on the other hand, he notes gravely that they are being regaled from a bottle of supermarket plonk, while on a calamitous evening with Isaac Bashevis Singer he finds himself trapped in a restaurant where water and apple juice are the only drinks served. His gastronomic enthusiasm leads to a breach with the critic George Steiner. After chairing a lecture given by Steiner at Hay-on-Wye he drives to a restaurant twenty miles away for dinner. Steiner, in the car behind, keeps flashing him down and demanding how much further there is to go. At the end of the evening he opines sharply that to drive so far for dinner is a sign of 'mental derangement'. This seems a harsh judgment, but Maschler's interest in food did once, he tells us, endanger his life. Stuffing himself with chicken tikka at a party for Rushdie, he got a bone lodged in his throat and had to be rushed to hospital.

Celebrities are his other passion. Just getting into their vicinity is cause for excitement. At a circus, he once sat near Princess Grace of Monaco and Charlie Chaplin. He managed to get himself photographed with Muhammad Ali, caught a glimpse of Cecil Beaton from an upstairs window, and almost met Yves Saint-Laurent. Most joyfully of all he was at a party attended by Princess Diana, and saw her give his mother-in-law a 'magical smile'. No doubt the psychologically inclined would read all this as a sign of insecurity. But from the little we learn of his early life he seems to have been remarkably self-assured even as an adolescent. After public school he gained a place to read PPE at St Edmund Hall, Oxford. But when he interviewed the college principal he got the impression that the man had admitted him only because of his brilliance at squash and tennis. So he renounced university and hitch-hiked round America instead. Keen to spend a summer on a kibbutz in Israel, he wrote to Ben Gurion, the prime minister, asking him to facilitate his passage out. When he joined up for national service in the RAF, he was appalled to find himself doing drill and digging trenches with the other recruits. For someone of his quality these pursuits were 'intolerable', so he went on hunger strike. When the sergeant remonstrated, 'I spoke quite softly and asked him kindly not to shout'. He was sent to a lunatic asylum for three weeks, then discharged as unfit.

It must be added that Maschler has clearly stirred warm and deep affection in many of his authors. When, in the late 1980s, he suffered from clinical depression, he received loving, supportive letters, which he reprints, from Lessing, Dahl and Vonnegut, among others. The only surprise is that, with so many friends in the literary world, none of them persuaded him not to publish this book.

Untold Stories
Alan Bennett, 2005

U*ntold Stories*, a follow-up to *Writing Home*, gathers Alan Bennett's miscellaneous prose from the past ten years. He compares it to the Christmas annuals that used to absorb him as a boy. But it is also, in its freewheeling way, an autobiography, and charts a feat of social mobility – the butcher's son who, via the eleven-plus and Leeds Modern School, won a scholarship to Oxford, got a first, nearly became a medieval historian, but instead shot to fame in *Beyond the Fringe*, and, when it transferred to Broadway, found himself at parties trying to make small talk with stars who, not so long ago, he had been queuing up to see at the Picturedrome on Wortley Road.

Bennett does not tell it as a success story, and doubts, in glummer moments, if it is one; 'Living is something I've managed largely to avoid.' Rather, he inspects his past to discover how he came to be himself – fastidious, buttoned-up, an inveterate outsider. It began at school. While his classmates sprouted alarming signs of manhood, he remained virginally undeveloped, and felt their pity and contempt. At sixteen, he came to the conclusion he was homosexual, which seems to have caused temporary dismay ('a fate that ruled out any possibility of happiness'), but also defiance. He has always, he says, resented all-male parties and gay talk, because they make assumptions about him that he finds offensive. 'Homosexuality is a differentness I've never been wholly prepared to accept in myself.'

Being categorised at all is what he resists. He laments his constant sense of being shut out, but when he looks at those he might be shut in with, being shut out is clearly his preference. 'I have never found it easy to belong. So much repels.' In 1988, he refused a knighthood, seemingly because he felt it would impair his separateness. Besides, it would have counted as swank, a fault his parents had taught him to despise. He thinks of them as singular, but they seem pretty standard in their values, as well as thoroughly admirable. Like most lower-middle-class couples at the time, they believed in keeping themselves to themselves and avoiding anything 'common', articles of faith their son has inherited. It would do, he suggests, as a definition of what has gone wrong with England in the past twenty years, to say that it has got common. Unfashionably ready to call vulgarity and stupidity vulgarity and stupidity, he picks out, in an anti-paedophile mob on a

Portsmouth housing estate, a tattooed mother with a fag dangling from her lips and a baby in her arms, proclaiming how concerned she is for her kiddies. Modernity appeals to him very little. Still a medievalist at heart, he envies the life of a fifteenth-century Carthusian monk and admits, though with shame, in his diary for 2000, that he is more outraged by the sacking of the monasteries at the Reformation than by anything happening in Yugoslavia or Sierra Leone.

His father taught him to distrust affectation ('splother', he called it), and Bennett proved all too apt a pupil. When his auntie Myra, always a show-off, fell ill, he was convinced it was just bad acting, and even her death, which quickly followed, struck him as not quite sincere. He has an unerring ear for verbal falsity – the archbishop of Canterbury at the Queen Mother's memorial service referring to her as 'someone who can help us to travel that country we call life', or Tony Blair saying 'I honestly believe' rather than just 'I believe'. The modern jargons we invent to keep reality at bay arouse his scorn. You sense the struggle when he refers to Rupert Thomas, who now lives with him, as 'my partner, as the phrase is'. He has trained himself, or maybe it was just a gift, to hear and see what is actually there, not what convention dictates, and in his prose as in his drama this literalism makes even ordinary idioms – 'the doctor has put her on tablets', or 'a proper wedding would run to bridesmaids' – shimmer with a kind of comedy.

The rawness of telling it as it was spreads through the two most harrowing items here, a description of his mother's periodic descents into madness, and an account of his treatment for bowel cancer in 1997. They avoid, respectively, the pieties usual in discussing mental illness, and battle-against-cancer heroics, and in both cases the lack of pretence brings the horror unnervingly near. These come first and last in the book. Elsewhere his incisiveness is less alarming, and often pleasingly sceptical. Puncturing reputations is a speciality. He comments wryly on the 'canonisation' of Iris Murdoch, whose famed unworldliness somehow did not prevent her accepting umpteen honorary degrees and a damehood from Mrs Thatcher. Sir Isaiah Berlin and Anna Akhmatova are also put through the mill – the one not much good at thinking, the other not much good at poetry, and both too pleased with themselves. A phrase is enough to destroy a treasured image of an immortal – Brylcreemed Sir Malcolm Sargent with his carnation buttonhole and 'wolfish smile'; Auden's 'harsh, quacking voice'.

But it is in writing about art that his eye for what is actually there is at its funniest. He was made a trustee of the National Gallery in 1993, an honour he treasures because it allows him to view the pictures after hours, when the crowds have gone. Having read of the raptures Bernard Berenson experienced before artworks, he felt at first he was failing some sort of sensitivity test. But as he came to know more of Berenson he decided he was 'both intolerable and silly', and that his own way of looking at the pictures has more human interest. Why, he wonders, in pictures of the Crucifixion, does only Jesus have visitors, and why does not a member of the Holy Family occasionally walk over to pay one of the other crosses a visit? Again, how is it that God has sent his only begotten son into the world with no trace of underarm hair? Then there is the matter of Joseph. Why, in nativity pictures, is he so sidelined? He imagines a conversation among the Wise Men: 'Who's the guy with the grey hair?' 'That's the husband.' 'Oh my God!'

Untold Stories contains far more than any review can tell – Bennett's experiences during national service, for example, or his brushes with the public ('It had better be good,' a pair of pensioners warn him in the foyer of the West Yorkshire Playhouse. 'We're big fans of yours'), or his friendships with Alec Guinness, John Gielgud, Maggie Smith and others. I have never read a book of this length where I have turned the last page with such regret. It is intelligent, educated, engaging, humane, self-aware, cantankerous and irresistibly funny. You want it to go on for ever.

Grayson Perry: Portrait of the Artist
as a Young Girl
as told to Wendy Jones, 2006

Grayson Perry was the first transvestite to win the Turner Prize, arriving at the award ceremony in 2003 in his best frock, with a bow in his hair. Pottery, his chosen medium, is not, he regrets, much good for conveying complex ideas, so this book is intended as a supplement and explanation. He wants it to be heard in the background, like 'the hum of my artistic engine', when people view his work. No doubt it would be good for that. However, in its own right, this is one of the most gripping and intelligent accounts of an artist's growth I have ever read. Pared down by Wendy Jones from tape-recorded interviews, it is also lithely succinct and splinter-sharp.

Born in 1960, Perry grew up in a council house in rural Essex and, most importantly, in the shed at the back. This was his father's 'male nest', a wonderland of neat tools and intriguing little drawers, where practical, masculine tasks offered an escape from the muddle of personal relationships. It was here that his artistic obsession with detail began, and his awareness of colour. There were no pictures in the house, except a print of a sailing ship given away with washing powder. But his father, when home-decorating, tried out colours in brushstrokes on the shed wall, and so introduced his son to abstract painting. He still thinks of his art as a 'mental shed', a place of action, but also a refuge, with a window for safely viewing the world.

This idyll ended abruptly when he was five. His mother became pregnant by the local milkman – a busy roundsman, who already had two other customers pregnant – and his father left for good. For Perry it was the most disastrous event of his life. He and his sister seemed to be forgotten. It felt, he recalls, as if nobody was adult enough to care. The milkman, whom his mother went on to marry, was a part-time wrestler and nightclub bouncer, and was soon trying out his combat skills on his new family. Perry's mother would implore her small, terrified son to rescue her when she was being battered, and took to sleeping with a chopper under her pillow in case she was attacked at night. When his stepfather started business as a news-agent, Perry was bullied into helping, and had to get up at 5.30 every morning to deliver papers for two hours. He won a place at King Edward VI Grammar School in Chelmsford, and did brilliantly at first, but started falling asleep in class, which aroused his teachers' suspicions, and they called in the NSPCC.

As an inner sanctuary from these ordeals he evolved an elaborate game, which lasted many years, and was his first multimedia artwork. It centred on his teddy bear, Alan Measles, a dashing and intrepid father-substitute, whose phlegmatic second-in-command was a tortoise knitted by Perry's aunt. Perry was the group's designer and engineer, making guns, ships and planes out of Lego to Alan Measles's orders. They were fighting a cunning and protracted guerrilla war against the far mightier German army, a fictional version of Perry's stepfather, and Perry's bedroom was a secret valley to which Alan Measles returned after each campaign. Its walls were cliff faces, and its candlewick bedspread was the field where the guerrillas camped.

With the onset of puberty a sexual element entered this game. The Germans managed to capture Perry more and more frequently, and subjected him to bondage, dressing him as a girl to make it more humiliating. He has come to see cross-dressing as a cry for a specific kind of attention. A man puts on a little girl's dress because he wants to be free of responsibility, and worshipped just for existing, as little girls are. Bondage, he explains, has a similar appeal, because it always has an element of caring, like being kept as a pet, or hugged. He foraged for women's clothes wherever he could find them, and at the age of fifteen first dared to cross-dress in public, tottering round Chelmsford's central park on high heels, wearing his mail-order auburn wig. It was risky, because he had to change in public lavatories, leaving the gents dressed as a lady and vice versa. This part of his story is as exciting as a spy thriller, and more enlightening, because of Perry's psychological commentary.

Eventually he was rumbled. His sister found his diary, which recorded his transvestite forays, and grassed. There was a terrible hoo-ha. His mother, his stepfather, his father, whom he was now seeing again, and his father's second wife, who had deserted her own children, all erupted in virtuous disgust. It evidently occurred to none of them that their own behaviour as parents and adults hardly qualified them to take a moral high line about a boy's completely harmless desire to dress as a woman. His stepfather, unwilling to lose Perry's labour, allowed him back into the house temporarily, but when he began his art-student course at Portsmouth Polytechnic he was instructed never to return.

Luckily his girlfriends at college, of whom he soon had a lot, were not so stupid. They screamed with laughter when he made a big thing of confessing his transvestism, and eagerly helped to kit him out in frills and flounces. At art school he learnt by his mistakes. One mistake was treating art as work, instead of as a game that absorbed his whole life as Alan Measles had. Another mistake was taking LSD, which, he says, polluted his imagination. And the third mistake was becoming obsessed with fame and fashion. In squats in Portsmouth, and later in London, there were endless fancy-dress parties, with everyone dolled up as pirates or poets or highwaymen, like 1920s Bright Young Things. He got sick of 'hanging out with groovy people' and took up pottery just because it was uncool and down-to-earth.

A sturdy conservative streak shows through. His ideal couple was his Aunt Mary and Uncle Arthur, who lived in a spotless council house, made perfect Marmite toast and gave him Arthur Mee's *Children's Encyclopaedia* – far superior, in his view, to its slick and gaudy modern counterparts, where acquiring knowledge is treated as something you do to get a job, 'instead of the lovely, mysterious adventure in a foreign land that learning seemed to me'.

This volume ends when he is twenty-two, and has just made his first plate. Since then he has been into and come out of therapy, married, had a daughter, and learnt to use pottery as 'a mode of self-psychiatric medication'. With luck we shall hear more about that in volume two.

Naked at Lunch: The Adventures of a Reluctant Nudist
Mark Haskell Smith, 2015

How would you feel walking naked into a roomful of naked strangers? What sort of people do it for fun? Investigating these questions takes American Mark Haskell Smith on nudist holidays in California, Florida, Spain and the South of France. He also joins 1,860 other naked tourists on a Caribbean cruise run by the nudist travel agency Bare Necessities. Though not a nudist himself, he comes from 'the hipster epicentre of Eastside Los Angeles' and has a special feeling for subcultures of all varieties. His last book was about illegal cannabis growers.

His research into nudism met with initial snags. His dermatologist warned him he had sensitive skin and exposing himself to the sun could be fatal. Also, his wife refused to accompany him, and most nudist resorts will take bookings only from couples. He managed to get a Palm Springs concern to waive this rule in his case, only to find that sunbathing nudists are suspicious of a lone naked male skulking in the shade with a notebook. They were clearly unlikely to help him with his enquiries.

But even at a distance he could pick out their most salient feature, which was that they were nearly all old. In America nudism is mainly for retirees. Observing family groups, Haskell Smith notes that while the aged have no hesitation baring their 'fat and saggy' bodies to the elements, youngsters cover up with as many layers of clothing as possible. Explanations for this vary, but one is that the young are daunted by the images of bodily perfection consumerism surrounds them with, whereas the old are past caring what anyone else thinks.

Rules in nudist resorts turn out to be fairly standard. To avoid being shut down as immoral or obscene, they stress that they offer only 'non-sexual' nude recreation. Overt sexual behaviour is banned, as are photography and, of course, swimsuits. At meals you are expected to place a towel between yourself and the chair, but otherwise you remain naked while waiters and staff are clothed. The exception among the venues Haskell Smith visits is the Vera Playa Club in southwest Spain. Unlike most nudist resorts it is not hidden behind high walls and locked gates, but open to everyone. It welcomes families with children – the British are the largest foreign contingent – and nakedness is optional. Clothed and unclothed mingle freely, and no one seems to care. Haskell Smith finds himself getting so used to nudity that to see a crowd of naked people around a swimming pool is 'almost boring'.

At the American Nudist Research Library in Florida, he bones up on the origins of the movement, and finds that modern nudism began in Britain in the 1890s. It spread to France and Germany, where roaming naked through wild terrain became fashionable in the 1920s, and it reached America by the end of the decade. Historically, nudists have tended to be high-minded and self-righteous. They have eagerly embraced progressive causes such as pacifism, vegetarianism, animal rights and religious tolerance. In Germany, however, anti-Semitism became part of the mix. Hitler closed down nudist clubs with unacceptably liberal views and, in 1934, opened new, Nazi-approved clubs, dedicated to clean living and pure breeding.

What teaches Haskell Smith most about clothes and nakedness is not historical research, though, but a week's hiking in the Austrian Alps. The Naked European Walking Tour, founded by a Brit, Richard

Foley, arranges hiking holidays for groups of about twenty adults – male and female, and of various nationalities – who live together naked in a mountain hut and hike every day wearing just boots and a sun hat. Joining them, Haskell Smith at last sees the point of nudism. It is July, and the going is often tough, but his skin, he finds, acts as a natural thermostat. His body remains dry and free, instead of trapped in sweaty clothes as it usually is on hikes. It puts him in mind of Walt Whitman's paean to the 'Adamic air-bath' of outdoor nudity.

On their longest hike – thirteen miles, climbing 2,400 feet – his knee gives out. Limping home in serious pain, he realises that he no longer wants to be naked. Putting on a pair of shorts, though it does not mitigate the pain, seems to give him a kind of psychological protection. On their last evening, packing up to leave, he discovers something else about clothes. The group has lived together naked for a week, and the subject of sex has never arisen. But when one of the young women, who is driving back to Italy that night, comes out dragging her suitcase, he does a double take. She is wearing a sundress and sandals, and he instantly thinks how sexy she looks, though when she was naked he never saw her like that.

This episode is easily the best thing in Haskell Smith's book. Elsewhere he has trouble striking the right tone. His attempts at humour can be puerile and facetious, and his interviews with nudist officials and spokespersons are often tedious, not least because he tries to liven them up by detailing his interviewees' height, weight, hair colour, clothing and what they eat or drink while talking to him.

He does not convert to nudism at the end of his investigation, but he takes a generous view of nudists' aims and beliefs. In his final esti- mate they are not freaks or weirdos but a persecuted minority, and victims of American puritanism. Naked bathing is now illegal in some states. In Montana a third offence can land you in prison for life. Even San Francisco banned public nudity in 2013. Nudist numbers are in decline. In America there are 30 per cent fewer nudist clubs than in 2003. Membership of British Naturism has halved in the last decade to around 10,000. However, nudists are fighting back. There is now a World Naked Bike Ride and a World Naked Gardening Day. We should all be glad. When the last nudist covers up, a living cell of liberty will have died.

Ahead of the Class: How an Inspiring Headmistress Gave Children Back Their Future
Marie Stubbs, 2003

When she arrived with her task force of two trusty former colleagues, things could hardly have been worse. Violence against teachers, fights, confrontations and disruptive behaviour were commonplace. Pupils wandered the corridors chattering into mobile phones and refused to go to classes. Epidemic absenteeism went unchecked. The staff were sunk in rancour and self-pity. One of them described the children as 'scum'. During breaks and lunch hours they barricaded themselves in the school, leaving the children to the mercy of the elements in the playground, a bleak stretch of tarmac encrusted with chewing gum.

Stubbs sailed into this sorry mess like a pocket battleship. There were no compromises. She insisted on pupils standing up and saying 'Good morning, Headmistress' when she entered a room. When they addressed her in their standard mixture of obscenity and moronic pseudo Americanism, they were requested to translate their utterances into decent grammatical English.

After initial disbelief, they complied. By relentless harrying she got them all out of their default mode of denims, baseball caps and trainers, and back into school uniform. She attacked the school buildings and playground to make them bright and welcoming. Corridors were repainted in primary colours and enlivened with flowers and potted plants. The reception area had comfortable chairs and excited pupils on duty to welcome visitors. Electronic signs flashed up announcements and birthday greetings in different languages (52 were spoken by the school's 600 pupils). The playground was marked out for basketball and football, and every year-group had a quiet area with tables, benches and container plants where they could read or eat sandwiches. To the horror of the old guard, the school was thrown open at lunch so that pupils could come in and enjoy its new look.

As St George's was a Catholic school, feeding the spirit was the first priority. Only a third of the pupils came from Catholic families, but a charismatic chaplain, brought in by the new headmistress, welcomed all faiths. A prayer room was set aside for Muslims during Ramadan, so they would not have to watch others eating while they fasted. The overall aim was to make every pupil feel valued, and it was on this issue that the decisive face-off with the old guard occurred. One of Stubbs's first announcements was that, for pupils coming to the end of their GCSE year, there would be a May ball in a top London hotel. To the diehards, this was lunacy. It would give the 'kids' ideas above their station. Besides, let loose in a hotel they would run amok. The pupils, by contrast, were thrilled. They set up a committee to plan the event and spent hours discussing what to wear. Then, on the day of the ball, the staff announced that they would be boycotting it *en masse*. Disaster loomed. But extra adults were drafted in to meet the hotel's regulations, and the ball went ahead. It was a dazzling success. The pupils looked stunning and behaved beautifully. Compliments on their manners arrived next day from the hotel management.

The staff's action seems inexcusable. But it is hard to deny them some sneaking sympathy. Many of their charges had little English, some none. Literacy levels were low. Disastrous family backgrounds and intractable social-welfare problems abounded. Refugee children came and went without warning. In effect, staff had to provide a different kind of teaching for each individual child. It must have been maddening for them, in the midst of all this, to find themselves being chivvied by a terrifying, high-heeled, smart-suited little dynamo with a will of steel and a nonstop smile, who tweaked them about their slovenly clothes, demanded that they set out clear aims for every lesson, and even made jokes about their 'fragile health' when they treated themselves to long stretches of sick leave on grounds of nervous exhaustion. After the ball most of the malcontents resigned. Meanwhile the school's facelift continued apace, sometimes by unconventional means.

Pupils giggled delightedly at their 'mad' headmistress when she issued each habitual latecomer with an alarm clock, and acted out a little charade with two chairs and an overcoat to demonstrate how you got out of bed when it rang. Prefects, library monitors and litter patrols were appointed, and accepted responsibility keenly. A new teacher transformed the art department, displaying pupils' paintings. Choirs and a drama group came into being. Since some pupils clearly arrived unfed, pre-school breakfasts were served in the cafeteria. A homework club gave space and quiet to pupils whose homes lacked them. In response to popular demand for sports fixtures with other schools, permission was obtained for St George's to use Harrow's cricket and soccer pitches, and the Rotary Club donated a minibus for team-transport. Rugby was added to the sports agenda, and a school cadet force started up under a TA officer – both, in Stubbs's view, useful channels for aggression, of which St George's had plenty. At her invitation, a stream of celebrity guests (Kevin Keegan, Ralph Fiennes, Cherie Blair) came to talk to the pupils. At the year's end, St George's had its first ever speech night, where the prizes were distributed by Frank Bruno.

The school governors stayed away. The black side of this story is the lack of support Stubbs says she received from those who were officially supposed to back her up. She found the governors high-handed, remote and unaware of their responsibilities. The

147

attitude of the Roman Catholic Diocesan Education Board ranged from neglect to downright hostility. She learnt at third hand that the LEA 'had a problem' with her and considered her 'conceited and stubborn'. Presumably, now she has blown the whistle, we shall hear the baddies' side of what looks, on the face of it, like shameful dereliction of duty. Meanwhile this vivacious and spirited book leaves one in no doubt that what they all deserve is to be put in the stocks and pelted with school dinners and poster paint.

Worrying: A Literary and Cultural History
Francis O'Gorman, 2015

It is 4.06am. Francis O'Gorman is in bed. His partner and three cats lie fast asleep beside him. But he is awake, worrying. So begins this subtle, exploratory, completely original book. He is worrying about meeting a colleague the next day (O'Gorman is a professor of English at Leeds University). But the reason for his worry does not really matter. His book is about the irrational, trivial worries that bedevil worriers' lives, and would seem ridiculous to anyone else. It is hard to tell how many habitual worriers there are because people are often ashamed to admit their worries. But I'd guess O'Gorman is right to recognise worry as 'a great but buried human trouble'.

Writing a book on an untouched subject would be worrying, even for a non-worrier. O'Gorman concedes at the outset that his topic is 'fuzzy' and its parameters porous. Worry as he experiences it is not exactly a clinical condition, yet it eats away at happiness. 'One thing's pretty sure,' he admits disarmingly, 'I am going to get things wrong.'

Self-doubt on that scale could be crippling, but it frees him from dogmatism. He is not afraid to contradict himself, and he equates changing his mind with seeing both sides of the question – which worriers are good at. So he backtracks even on big issues, such as when worrying began.

He starts by thinking it quite modern. The verb 'worry' in its current sense did not emerge until the late nineteenth century. In earlier usage it meant something like 'maul'. Shakespeare uses it only once, in *Richard III*, about dogs worrying lambs. The Victorians, who first used 'worry' as we do, attributed it to the pressures of modern city life. A 1907 book called *Worry: The Disease of the Age* concluded that only Britons and Americans suffered from it, and that it was really rather distinguished. Spaniards, Greeks and Italians, it observed, were not worriers because they were too idle and did not use their brains enough. Modernist writers quickly seized on the fashionable topic: James Joyce's *Ulysses* and T.S. Eliot's *The Love Song of J. Alfred Prufrock* are both about worriers.

But even if they did not use our word for it, earlier ages must have worried, O'Gorman works out, and he widens his account of human development to take this in. Worrying involves imagining possible futures, an ability that distinguishes us from other animals, and must be almost as old as the act of thinking. For early man, survival depended on worry – about finding food and water, about evading predators. If you did not worry, you were dead.

Not that the evolutionary explanation of worry necessarily, for O'Gorman, rules out other alternatives. The Freudian explanation, that worry is rooted in the trauma of birth and loss of the womb, attracts his attention. So does the idea that worry stems from maternal neglect. He refers to an experiment in which baby rats that had been handled by humans grew up more confident than their siblings that had not been. It emerged that their confidence did not come from human contact, but from the fact that the mother rat, when they were returned to her, licked them all over to remove the human taint, and this made them feel cared for.

The fact that, whatever the cause, worriers can't help worrying doesn't, for a true worrier, make it excusable. If your children are out late and don't phone to say where they are, is your worry a measure of your love for them or mere selfish concern for your peace of mind?

O'Gorman seems too worried to decide one way or another. But it is a good instance of how his approach dissolves what we take to be certainties, such as our love for our children. He is extremely funny about the self-help books that offer to cure worry. What they all insist on is that you must exercise your willpower. You must simply stop telling yourself that you are unsuccessful or inadequate or fat. But what, mutters the worrier, if I am?

He quite sees what is wrong with worry. It is pointless and talking about it can be boring. He remembers evenings in pubs when he has watched friends drink themselves blotto to escape from his painstaking unpicking of his anxieties. All the same, he contends that worry is better than its opposite. It is more thoughtful, serious and genuine than the glossy cheeriness of the happiness industry. It is also more realistic. Given the horrors of human history, an unworried contemplation of the future would be idiotic. It is true that the kind of worry he is writing about arises from trivial, humdrum concerns. But this, he argues, is a point in its favour, since it diverts our minds from catastrophic world events that we can do nothing about.

His personal release from worry is into the past. Holidays give him more pleasure when they are over, and he can replay them in his mind without the fuss and bother they actually entailed. Old photographs are another comfort, because the people in them are released from whatever worries they once had. Worriers, 'trying to get away from the noise in their heads', turn to art or music. When in Venice, he spends hours before Giovanni Bellini's triptych in the church of the Frari because it takes him back to the certainties of the age of faith. Its people 'confidently know what's planned for them'. O'Gorman is a musician as well as a literary critic, and for him contrapuntal music is the best antagonist against the fretful landscapes of worry, particularly the music of J.S. Bach that expresses the confidence that 'everything, whatever happens, fits'.

But is art's reassurance won through worry? As worry is a feat of the imagination, it has the same source as creativity. If we collected all the evidence, would it suggest that the great writers and artists, whatever their differences, have all been worriers? It would be an intriguing subject for O'Gorman's next book.

Alamein to Zem Zem
Keith Douglas, 1946

K eith Douglas was at Oxford when war broke out. He quickly enlisted, was commissioned in the Sherwood Rangers and posted to the Middle East. On 23 October 1942, when the Battle of Alamein began, he was in Cairo, seconded to Divisional HQ. Eager not to miss the action, he took a truck and, against orders, drove to rejoin his regiment. He served as a tank commander throughout the whole of the Allied advance across North Africa, and witnessed the German surrender in Tunisia. *Alamein to Zem Zem* is his story.

Boyishness and inexperience give it flashbulb immediacy. On his first day in action he notices a plane floating high above and watches a succession of silver droplets fall from it, as gracefully as a shower of rain. Just in time, he realises they are bombs and dives into his tank's turret. The strange conditions of tank warfare are graphically conveyed. The regiment rides in Mark III Crusaders, low-slung tanks with long sloping lines that look like speedboats as they race across the desert trailing dust-clouds. Pulverised sand coats everything. Trucks, stores, tanks are dust-colour. Everyone wears a white dust-mask, like a clown. Wounds, even scratches, fester into monstrous desert sores.

An effect of the shattering engine noise inside the tank is that the world outside seems like a silent film. Men shout, vehicles move, shells burst, all soundlessly. Tank battles are remote and impersonal, like space wars. Douglas's first engagement happens when some blotches on the horizon, shivering in the heat haze, are identified as an enemy squadron. The whole regiment opens fire, Douglas feverishly loading rounds into the six-pounder while the turret fills with hot shell-cases. He sees nothing of the combat, learning only later that a victory has been won. The long periods of inaction add to the sense of detachment. For hours the tank crews huddle in their turrets, smoking, nibbling biscuits, reading. Douglas gets through a 'libraryful' of novels in the eight-month campaign.

Outside in the desert sprawl the dead, Germans, Italians, Libyans, New Zealanders, covered in flies. Douglas observes them in wonder, noting how their clothes tend to cover the places where arms or legs should have been, 'as though with an instinct for decency'. A company of Italian Bersaglieri lie 'like trippers taken ill', the breeze fluttering their plumed helmets, their corpses surrounded by picture postcards of Milan, Venice, family snapshots, and other 'pitiable rubbish'. It was this kind of scene that Douglas immortalised in his most famous poem, 'Vergissmeinnicht'.

Loot is plentiful. As the retreating enemy vacate their positions, the tanks of Douglas's regiment take on cargoes of luxuries – crates of cherries, Macedonian cigarettes, cigars, straw-jacketed bottles of Chianti. Their commanders are festooned with Luger and Biretta pistols and German binoculars. 'We shared out the plunder with the immemorial glee of conquerors.' That rather grandiose appeal to history suggests a tinge of guilt. But you do not, as you read, begrudge them their pickings, because their zest is so understandable and their danger so acute. Sitting in a tank, packed with high-explosive ammunition and fuel, and being fired at, requires abnormal neglect of personal welfare. The effect of tanks burning punctuates the narrative with unforgettable scenes of horror.

Within the regiment, personal tensions crackle. The regular yeomanry officers are old-style country gentlemen, with a cavalryman's disdain for rules and procedures. They go to war fragrant with pomade, wearing suede boots, beautifully cut cavalry twill trousers, doeskin waistcoats, silk stocks with gold pins. Other ranks are treated with impeccable politeness, as if they were family retainers. Douglas, like the other new officers, fumes at these lordly throwbacks. Yet he respects them too, for they are utterly fearless and born to command. In his poetic tribute to them, 'Aristocrats', he celebrates them as unicorns – elegant, chivalrous, doomed.

There is no hatred for the enemy. Both sides treat prisoners well. Chatting with some, Douglas finds that one was at Cologne University and competed in athletics against Cambridge before the war. Another was an opera singer in Milan. Everything, from flowers carpeting the desert in winter to vanquished enemies, is seen with a poet's eye and the generosity of youth. Few battle narratives are so exuberant or so sensitive.

Despite being blown up by a mine at Zem Zem and briefly hospitalised, Douglas survived the campaign. He later took part in the D-Day landings. Three days after arriving in Normandy he was killed by a mortar bomb, aged twenty-four.

ANTHROPOLOGY

Feast: Why Humans Share Food
Martin Jones, 2007

The captivating thing about Martin Jones's book is that it makes you feel like an archaeologist without going to the trouble of learning to be one. Each section begins with a detailed reconstruction of an actual meal from the past. The exact dates are impossible to fix, but almost everything else can be pinned down. About 46,000 years ago, in a cave in southern Spain, a group of Neanderthals roasted horse meat. Some 35,000 years later, beside the Euphrates in Syria, a matriarchal community of hunter-gatherers prepared mustard-seed cakes and lentil stew. After another 5,500 years, a large number of Iron Age Britons congregated for an almighty binge and blowout on Hambledon Hill in Dorset. Some two millenniums later, a ceremonial banquet was staged in a palace in Mycenaean Greece. In Roman Colchester, around AD 45, a high-ranking officer threw a dinner party for friends.

After each reconstruction (there are ten in all) Jones takes us through the rigorous detective work that made it possible – the collection of sediment, debris and bone fragments, the investigation of ash and pollen, the use of electron microscopes to identify minute traces of food molecules, including DNA, on grinding stones and cooking vessels, the analysis of fossilised human faeces (revealing, in the case of the Colchester Romans, that their fare included goat, hare, oysters, scallops, raspberries, grapes, figs, dates and, surprisingly, sticklebacks, although Jones thinks these may have been table decoration).

A typical early-human meal, with people sitting round a fire, talking and sharing food, would, Jones points out, be inconceivable for any other species. To most other animals, direct eye contact and opening the mouth to expose the teeth are signs of hostility, fire is terrifying, and placing food midway between several individuals would trigger violence. So how have our strangely abnormal eating habits evolved? Jones searches for clues among his selection of meals from the archaeological record. The key to human survival, he believes, was the enlargement of the feeding group, which increased our ability to respond to changes in climate and environment. An average group size for chimpanzees and gorillas is sixty to seventy. But for Neanderthals and later hunter-gatherers the number rises to 150. To allow group cooperation on this scale the brain's neocortex had to grow, which meant that some other part of the body had to contract, and that part, seemingly, was the gut.

Direct evidence that the gut was larger in early human species is hard to find. But fossil skulls show that the teeth were certainly bigger, so it seems reasonable to suppose that the whole digestive apparatus shrank as humans evolved. What allowed it to shrink, researchers now suggest, was the invention of cooking. Cooking breaks down the fibres in food, and so effectively predigests it. This means the gut can get smaller, and energy saved on digestion allows the brain to grow. Neanderthals cooked their food and had big brains. However, they were not modern humans. Something else was needed, namely eye contact and talk. It is difficult to tell from the remains of a prehistoric meal whether dinner-party conversation occurred. But a clue, Jones suggests, is jewellery. Beads and other adornments invite the gaze, so where they are found we can assume eye contact and the opening up of minds that goes with it. In the more recent, upper-layer deposits in the Spanish cave where the Neanderthals roasted their horse meat, beads made of pierced shells and teeth were found, announcing the arrival of a new kind of diner – our own species, *Homo sapiens*.

The next step on the road to modern eating habits seems to have been the invention of weaving, which produced baskets and similar containers. These allowed grains and other plant seeds to be harvested, and so brought about a revolution in human diet. Jones thinks the transition from hunter-gatherers to agriculture was gradual, taking many thousands of years. The women baking mustard-seed cakes in the Euphrates valley 11,000 years ago were still at a halfway stage, and analysis shows that they gathered and ate a wide range of wild plant seeds as well as nuts, fruits and herbs. But by the time of the palace banquet in Mycenean Greece (1200 BC) the monoculture of domesticated cereal crops was well established.

It had, Jones points out, various harmful results. The pollen record shows that the introduction of vast, controlled arable landscapes led to wholesale loss of trees, and the collapse of woodlands brought widespread soil erosion. It was also bad news for women. The preparation of grains and seeds required hours of back-breaking toil, grinding with a quernstone, and this was evidently not a task for which men volunteered. Female skeletons show curved thigh bones, arthritic knee joints, compression of the lower spine and deformed feet, consistent with kneeling for many hours driving the body back and forth.

Cereal monoculture also transformed politics, making centralised government possible. Grain harvests are measurable, transportable and taxable. Archaeologists excavating the Mycenean palace found a vast complex of storerooms, magazines and silos that housed the grain, wine and olive oil extracted from the population as tribute to the palace's royal occupants. Social stratification was reflected, too, in the different and inferior foodstuffs and drinking vessels provided for the humbler participants in the banquet. All this contrasts with the British Iron Age revellers on Hambledon Hill 1,000 years earlier. They still enjoyed a mixed diet of grain, hazelnuts, milk, grapes, a lot of roast beef and, occasionally, human flesh. Nobody taxed or stock-piled any of this, and they did not have a king or authoritative leader. They lived in matriarchal bands that met periodically to feast and fight.

It is possible that the distinction between rich and poor came only with cereal monoculture, and was unknown in hunter-gatherer communities. Science can detect signs of starvation in ancient skeletons – arrested bone growth and a porosity in the eye sockets caused by anaemia. No such traces have been found in hunter-gatherer skeletons, suggesting that modern agriculture brought population growth, poverty and hunger. Admittedly, it might also suggest that hunter-gatherers had many quicker ways to die than starvation.

Jean-Jacques Rousseau would have been pleased to read Jones's book because, in his *Discourse on the Origin of Inequality* published in 1754, he, too, argued that poverty and inequality came only with agriculture, and that when hunter-gatherers roamed the wild everyone was equal. But what in Rousseau was an imaginative leap is subjected in Jones to intricate scientific testing. As a professor of archaeological science at Cambridge, he might be expected to regret the reduction of the old-style human meal to a group of silent munchers watching television. But he holds, on the contrary, that the flickering television screen is closer to the ancient campfire than the Victorian dining-room table ever was, and that the exchange of conversation that has always accompanied human eating becomes, with television, virtual and worldwide. Whether you agree with that or not, it is typical of Jones's genius for giving food a new look.

The Reinvention of Humanity: A Story of Race, Sex, Gender and the Discovery of Culture
Charles King, 2019

Charles King's new book is about an intrepid group of women and their quest for truth. The man who was astute enough to see their potential, Franz Boas, was born into a wealthy German Jewish family in 1858. He was a dedicated researcher, but none of the existing academic disciplines satisfied him so he created his own, inventing modern anthropology. At the time anthropologists such as J.G. Frazer, author of *The Golden Bough* (now remembered, if at all, as a source for T.S. Eliot's *The Waste Land*), built their theories on mythology and other ancient stories. But Boas decided to investigate real human beings. In 1883 he travelled north to Baffin Island and lived there with the Inuit, learning their language and recording everything he observed, from their migration patterns to how they built igloos. Discovering that he was helpless in the darkness and cold, and depended for survival on a race who were despised in the West as savages, confirmed his lifelong belief that humanity is a single entity and that categories like race – and, he came to believe, gender – are artificial constructs.

In 1887 he emigrated to America, but his revised version of anthropology made him unemployable at first, so he took various dead-end jobs. At the 1893 Chicago World Fair he organised the anthropology exhibit, which attracted little attention compared to the fair's other new inventions such as the zip fastener and chewing gum. But his reputation spread, and in 1899 he was appointed professor of anthropology at Columbia University, where he taught for the rest of his life. His star students were all women, and in 1925 he sent Margaret Mead, now the best known of them, to Samoa to find out whether teenage rebellion was a problem among 'primitive' people as it was in the sophisticated West.

Mead reported that it was not, because Samoan teenagers had nothing to rebel against. Samoan sexual norms were fluid. Virginity was not considered of much importance, same-sex relationships were common and strict fidelity in marriage was unusual. Published as *Coming of Age in Samoa* (1928) these findings are sometimes credited with promoting the mid-century sexual revolution (though arguably the contraceptive pill should take some of the credit). On a later field trip to New Guinea Mead came upon a society in which, she found, females occupied the dominant positions while males spent their time 'primping' and decorating themselves. The follow-up book, *Sex and Temperament* (1935), has been seen as a cornerstone of the feminist movement.

Boas's other students, though less famous, all made original contributions to anthropology. Ella Cara Deloria was born on an Indian reservation and her linguistic skills revolutionised Western understanding of Native American cultures. Zora Neale Hurston, novelist, civil rights activist, and a leader of the interwar Harlem Renaissance, studied voodoo in Haiti, and was the first researcher to photograph a 'zombie' – that is, a reanimated corpse – vouched for by family members as genuine. Ruth Benedict was one of Mead's sizeable contingent of male and female lovers, but as an anthropologist she studied the Pueblo of New Mexico and published a classic text, *Patterns of Culture* (1934). It popularised the term 'cultural relativism', which meant understanding a society's beliefs and values in the context of its own culture, rather than judging it from some external standpoint. This would, Benedict hoped, persuade people to accept 'the coexisting and equally valid patterns of life which mankind has created'.

These were central beliefs of Boas and his group. But far from increasing tolerance cultural relativism enraged conservatives. How, they demanded, can we tell right from wrong if everything is relative? It is a good question, and one that King might have examined more carefully. For it turns out that both he and the anthropologists he studies do in fact, when it comes to the crunch, believe in right and wrong as moral absolutes. He cites, for example, 'genocidal fascism' as a 'great moral evil'. Few would disagree, but a cultural relativist would have to point out that to genocidal fascists it seemed the right and proper course of action at the time. To condemn them from our external standpoint is to refuse to see their behaviour as one of the 'coexisting and equally valid' patterns of life humans have created. So cultural relativism, it emerges, is itself relative. Allowable in some contexts, it is monstrous in others, and it would have saved King's readers puzzlement and exasperation had he made it clear he meant that from the start.

A powerful section of his book points out how far Nazi racist theories originated in America. A work called *The Passing of the Great Race*, published in 1916 by the American lawyer and zoologist Madison Grant, lamented the contamination of America's pure white race by hordes of multicoloured mongrel immigrants. Hitler wrote enthusiastically to Grant, calling his book 'my Bible', and the theory of 'racial poisoning' elaborated in *Mein Kampf* adopts Grant's ideas with the simple substitution of Jews for coloured races. Grant's eugenicist programme was, King notes, widely accepted in America. In the interwar years three quarters of American universities introduced courses on eugenics, many using Grant's book as a set text. By the early 1930s twenty-eight of the forty-eight American states had laws authorising the compulsory sterilisation of people the authorities deemed unfit to breed.

A weakness of anthropology as practised by the Boas group is that it depends on hearsay, which excludes it from usual definitions of science. Whether to believe informants was always problematic. A later researcher (relegated to a footnote by King) tracked down and questioned one of Mead's original interviewees who admitted that the stuff Mead had been told about sex in Samoa was just a hoax. A later researcher in New Guinea found no evidence of the gender roles Mead described. However, these doubts do not detract from the courageous idealism of the Boas group, or from King's hugely informative and adhesively readable account of them.

Don't Sleep, There Are Snakes: Life and Language in the Amazonian Jungle
Daniel Everett, 2008

Over the past thirty years, Daniel Everett has spent long periods in one of the earth's remotest places, pursuing something still more remote, the origins of human language. In 1977, he, his wife Karen and their three young children went to live with a hunter-gatherer tribe called the Piraha, who occupy a few scattered jungle villages on the banks of the Maici, a tributary of the Amazon. It is not a place many would choose as home. In the river, hazards range from 30ft anacondas to microscopic fish keen to enter your bodily orifices. On land, there are tarantulas, scorpions and swarms of mosquitoes that darken the air and bite through your clothes. Everett and his wife went there as missionaries, aiming to translate the Bible into Piraha. Others had tried to do this, on and off, for 200 years, but they had all given up, finding the Pirahas recalcitrant and their language impossible. It does not even sound like a language – more, it has been said, like the melodic chattering of exotic songbirds.

Everett, however, was resolute. The son of a drunken Texan cowboy, he had played guitar in rock bands and was into drugs until, at high school, he met Karen, whose parents were missionaries, and became a born-again Christian. Although Karen and their eldest daughter almost died of malaria in the first few months, he – and they – stuck it out, and he has become not just the world's first non-Piraha Piraha-speaker, but a professor of linguistics whose discoveries question basic modern assumptions about what language is.

Far from finding the Pirahas recalcitrant, he liked them from the start, perhaps because of his own easy-going youth. They are, he reports, patient, kind, peaceful and contented. They care for the elderly and handicapped and laugh a lot. They have no chiefs or authority figures, and are admirably laid-back. There is no trace among them of the colourful rituals or the rich oral history that primitive peoples are supposed to have. They do not paint themselves or wear feathers or have ceremonies. The dead are buried haphazardly and there is no such thing as marriage. Couples live together, and when one of them tires of it he or she goes and lives with someone else. They have no myths about how the world began, no fictions and no art except necklaces made of seeds, teeth and drink-can pull-tabs, which women wear to ward off evil spirits. They live for the present, incurious about the past and uncaring for the future. They never preserve food, and although they make rudimentary tools and weave palm-leaf baskets they throw them away once used and make new ones next time. They are fit and lean and, as Everett's photographs show, have beautiful, broad, innocent faces, like beings straight out of Eden.

True, they can seem callous. Women are left to give birth alone and when things go wrong they are not aided. Everett heard of a young mother who screamed for help for hours until she and the baby died, while the Pirahas sat passively by. When he and Karen adopted an orphaned newborn baby, feeding it hourly through a plastic tube, the Pirahas waited until they went out and then poisoned it. Everett attributed both incidents to a kind of Darwinian realism, which he came to regard as healthy. The Pirahas, he deduced, believe you must be fit to survive, and see no point in prolonging the existence of the unfit. But perhaps the baby incident also revealed resentment of his interference, in line with the Pirahas' normal hostility to intruders. Once, when a number of them got drunk on liquor supplied by a river trader, he overheard them plotting to murder him. He marched into their hut and confiscated their weapons, and they were seemingly too drunk or cowed to resist. Next day they apologised.

Piraha is unrelated to any known language, and is at once simple and unfathomably complex. It has one of the smallest sets of speech sounds in the world, consisting of three vowels and eight consonants for men (three vowels and seven consonants for women). It has no comparatives, and its nouns do not have different plural and singular forms. Each verb, on the other hand, can have up to sixteen suffixes that modify its meaning, with the result, Everett works out, that there are 65,536 possible forms for every Piraha verb. It has no fixed colour terms, no numbers and no words for 'all' or 'every'. Its sentences are simple assertions containing one verb and they never have relative clauses embedded in them. According to the theories of Noam Chomsky, the dominant force in modern linguistics, embedded relative clauses are a vital feature of all human language, distinguishing it from animal noises, and this is one reason why Everett's revelations have caused such a furore.

His disagreement with Chomsky goes further. He does not believe that humans have a 'universal grammar' hard-wired into their brains. On the contrary, he argues, grammar and all other features of a language evolve within a culture and reflect its mind-set. In his view, an 'immediacy of experience principle' (IEP) underlies the Pirahas' life and language. They have no interest in the past and their language has no perfect tense. They have no words for numbers or colours because these are general and generalisation violates the IEP. For Pirahas, a thing is its own particular colour, not 'red' or 'green'. Five men and five Brazil nuts have nothing in common, though our generalising mentality thinks they have. Everett ran numeracy and literacy classes that the Pirahas eagerly attended, but none of them ever learnt to count up to ten, or to understand that the random marks they made on paper were different from the words Everett wrote out for them to copy.

What they can do is, however, far more fascinating than what they cannot. Their language has a wide array of tones, stresses and syllable lengths, and its speakers can dispense with vowels and consonants altogether and convey their meaning by whistling, singing or humming. Hum-speech is particularly used by mothers talking to small children. Perhaps hearing this is something like hearing the very beginning of language, when it was just emerging from the rhythmic noises made by our human ancestors.

Everett did not convert the Pirahas to Christianity. The IEP dictates that they believe only what they see, or hear from a reliable eyewitness, and once they realised Everett had not met Jesus they lost interest. He, however, found their viewpoint so persuasive that he abandoned his religious faith. To an outsider this seems odd, particularly as his decision meant the end of his marriage to Karen and the break-up of his family. For one thing, although the Pirahas have no word for God, they believe in spirits and see them frequently, so they are not a good model for the rational atheism Everett has embraced. Further, he stresses the vital importance of caring about other cultures and languages, especially endangered ones such as the Pirahas, of whom barely 300 remain alive. Yet it is a leading Piraha characteristic that they despise other cultures, calling themselves 'straight heads' and speakers of other languages 'crooked heads'. It is impossible to imagine them taking an interest in comparative linguistics, and if they are wrong on this it is not apparent why Everett thinks them right in religion. However, these quibbles do not in the least detract from the power of his remarkable book. It is written with an immediacy even a Piraha might envy, and its conjunction of physical and intellectual adventure is irresistible.

Letters to Lily on How the World Works
Alan Macfarlane, 2005

Alan Macfarlane is a professor of anthropology at Cambridge, and he has a granddaughter Lily, aged seven. He has written these letters for her to read when she is seventeen, and I hope she finds them less confusing than I do. His purpose, he says, is to tell her what human beings are really like, and to demonstrate how odd, anthropologically speaking, she and everything she believes in are. At seventeen, she will be a young woman with an individual identity and legal rights. She will consider herself the equal of any man, and will be free to choose her own husband, job, religion and political affiliation. In all these respects, her grandfather admonishes her, she will be highly untypical. In most other cultures throughout the world she would have been married already and probably have several children. Her inferiority to men would be obvious and unquestioned. She would have no legal rights. Her husband would have been chosen for her. Her childhood from the age of five would have been spent slaving in the fields, and she would be sick almost all the time, suffering from septic sores, coughs, diarrhoea and intestinal worms, if nothing worse.

No doubt Lily will accept the sad truth of all this. But what will surely strike her as strange is that her grandpa believes these other cultures, with their horrible injustices and cruelties, are just as good as her own Western culture. He is not, she will know, a cruel man. He maintains that rearing animals for food is equivalent to 'cannibalism'. He even worries about the propriety of killing slugs in the garden. Yet his anthropological training has convinced him that all human cultures are equally 'valid', and none is 'intrinsically morally better' than any other. Ideals such as democracy, equality before the law and human rights are just 'local traditions', developed in Britain and America, and there is no reason to prefer them to their opposites, which are far commoner worldwide.

Lily will, I think, be especially surprised by her grandpa's favourable estimate of witchcraft. Most human societies today believe in witchcraft, he tells her, and it is 'intellectually and socially attractive'. Its advantage is that, when misfortune happens to you, you can identify whose bad magic is responsible and punish or kill them. The alternative is to believe that misfortune is just misfortune, which is 'unsatisfactory', compared to torturing and killing a witch. Lily may notice that, elsewhere in the book, he grows indignant about the thousands of innocent people who were hanged and burned as witches in sixteenth-century Europe, and he likens this to America's current 'witch-hunt' against the so-called 'axis of evil', of which he disapproves. Yet if believing in and hunting down witches is such a good idea, it is hard to see what he is complaining about. Further, it is clear from the parts of the book where he writes about Western science that he thinks scientific research is the only true path to 'reliable knowledge', and knows that witchcraft is an illusion. So how can it be intellectually attractive? It is all very muddling.

Lily will learn from the book that in most other cultures in the world she would have no individual identity, but would exist only as a member of a family group. Loyalty to family would be paramount, and would far outweigh Western superstitions such as justice and the rule of law. If she were brought before a court she would naturally lie to protect family members. She would expect jobs and privileges in the family's control to be distributed within the family, not outside. In the West, this is what we call 'corruption'. But for Macfarlane that is a very parochial view. Globally, corruption is the dominant practice. True, it leads to a breakdown of state control. But the functions that we expect the police and courts to fulfil are carried out in other cultures, Macfarlane explains, by criminal gangs. In Russia, India, southern Italy and elsewhere, mafia-style organisations 'provide the assurances and security that the state cannot provide'. Nor, Macfarlane assures us, are they as bad as they are painted. They may sometimes have to resort to murder, but more often a mere gesture, such as killing your favourite pet and leaving it on your pillow, will be enough to persuade you to accept their authority.

I imagine Lily may find this upsetting, and at the least she will surely want to ask grandpa why our Western culture is not morally better than one where criminals run the justice system. She may inquire, too, how his accounts of tribal customs among the Yoruba of Nigeria, the Yanomamo of Venezuela, and other exotic peoples, are meant to affect her own conduct. In almost all the world's cultures outside England and America, he says, it is considered reasonable for a man to strike his wife, and unreasonable for her to strike back. Suppose (which heaven forbid) Lily were to marry a man who beat her. Should she reflect that this is an almost universal practice and refrain from retaliating, or should she, at the risk of being anthropologically incorrect, kick him in the crutch? Her grandpa is of no help in resolving such dilemmas. As an anthropologist he is, it seems, disqualified from making any useful judgments at all, and the most he can tell her is that some people think one thing and some another.

I suspect, however, that seven-year-old Lily will already be shrewd enough to see through his posture of academic impartiality. Whatever he says, she is unlikely to believe that he considers his own views no more important than those of a Nigerian Yoruba, or of the eco-friendly, witch-hunting Nepalese villagers among whom he has lived while pursuing anthropological research. His pride in being a fellow of King's College, Cambridge, and walking on the lawns, from which the common people are debarred, is patent even to readers of this book. His advice to Lily to visit his website, where she will find 'lectures I've given and television films I've been in' does not suggest a shrunken ego. He extols the English for inventing and exporting democratic politics, religious toleration and equality before the law, which would make no sense if one culture were really no better than another.

In the past, he believes, the backbone of English liberty were the independent 'yeomen', to whom he feels some affinity, living as he does in a seventeenth-century yeoman's house, and he advises modern readers that they will find the archetypal English yeoman in J.R.R Tolkien's depiction of Bilbo Baggins, Frodo and their friends. It may come as a surprise to Lily that her academic grandpa is a hobbit at heart. But at least Bilbo, waging his war on terror against the evil Mordor, would have had no truck with anthropological blah about the equal validity of all cultures.

BIOGRAPHY

The Fortunes of Francis Barber: The True Story of a Jamaican Slave Who Became Samuel Johnson's Heir
Michael Bundock, 2015

Francis Barber was Dr Johnson's Black servant. He turns up in every biography of Johnson, but this is the first he has had all to himself, and it is a joy – elegant, precise, formidably informed. Michael Bundock clears away a fog of falsehoods and rebalances the story, not always in Johnson's favour.

Born a slave on a Jamaican sugar plantation, Barber was brought to London in 1750, when he was seven or eight, by the plantation owner Colonel Bathurst, whose son Richard was a friend of Johnson. Bathurst had the child baptised (which suggests Barber might have been his own son by a woman slave), then packed him off to a boarding school in Yorkshire. Two years later, Johnson's wife Tetty died, he was overwhelmed by grief, and the Bathursts evidently thought a child's company might lift his spirits. So young Barber was retrieved from Yorkshire and given to Johnson.

It could have been disastrous. Johnson was a grotesque figure, sometimes alarming even to adults, and the shifting population of oddballs and derelicts he shared his house with were scarcely ideal kindergarten staff. However, it worked, up to a point. Trust and affection between master and servant grew. Young Barber was evidently allowed into the upstairs workroom in Gough Square where the great dictionary was prepared. Some spare dictionary sheets survive on which he has practised writing his name.

Then, in the summer of 1756, he walked out of Johnson's house, seemingly after a quarrel, and got work and lodging with an apothecary in Cheapside. Bathurst had died the previous year, and in his will he had left Barber a sum of money and his freedom. It may be that up to then Barber thought himself Johnson's slave, rather than his servant, and deduced that he was not free to leave. That would be a quite reasonable assumption. Slavery was far from extinct in eighteenth-century England. Newspapers advertised slaves for sale and offered rewards for the return of runaways. Slave collars were still in use, and Bundock cites a goldsmith who advertised 'silver padlocks for blacks or dogs'.

Johnson was dismayed. 'My boy is run away,' he wrote. He regarded slavery as a 'dreadful wickedness', partly, Bundock suggests, because of what Barber had told him of plantation life. For him, Barber was more a son than a slave. He put a notice in the *Daily Advertiser* to say that 'Francis Barber, a black boy, has been for some months absent from his Master', and would be 'kindly received' if he returned.

Apparently Barber got in touch and there was a reconciliation. But after a year with the apothecary he chose not to return to Johnson's house. Instead he joined the navy. Friends of Johnson saw this as gross ingratitude. But it was, Bundock points out, an intelligent decision. In the navy professional skill mattered more than colour. Black sailors ate the same food, wore the same clothes and shared the same quarters as whites, and consequently Black people were far commoner in the navy than in the population at large. In his two years as a sailor Barber saw active service aboard the frigate *Stag* and, so far as we know, was happy and fulfilled.

But Johnson robbed him of his chosen career. He had an irrational prejudice against the navy, and pulled strings to get Barber discharged, on the grounds that he had been press-ganged, which was untrue. He wanted Barber to be a scholar, like himself, and sent him to learn Latin and Greek at a celebrated grammar school in Bishop's Stortford. Barber was twenty-six by this time, and thrusting him into the daily company of schoolboys seems a crassly unimaginative act. However, Barber stuck it out, though he made little progress in the classics.

After this he evidently resigned himself to staying with Johnson. In 1773, he married a young white woman, Elizabeth Ball, and she came to live in the house, too. The mixed marriage sparked racist bigotry in Johnson's circle, and when Elizabeth gave birth to a white daughter the more malignant gossips, such as Johnson's friend Mrs Thrale, took it as proof of her adultery. Johnson, though, cherished Elizabeth and gave her a treasured prayer book that he had once given Tetty. Pleasingly, Bundock finds no reliable evidence to support the rumours that the Barbers' marriage was unhappy. Their son, born in 1783, was christened Samuel, after their friend and benefactor.

In his will Johnson left Barber the bulk of his estate. However, he did not receive the proceeds directly. Johnson appointed three trustees to manage the bequest and pay Barber an annuity. So even this final generosity carried with it the implication that Barber was not fit to make decisions for himself. It brings to mind Mrs Thrale's recollection that when Johnson 'spoke of negroes, he always appeared to think of them as a race naturally inferior'.

Of course, that might just be Thrale's prejudice talking. But it is typical of Bundock's candour that he does not merely discount it. He is a lawyer by profession, and one of the great pleasures of reading his completely captivating book is to watch him gathering all the evidence and teasing out the truth, even when it would be nicer to believe something else. Reluctantly, for example, he decides that

Joshua Reynolds's soulful *A Young Black*, often taken to be a portrait of Barber, actually depicts Reynolds's own servant.

If Johnson did doubt Barber's financial acumen, he was not wrong. After his master's death Barber took his family to Johnson's birthplace, Lichfield, in Staffordshire, and prospered at first. He ensured young Samuel had a good education, and even opened a school himself. Bundock believes he might have been England's first Black schoolmaster. But long before his death in 1801 he was reduced to borrowing from, among others, James Boswell. In return he provided Boswell with invaluable information for his *Life of Johnson*, published in 1791. Bundock's is one of the very few books about Johnson worthy to stand beside that classic.

Sarah: The Life of Sarah Bernhardt
Robert Gottlieb, 2010

Sarah Bernhardt makes today's celebrities look piffling. She was as showy as the aurora borealis and as promiscuous as a bedbug, and at her funeral half a million mourners lined the streets of Paris, weeping and kneeling.

Her story is a mushroom cloud of gossip, rumour, scandal and scholarship, and condensing it into 236 pages requires rare self-restraint. But Robert Gottlieb, a distinguished American publisher and a former editor of *The New Yorker*, has produced a book that is wise, funny, affectionate and enjoyable as well as blessedly compact.

Glamour was Bernhardt's element but her roots were in the squalor and corruption of the second empire. Her mother, Youle, the daughter of a Jewish oculist in Amsterdam, ran away to Paris as a teenager and set up as a high-class prostitute. Rossini and Alexandre Dumas were among her clients, but the most important was the Duc de Morny, the brother of the emperor Napoleon III. Who fathered Sarah is unclear, but it was probably an obscure naval officer called Morel.

Youle's profession left little time for motherhood so, soon after giving birth in 1844, she packed Sarah off with a nurse to a farm in Brittany. Later she sent her as a boarder to a Paris convent. She began grooming her and her two sisters for careers in prostitution as early as possible. The great Parisian gossipmongers the Goncourt brothers recorded that Youle 'made whores of her daughters as soon as they turned thirteen'.

That Sarah should become an actress was de Morny's idea. He entered her for the Paris Conservatoire, and a note bearing his signature, passed among the judges at her audition, ensured her acceptance. She did badly there, but at the end of her course de Morny intervened again to get her a coveted job at the Comédie-Française. Once more she was a failure. She had a weak voice, and people joked about her thinness. If she swallowed a pill, they said, it made her look pregnant. After eight months she tore up her contract and walked out. For the next two years she lived by prostitution, setting up a 'court' of wealthy lovers in her white-satin salon. She contrived to look flushed and tubercular, and would prick her gums with a needle and show her lovers her blood-speckled handkerchief to extract donations.

Her sister Régine died aged nineteen after a miserable life of prostitution and neglect. What saved Sarah was giving birth to a son, Maurice. She boasted that his father was a Belgian prince, but many doubted this, including the prince. So she resolved to bring him up unaided. She got work at the state-owned Odéon theatre, thanks, once again, to de Morny's corrupt interference. The manager told her, on arrival, that he would never have taken her on unless coerced. But this time she flourished, scoring her first triumph as a troubadour in a flowery romantic piece called Le Passant. Among her great roles were Racine's *Phèdre*, Marguerite in Dumas's *La Dame aux Camélias* (which became Verdi's *La Traviata*), and *Hamlet*.

It was at the Odéon that she started her lifelong habit of sleeping with her leading men. Her non-professional lovers included Charles Haas, the model for Proust's Charles Swann, and, perhaps, Napoleon

III. Her weak voice, now proclaimed 'silvery', enchanted audiences, but it was her passionate intensity that most impressed. She acted, one critic wrote, 'with her heart and entrails'. Not everyone liked it. According to Chopin's mistress George Sand she was a 'great tart' and 'definitely stupid'. But that was a minority view. During the disastrous Franco-Prussian war of 1870 she turned the Odéon into a military hospital where she personally tended the wounded and dying, remaining at her post throughout the bombardment of Paris and the Commune. It made her a national icon.

With the peace, Victor Hugo returned from exile, aged seventy, and joined her retinue of lovers, sharing her favours with the artist Gustave Doré, the Prince of Wales and many more. Paris police reports of the 1870s specify her highly respectable clientele – businessmen, MPs – with details of the jewellery they gave her and how much she charged. She toured Europe with her own acting company and was showered with gifts by the tsar of Russia, the emperor of Austria and other royals. She undertook nine American tours, the last during the First World War when she was seventy-three and had had one leg amputated. In Paris she ran her own theatre, its walls lined with yellow velvet, with her name spelt out high on the facade in 5,700 light bulbs.

Her genius for self-advertisement told her exactly what would catch people's attention and keep her in the news. Early in her career she began collecting animals – a monkey, a cheetah, a lynx – and when extra publicity was needed, she added a new recruit to the menagerie. There was a tiger cub ('Don't hold him too near,' she warned visitors, 'he has a way of dabbing at your eyes') and an alligator that she used to take to bed until it drank too much champagne and died. She acquired a silk-lined coffin and had herself photographed sleeping in it, clasping a spray of lilies. In 1878 she went up in a hot-air balloon and wrote a book about it that was an instant bestseller. She took up sculpture (her studio in the Boulevard de Clichy was later Picasso's), and posed for the press beside one of her portrait busts, wearing a natty white silk trouser suit, presumably envisaged as a sculptor's working gear. On and off stage she was dressed by the leading couturiers and designers and glittered with jewels.

Purists were disgusted. Henry James dubbed her 'the muse of the newspaper'. She was not an actress, he spluttered, but followed 'the trade of a celebrity, pure and simple' (not, surely, adjectives he would have applied to Sarah had he thought for a moment). What she was really like as an actress is impossible to say. Thousands of eyewitness accounts survive but even professional observers seem to take leave of their senses when describing her. Ellen Terry said she was 'as transparent as an azalea, only more so'. In the contemporary photos Gottlieb reproduces she looks dismayingly hammy, but that was the manner of the time. George Bernard Shaw deplored her 'childishly egotistical' way of acting; she did not enter into a character, he objected, but 'substituted herself for it'. She was inordinately fond of death scenes because they focused the sympathies of everyone in the theatre solely upon her. In play after play she was poisoned, stabbed, garrotted, burnt to death or slowly consumed by TB, and she visited hospitals, morgues and even executions to make her pangs more accurate.

What her adoring fans responded to was not just her art but her indomitable spirit. Only months before her death in March 1923 she was still acting and rehearsing. At last, another actress had to play her role, and she lay in bed on the opening night mouthing her lines when she knew the curtain had gone up. Not long before that, an outspoken friend had asked her when she planned to give up love. 'With my dying breath,' she said.

Bulwer Lytton: The Rise and Fall of
a Victorian Man of Letters
Leslie Mitchell, 2003

His high-society melodramas thrilled the middle classes. His novels glamorising criminal types soared to bestsellerdom on an inflammable cloud of moral outrage ('a disgrace to the writer, a shame to us all', *The Times*). His apocalyptic spellbinder, *The Last Days of Pompeii*, romped through thirty-two editions. His farragos of fake-medievalism out-Scotted Scott.

Yet nobody reads him now. Leslie Mitchell blames his eclipse on the reaction against Victoriana after the First World War. That may be so, but there are good reasons for not reading Lytton. He wrote turgid, prosy prose. He could not create characters, producing instead improbably chivalric heroes, and heroines so pure and childlike they appear mentally retarded. His critical opinions suggest he did not understand what literature was. He had doubts about *Middlemarch* ('a poor book') and believed the true spark of genius resided in dashing blades like himself, rather than 'among the village gossips of Miss Austen'.

Mitchell concentrates on the man not the writer, which is the right choice, for he was a fascinating if disastrous human being. His father, a fiercely philistine general, died when he was four, and his mother, who came from a line of dreamy eccentrics, smothered him with affection. She tried him at various schools, but decided he was too precocious for education, a view the schools shared. At Cambridge, he found Trinity offensively serious, and quickly moved to a less demanding college. He sported magnificent side whiskers and the full peacock rig of the Regency dandy, fashions that, to the delight of Victorian caricaturists, he never relinquished. Vanity was his master passion. He once remarked, with unusual self-knowledge, that he was the vainest man who ever lived. On his father's side he traced his ancestry to the pre-Norman kings of Britain, and he decorated

Knebworth, the country house near Stevenage he inherited from his mother, with a formidable array of gargoyles, turrets and heraldic beasts to match his own antiquity.

At twenty-four, he married a famous Irish beauty, Rosina Wheeler. His letters praised her 'genius for kissing' and expressed his devotion through doggy infantilism. She was 'Poodle'; he, 'zoo own puppy'. A son and a daughter duly arrived, but it was soon apparent that Lytton found Rosina a bit of a handful, though he warmly denied it ('me does not wish oo to be a bit more stupid than oo is'). His mother, meanwhile, disapproved of the match and discontinued his allowance. Poverty drove him to authorship, which he would otherwise have considered beneath him, but Rosina refused to economise, insisting that 'the vile details of household affairs' must be left to the servants. Tension mounted. She complained, truthfully it seems, that he beat and kicked her even when she was pregnant, and his infidelities aroused her furious resentment. Lytton's were the ethics of the rabbit warren. Servant girls, milliners, women of fashion, aspirant authoresses, came and went in an unending stream, and he enriched the nineteenth-century gene bank with a plenteous crop of illegitimate children.

They separated after seven turbulent years, and Rosina devoted the rest of her life to vengeance. She pursued Lytton with lawsuits and mounted a campaign of public defamation. Volleys of letters, sometimes as many as twenty a day, arrived at the clubs and hotels he frequented, addressed to 'Sir Liar Coward Bulwer Lytton'. She published a string of novels, starting with *Cheveley* in 1839, in which the shortcomings of her husband and the whole Lytton clan were derisively exposed. When he stood for parliament she broke into the election meeting and made a speech from the hustings claiming he had murdered their daughter Emily (who had died at nineteen), possibly after an incestuous relationship. She wrote to Queen Victoria advising her that Lytton had committed sodomy with Disraeli. In retaliation Lytton had her briefly committed to an asylum, but there was a public outcry and she had to be released.

The real victims were the Lytton children. Neither parent had the least regard for them. Rosina admitted she did not understand what maternal love meant. They were brought up by carers, and Lytton, while never stinting his own comforts, kept them on short-commons. Emily died alone, probably of TB, in a Brompton Road lodging house, wearing, it was rumoured, a borrowed nightdress. Robert survived, and rose to be Viceroy of India, but his early years make bleak reading. For Lytton, the hullabaloo Rosina stirred up was above all an affront to his dignity. Artists, he believed, were a race apart, and it was intolerable to have his doings dragged before the vulgar gaze. His interest in spiritualism, mesmerism and mystical enterprises confirmed his sense of his own distinction. There was, he found, a 'sort of electric link' between creative persons like himself and God. It was revealed to him in a dream that the afterlife would be selective. No tradesmen or peasants would be admitted. Gentlemanly quiet would prevail, and coffee would be served.

By contrast with his private life his political career was, Mitchell shows, highly creditable. As a radical MP he espoused all the right causes – the emancipation of slaves, universal education for boys and girls of all classes, freeing Ireland from the depredations of English landlords. As secretary of state for the colonies he understood that without its colonial empire England would become a 'third-rate nation', but refused to countenance maintaining colonial rule by force. If the colonies wanted to be free they should be. Even his mistakes were idealistic. He opposed the repeal of the Corn Laws because he saw that cheap imported wheat, while it would feed the starving poor, would destroy the centuries-old life of the English countryside. He believed the Crimean War should not have happened. Tsar Nicholas was, he agreed, a tyrant, but the war's aims could have been effected by diplomatic means. It riled him that Palmerston, the prime minister responsible, was fêted 'like Mama England's spoiled child', instead of being brought to book. It has a strangely familiar ring.

Mitchell's biography is richly entertaining and full of new insights. In dusting down and touching up a Victorian monument, it opens perspectives on the whole era, especially its sexual freedoms, its superstitions and its love of scandal. He omits, perhaps because he thinks it too familiar, the one thing most people know about Lytton, which is that when his friend Charles Dickens showed him the proofs of *Great Expectations*, he persuaded Dickens to change the ending. In the original version Pip and Estella remain lonely and apart. It was on Lytton's advice that Dickens introduced the heart-stopping moment when their hands touch, and Pip says: 'I saw no shadow of another parting from her'. Set against that intervention, Lytton's own literary output counts for little. But that one critical feat should earn him the gratitude of readers as long as English lasts.

Damned to Fame: The Life of Samuel Beckett
James Knowlson, 1996

Samuel Beckett: The Last Modernist
Anthony Cronin, 1996

The World of Samuel Beckett, 1906–1946
Lois Gordon, 1996

James Knowlson's *Damned to Fame: The Life of Samuel Beckett* is a literary biography of supreme distinction. Knowlson knew Beckett for more than twenty years, they corresponded regularly, and Beckett chose him as his official biographer. The depth of detail he commands is formidable, and instantly puts other Beckett studies in the shade. If he sometimes hagiographs, he also convinces you that Beckett was unusually hagiographable. You end up feeling he would have made a marvellous Pope. True, he was a Protestant, and did not believe in

God. But these incidentals apart, he had all the qualities a great pontiff needs – cast-iron integrity, boundless generosity, saintly self-denial. He hated the body and its pleasures as intensely as the most austere desert Father. His art pursued a spiritual ideal that demanded the renunciation of virtually all recognisable human qualities. His wit would have been a wow on Papal walkabouts. Once when a bystander asked him if he minded that she had named her dog after him, he riposted: 'Don't worry about me. What about the dog?'

Like many saints, he came from a rather worldly background. Father was a prosperous quantity surveyor, and they lived among doilies and finger bowls in a smart new Tudorbethan villa, with tennis court, in the Dublin commuter belt. At public school (Portora) young Sam excelled at boxing, golf and cricket. He is the only winner of a Nobel Prize for Literature to appear in Wisden, scoring eighteen and twelve for Dublin University against Northants in 1926. The philistine atmosphere at home does not seem to have bothered him in the least. He enjoyed Sexton Blake and Gilbert and Sullivan, whose operas he knew by heart, and drove a natty sportster, his father's gift. Apart from the death of a pet hedgehog, nothing occurred in his formative years to justify the universal pessimism he later specialised in.

It was higher education that put paid to this idyll. At Trinity College Dublin he became fascinated by avant-garde literature, painting and theatre. In Paris he met James Joyce, and joined his circle of worshippers, learning to hold a cigarette in the same way, and wearing uncomfortably narrow shoes. Compared with Parisian café life, the prospect of paid employment seemed uncongenial. He tried lecturing at Trinity but hated it and despised the students. His decision to become a writer upset his parents, who found his efforts either impenetrable or shockingly rude, a view shared by most of the publishers he approached. Though determined, he felt guilty about letting his family down. He started to drink heavily, and his health gave way. Palpitations, night sweats and abcesses, which chose the most distressing places to appear (scrotum, roof of mouth) were to plague him for the rest of his life. In the midst of this dismal time, his father died suddenly of a heart attack, his last words, 'What a morning!', providing a fine example of Beckettian irony.

Devastated, Beckett succumbed to depression, and his mother sent him to London for two years' psychotherapy. In retrospect, he saw this as a turning point. On the analyst's couch he came to repent of his 'boozing, sneering and lounging' and his 'arrogant otherness'. But it was the Second World War that really changed him. In 1936–37 he spent seven months in Germany (his lost diary of the trip has been recovered by Knowlson), where talk with artists and intellectuals alerted him to the menace of Nazism. Returning to Paris when war broke out, he joined the Resistance, typing and translating for an intelligence-gathering cell belonging to the British Special Operations Executive. When the cell was betrayed (by a Catholic priest), he and his partner Suzanne Déscheveux-Demesnil escaped from the Gestapo to a remote village in Provence, where Beckett worked as a farmhand, enduring drudgery and near starvation. He rejoined the Resistance and patrolled with the local maquisards who were harrying the retreating Germans in the last weeks of the war. His courage earned him the Croix de Guerre. In later years, when his Resistance activities were mentioned, he dismissed them as 'boy scout stuff'.

Knowlson reckons that Beckett's war service, and his voluntary work in the early months of peace in a Red Cross hospital in Normandy, brought him closer to ordinary people. The conceited, shut-in young man of the 1930s became helpful and thoughtful for others. He opted to write in French, because it freed him from the dense allusiveness that made his English work inaccessible. No doubt there is something in this, but it can make Beckett sound altogether too user-friendly. He remained an uncompromisingly obscure writer, and frankly admitted that he did not care whether he could be followed or not. He was surprised by the success of *Waiting for Godot*, considering it largely the result of misunderstanding. Directing his own plays, he firmly vetoed any attempt by the actors to introduce human feeling. When *Play* was put on at the National, he insisted on the lines being delivered so fast they could not possibly be intelligible. This was not just perversity. He distrusted language because it falsified, he believed, the deepest self. His bleak vision of human ignorance, impotence and loneliness made communication an absurd endeavour. He could not, he said, write down any words without the conviction that they would inevitably be lies.

His morose insistence on human futility links him with a certain kind of religious fanatic. So does his fixation about textual purity. He defended the integrity of his own plays as if they were Holy Writ. Not a syllable must be changed; even the stage directions had to be obeyed to the letter. Furious on hearing that a Dutch company planned staging Godot with an all-female cast, he took them to court. When that failed, he imposed a total ban on productions of his work in Holland. He had a Puritanical contempt for luxury and display. Fame appalled him, because it made solitude more difficult. With money left by his mother, he built a dull little house at Ussy-sur-Marne, thirty miles from Paris, where he secluded himself, subsisting on rice and stewed prunes. Both he and Suzanne regarded the Nobel Prize as a disaster, because of the publicity involved. He gave most of the money away. Stories of his generosity abound. Once when a tramp admired his jacket, he took it off and gave it to him, without bothering to empty the pockets.

This, like his war record, would look good on a Papal C.V. His relations with women would need more careful presentation. He tended to dissociate love from sex, and resorted with some regularity to prostitutes and casual pick-ups – though Knowlson is sure he felt guilty and disgusted afterwards. There were also longer-term affairs, which sparked bitter quarrels with Suzanne, especially in the 1960s.

Anthony Cronin's *Samuel Beckett: The Last Modernist* is more severe about Beckett's tangled sex life than Knowlson, calling it 'algolagnic, infantile and voyeuristic'. Though his biography has the misfortune to appear in Knowlson's wake, it is by no means negligible. It draws on the published works, and on their critical reception, more richly that Knowlson, and is written with wit and drive. Lois Gordon's *The World of Samuel Beckett, 1906–1946* also has its own emphasis, vividly depicting the contemporary political and cultural context, and arguing that Beckett was more interested in politics than has usually been conceded. But her enthusiasm for Beckett's kindness and generosity, though valid, glosses over the complications, private torments and psychological black holes that Knowlson's branching forest of a book encompasses.

Eric Gill
Fiona MacCarthy, 1989

Fiona MacCarthy's *Life of Eric Gill* uncovers a lot that has not been made public before. It appears from Gill's diaries that he enjoyed incestuous relationships over a long period with two of his sisters and with his two eldest daughters. He also had sexual congress with the family dog. For a lay brother of the Order of St Dominic, who wore the girdle of chastity of the Confraternity of Angelic Warfare, this is obviously not a good record.

On the other hand, it is not entirely surprising. Gill's unusually robust sexual appetite has been common knowledge for a long time. Gill made no secret of his problem. Thoughts of sex, he admitted, filled every spare minute. The Catholic arts and crafts communities he presided over — first in Sussex in 1913, later in the Black Mountains and the Chilterns — usually had at least one of his current mistresses on site, apparently with his wife's connivance.

Nor were Gill's monastic aspirations hypocritical. The idea of a bare white cell really appealed to him. It was just that he needed regular sex as well. Most people would see this as inconsistent. But artists are not meant to see things as most people do. Gill was a great artist (or great artist-craftsman, as MacCarthy guardedly puts it) and the contradiction between rigour and voluptuousness, which made him look a fraud to outsiders, was vital for his work. In his nude studies the tension between clean, hard lines and luscious female roundness is the key to the eroticism. The same contrast excited him in real life. He preferred women in uniform. Nuns and nurses were his favourite.

Gill's treatment of women understandably riles MacCarthy. He did not think much of their minds, and on the Gill smallholdings the women did the menial work while the men busied themselves with intellectual talk. He did not think females worth educating, so his daughters never went to school. Their ignorance and isolation must have made it easier for their father to seduce them. His liaisons could be shamelessly exploitative. He particularly fancied skivvies and maids-of-all-work, who risked dismissal by resisting him.

However, there is not much point in deploring all this and at the same time applauding, as MacCarthy rightly does, the 'exquisite' art of Gill's nudes. For Gill's attitudes are quite clearly implied in his pictures. The young women he depicts are reduced to sexual icons. Individual features, like the face, are smoothed away, and the revealing poses the models are made to take up advertise their subjection. No one, surely, could claim to be much surprised that (as MacCarthy has discovered) Gill's wood engravings of his naked daughter, Petra, belong to the period when he was incestuously involved with her. Gill felt bothered by it all, of course. 'What does God think? Oh Dear!' he lamented in his diary. 'This must stop!' But if it had stopped his art would have stopped as well.

MacCarthy's occasional exasperation with Gill does not prevent her assembling a wonderfully detailed account of his personality – so vivid you feel you know just what it would have been like to visit him at one of his patriarchal communes. After trudging up the farm track, you would come upon a cluster of outbuildings, where Gill's young male acolytes laboured at stonecutting, printing and calligraphy.

Gill would greet you, dressed as usual in a short homespun smock and golfing stockings. He never wore trousers, believing them an insult to the phallus – though he kept a pair of red silk underpants for special occasions such as the Royal Academy dinner.

Having toured the chapel and the spartan living quarters, you might be taken outside to make water 'to the greater glory of God'. Gill, hitching up his smock, and sprinkling the grass, would explain that he could not see the point of bathrooms. If you were unlucky enough to be invited to dinner, you would face a long wait while the Gill women-folk struggled with a heap of damp logs on which they cooked. Gill, meanwhile, would smoke cigarettes, which he rolled himself, and talk incessantly about the evils of mass production, or birth control, or Bird's Custard Powder, which he considered a 'blasphemy'.

When the meal arrived there would be much splashing of holy water, probably supervised by Father McNabb, a rather demonstra-tive Dominican who sometimes embarrassed acquaintances by lying full length on the floor and kissing their feet. After dinner would come compline in the chapel and then Gill might show you his drawings of his own private parts in various states of arousal – exact in every detail, he would explain, the measurements having been taken with a footrule by his secretary Elizabeth Bill. This would naturally lead to an exposition of Gill's theory that Christianity and sexual intercourse were essentially the same. He would go on talking till 2 or 3am.

Gill's theories being what they were, the less they get into his art the better. His masterpiece, *Mankind*, is almost entirely impersonal – a huge, apple-smooth, naked female torso carved from two and a half tons of Hoptonwood stone. Carving it, Gill said, had been like undressing a girl, each layer of stone a garment: first one got rid of the rough woollies, then the delicate silk. But the result is hardly sexual at all: flesh has given way to classical anonymity. MacCarthy regrets this, preferring the more 'radical' work. But it is hard to agree because Gill's radicalism was so insensitive and posturing. His wood engraving *Nuptials of God*, for example, which shows Christ tastefully arranged on the cross while a woman with long flowing hair embraces him, seems, when you consider the realities of crucifixion, disgustingly unimaginative, like a comic drawing of Auschwitz.

Where everyone agrees Gill was supreme was in the typefaces he designed for the Monotype Corporation, and in these his theories had no chance of intruding. They were the work of his eye and hand, which were faultless. He was unable to draw an ugly line. Strictly, he should not have accepted the Monotype commission since it involved collusion with the world of industry, which he despised. But his objection to machines was always partial. He was crazy about railway engines and was thrilled when asked to design the nameplate for the *Flying Scotsman*.

His boyishness, even more than his odd clothes, sets him apart from the celebrities MacCarthy shows him consorting with – H.G. Wells, Shaw, Virginia Woolf, the Webbs. Beside such notables, he seems defenceless. His gaucheness, his zeal for honest craftsmanship and his tiresome theories, all add to the effect of innocence. A Dominican, dining with the Gills, once thought he saw a nimbus shining round Eric's head. Despite the sexual improprieties it unearths, MacCarthy's authoritative biography allows you to understand how someone might have thought that.

Betjeman: The Bonus of Laughter
Bevis Hillier, 2004

John Betjeman is remembered as a lovable eccentric, the nation's favourite walking talking teddy bear. But he emerges from Bevis Hillier's biography as exploitative, querulous, calculating and deceitful, his worship of wealth and rank sorting oddly with his earnest professions of Christianity. His snobbishness took root at

Oxford, where he panted after young aristocrats and grew ashamed of his parents' social class. Repelled by the stigma of trade, he refused, after he had been sent down from university, to take over his father's cabinet-making business, a decision that spelt ruin for its workforce of skilled craftsmen. Instead he entered the art world from a more refined angle with a job on *The Architectural Review*, and tried, meanwhile, to persuade various high-born maidens to marry him.

Hillier's second volume (there is a third still to come) opens in 1933, shortly after Betjeman had wed Penelope Chetwode, whose father Sir Philip was Commander-in-Chief of the army in India. The Chetwodes were far from enraptured with their new son-in-law, so the young couple were thrown on their own resources. Although lacking qualifications, and allergic to work of any kind, Betjeman managed, in the years that followed, to secure a succession of employments through adroit use of the old-boy net. His general policy, once in a post, was to do as little as possible and charm kindly colleagues into shouldering his burdens for him — 'Just look helpless' was his motto. Mostly his jobs were in journalism (film critic on the *Evening Standard*, literary editor of *Time and Tide*), so his slackness could do little harm. But it is more alarming to find him being appointed in 1943 to a senior post in the branch of the Admiralty responsible for shipbuilding and armaments, matters in which he did not even pretend to take an interest. As scandalous was his subsequent elevation to head of the books division of the British Council, where he treated his duties with open contempt, and disappeared from his desk for days on end.

The only job for which he showed any flair had come earlier, in 1941, when he was made press attaché to the senior British diplomat in Dublin. Since Ireland was neutral there were German diplomats about, so the atmosphere was strained. Betjeman had to keep Anglo-Irish relations sweet by dissimulation, and by ingratiating himself with those in power, arts he had long perfected. Playing the innocent buffoon, he once offered the Irish deputy prime minister a bite of his

Mars bar when they met in the street. He may, Hillier suspects, have been a British spy. The Irish thought so at the time. He was told, after the war, that in 1941 he had been put on an IRA hit list. Whatever his real role, the one thing about him that remained absolutely genuine was his self-pity, which allowed little awareness of the wartime afflictions others were enduring. 'I am in Hell,' he moaned. 'This eternal lunching-out is getting me down'.

Reading about Betjeman induces strong sympathy for his wife. Luckily Penelope, whom he nicknamed 'Filth', could hold her own when it came, as it often did, to marital disputes. Their German maid thought Betjeman's name was 'Shutup' because Penelope said it to him so often. Confident of her status, she had none of his hang-ups about class. If she did not care for the company at social gatherings she would read or darn socks. She was mad about horses, which he hated. When she was expecting their first child, Paul, she confided, 'I wish it could be a little horse.' Betjeman's incompetence threw all the chores on her. She ran a duck farm, a smallholding, and a café in Wantage that he had taken a lease on but soon neglected.

Becoming his wife had meant sacrificing her career as an Indologist. When, early in the marriage, she went to Berlin to pursue her studies, Betjeman had an affair with the maid and told her about it to pay her out. She was tolerant of his various 'pashes' and often made friends with the girls concerned. But a watershed in the marriage came in 1948, when she converted to Roman Catholicism after having a vision of the heavenly host while on holiday in Assisi.

Betjeman, a bigoted Anglican, who thought Catholicism had no place on English soil, went half-crazy with vexation. In front of the children he would ridicule his wife's Catholic prayers, adopting a heavy Irish accent ('Hooley Merry, methyr of Guard . . .').

Three years later he began his long liaison with Lady Elizabeth Cavendish, who seems gradually to have replaced Penelope in his life. As the daughter of the Duke of Devonshire she satisfied his social aspirations. She was also twenty years younger, and a lady-in-waiting to Princess Margaret. When Betjeman's London flat was damaged by fire he moved into a Rotherhithe apartment owned by Antony Armstrong-Jones, whose friendship with the princess was just beginning. To judge from the acknowledgement pages, Lady Elizabeth was not among those who helped Hillier with his research, so the precise nature of her relationship with Betjeman is unclear. But it evidently caused Penelope pain, while affording Betjeman the 'thrilling moment of triumph' with which this volume ends. This was the award of the Duff Cooper prize for his *Collected Poems* in 1958. The judges were all old pals, and the presentation was made by the princess, whose speech referred to Betjeman as 'a friend of mine', while he shed tears of grateful servility. A sardonic observer of the event was Maurice Bowra, who commemorated it in mock-Betjeman verses: 'Gosh, O gosh, your Royal Highness / Let me lick your lacquered toes.'

Hillier has devoted twenty-five years to this biography. It is based on extensive interviews with Betjeman, Penelope and all traceable acquaintances. The length is enormous, and so much detail is given about every character, major and minor, that you start to suspect some sort of biography-writing virus has run wild in the text. But the project is much richer than a mere life of Betjeman. It is an in-depth investigation of every section of the English upper middle class that he inhabited. The picture that unfolds is not appealing. Privilege dominates. Influence and string-pulling are rife. Betjeman liked this. It was the world he understood. The threat of social equality alarmed him. After 1945 his letters are sprinkled with jibes about the 'slave State' and the iniquities of taxation. It appears from one letter Hillier cites that he was caught out in tax evasion in 1958. It would be interesting to know more about this, and also about the fact, passed over in a sentence, that Penelope had insisted on his seeing a psychoanalyst to get rid of his persecution mania. But to demand more data when Hillier's supply is already so generous would be graceless, not to say masochistic. We can be sure that no more informed biography of Betjeman will ever appear.

Eileen: The Making of George Orwell
Sylvia Topp, 2020

Many things contributed to the making of George Orwell – his awful prep school; then Eton; then his service with the Indian Imperial police in Burma, which opened his eyes to what imperialism meant; then his resignation from the police and self-imposed penance, chronicled in *Down and Out in Paris and London* (1933). So Sylvia Topp's claim that marriage to Eileen O'Shaughnessy was the making of him is unduly grandiose. All the same, her book is a revelation, because it sees things from Eileen's viewpoint and shows that Orwell persistently failed to do so.

Eileen, born in 1905, came from a well-off family in South Shields. She became head girl at Sunderland Church High School, wrote poetry and won a scholarship to St Hugh's College, Oxford, where she read English. She wanted to be an academic, but got only a second-class degree, so drifted through various jobs, started her own typewriting agency and signed on for an MA in educational psychology at University College, London. It was at a party in the spring of 1935, given by another psychology student, that she met Orwell, and they were married on 8 June 1936.

Orwell was not a happy man, but he was marginally happier when away, preferably far away, from his fellow human beings. The marital home he chose for himself and Eileen was a dilapidated cottage in a remote Hertfordshire village. There was no electricity; the only running water was a cold tap; the lavatory was a lean-to earth closet. The kitchen flooded, the fire smoked, the stove malfunctioned. The corrugated-iron roof made a racket when it rained. Orwell was very happy there, and Eileen very busy. It was understood that her husband's writing took precedence over everything, so she did all the cooking and household chores, as well as helping with the goats, chickens, ducks and vegetable garden, which were components of

Orwell's sternly self-reliant ethos. When he was ill, which was often, Eileen managed everything.

Orwell's published writings project the image of a deeply moral man, a kind of puritan saint. But that image is misleading. Although he referred to his union with Eileen as an 'open marriage', it is not clear that she allowed herself extramarital affairs, whereas he unquestionably did. Perhaps he banked on their not having any long-term consequences, since he believed he was sterile – without, apparently, bothering to seek any medical evidence. From the few accounts that remain, it seems he was an inept and clumsy lover, liable to make a sudden lunge in the middle of ordinary conversation. His love letters could be oddly formal ('I would regard it as a privilege to see you naked'), while enjoining secrecy, lest Eileen got wind of them ('be clever & burn this, won't you').

As he became more famous and successful – a presenter at the BBC, an editor on *Tribune* – he seems to have regarded secretaries as fair game. Some of them resisted, apparently, some not. A woman friend recalled him speaking 'almost contemptuously' about an affair with one of them. When he and Eileen had been in Morocco for the sake of his health, during the winter of 1938–39, the 'exquisitely beautiful' Berber women attracted his admiration, and he begged Eileen to allow him to visit a local prostitute. She apparently consented. But since he later boasted to Harold Acton that he had 'never tasted such bliss as with certain Moroccan girls', he might have interpreted Eileen's one-off consent more generally. 'There is no evidence,' Topp remarks, 'that he noticed or even considered how Eileen might feel.'

Her courage and devotion had been evidenced during the couple's six months in Spain from January to June 1937. When Orwell joined the anti-fascist militia in Barcelona, she quickly followed him, and her presence of mind saved their lives when the secret police were on their trail. The personal qualities everyone who knew her remarked on were cheerfulness, good humour and a habit of witty exaggeration. Topp argues persuasively that these traits start to show up in Orwell's writing soon after they met. She detects them especially in *Animal Farm* (1945), which seems to have been almost a joint production. Eileen typed it, as she did all his manuscripts, and covered the back of each page with suggestions. They would laugh over its jokes in bed together.

Frequently ill himself, Orwell seems not to have noticed, or not to have wanted to notice, how tired and ill Eileen was becoming. She was shattered by the death of her brother Eric, a brilliant chest surgeon and army medical officer, killed in the retreat to Dunkirk. In the immediate aftermath she was bedridden for weeks. But Orwell's demands on her time and energy did not let up. He even offered her typing and editing services to friends. She knew she should have an operation, but put off consulting a surgeon, because Orwell wanted them to adopt a son, and if she were found to be seriously ill adoption might not be allowed. Orwell opposed the very idea of an operation, and she felt obliged to ask his permission, and apologise for wasting his money. Almost unbelievably, instead of staying with her and their newly adopted son at this perilous moment, he accepted an assignment from *The Observer* to go to Europe as a war correspondent for two months, leaving on 15 February 1945. On 29 March, Eileen died while being anaesthetised prior to a hysterectomy.

It is fair to say that, despite the outstanding merits of Topp's book, its first three chapters, about Eileen's ancestry, schooldays and undergraduate years, are tough going, full of trivia and unlikely conjectures, and best skipped. But it quickly improves once she has met Orwell. It draws on new and out-of-the-way sources, including some from Peter Davison's *The Lost Orwell*, and Davison, the editor of the great twenty-volume *The Complete Works of George Orwell*, provides a moving introduction. Topp's enterprise was crowdfunded by 372 people whose names appear at the end. They should feel proud.

The World Is What It Is: The Authorized Biography of V.S. Naipaul
Patrick French, 2008

The biggest surprise in Patrick French's colourful biography of Sir Vidia Naipaul is that its biographee should have allowed it to be published. For it exposes him as an egotist, a domestic tyrant and a sadist to a degree that would be farcical if it were not for the consequent distress suffered over many years by his first wife, Pat. The book is, in large part, Pat's tragedy. They met at Oxford, and their early letters are touchingly innocent, frank and hopeful. She defied her family in marrying him, but things soon started to go wrong. It was partly, it seems, that he was too fastidious to commit himself wholly to another person. He would not give her a wedding ring, though she pleaded for one and eventually bought one herself. But it was also that she did not attract him sexually. He felt sexual desire to be shameful, and could not associate it with love. They were both too embarrassed to discuss his problem, and he began to consort with prostitutes, while Pat saw her hopes of motherhood fade.

Then, in 1972, he met an Anglo-Argentinian woman, Margaret Murray, and felt an instant attraction. They soon found that what French calls the kinks in their personalities matched. She enjoyed being his slave and victim, while he was aroused by mistreating and dominating her. It gave him, he said, carnal pleasure for the first time in his life. Being ignorant and not very bright (he estimated that her vocabulary was limited to fifty words), she was of no interest to him except as a sex object. When they were apart he did not bother to read, or even open, her letters. But, for the next twenty years, they would meet in locations around the world to do things that, Murray said, it would have made her sick to do with anyone else, though she longed to do them again with him. She cherished the wounds he inflicted as signs of his passion. On one occasion he beat her, on and off, for two days, until his hand became painfully swollen and her face was too disfigured for her to appear in public.

She left her husband and three children, in hopes that he would marry her. But he still needed Pat to guide, support and mother him, so he shuttled between the two women, repeatedly threatening each that he would put an end to their relationship. It destroyed Pat. The effect of his 'hating and abusing' her, her diaries record, was to convince her of her own 'revoltingness and folly'. He would reduce her to tears in front of guests, yet demand to be cosseted like a child. When he told her of his affair, he expected her to comfort him for being apart from Murray, and she did. Her love and admiration seem to have been limitless. In her diaries she refers to him as 'the Genius'.

Murray became pregnant three times during their relationship. On the first occasion, Naipaul sent a cheque to cover the termination. 'I was quite happy for it to be aborted,' he explains. 'I would have had to give up so much.' The other two times he paid no heed, and left her to arrange what she called her 'little murders' herself. This was typical of his undeviating self-concern, which French traces to the humiliations of his early life. Descended from destitute Indian labourers sent to Trinidad to cut sugar cane, he was made to feel inferior even within his own extended family by the failures and mental breakdowns of his beloved father, whom he was to commemorate in *A House for Mr Biswas*. By dint of heroic swotting, he won a scholarship and escaped to Oxford. But beneath its affability, 1950s Oxford was a maze of invisible barriers that he felt, rightly, had been erected to stop people like him succeeding. He tried to gas himself, but the coin-in-the-slot meter gave out while he was still conscious. Post-Oxford London was even worse. Nobody wanted to employ small, asthmatic Indians. He applied for and failed to get twenty-six jobs, and came close to starvation, living on boiled potatoes and handouts from Pat, who was working as a schoolteacher.

To survive these setbacks, as French sees it, he had to cling to a belief in his inherent superiority. In Trinidad, his maternal grandmother, the family matriarch, had insisted that they were Brahmins, and whether this was true or not, pride in caste became, for Naipaul, a vital distinction, requiring him to be served special food and granted special privileges. Even straightening the duvet on his bed was beneath his Brahminical dignity. His 'malign jokes' about Black people can also be traced, French suggests, to his childhood in Trinidad, where the Black majority was felt by the Indians to be a threat, and where such joking was traditional. It even had a special name, picong. Which does not, of course, redeem it from being malign.

French's character analysis is not flattering, but it does justice to its subject's complexity. For Indians, too, fell far below Naipaul's standards. Highly sensitive to dirt, he complained that they defecated everywhere – on railway lines, on beaches, in parks. His first two books about India gave great offence. Yet it was, it seems, a kind of self-hatred. Long before he went to India, while he was still a child in Trinidad, his whole family of aunts, uncles and cousins had moved to a well-kept country estate, and reduced it to desolation, uprooting orange and mango trees and clearing the land for Indian peasant agriculture. The indoor WC was dismantled, as unacceptable to Hindu ideas of cleanliness, and a latrine was dug in the woods. It gave him an understanding, he says, of the ease with which a civilisation can be destroyed, and this became the dominant theme in his writing.

French's book is a magnificent achievement. He has mastered the huge Naipaul archive at the University of Tulsa, and has interviewed countless Naipaul friends and former friends worldwide. He took on the task only on condition that no direction or restriction should be imposed by Naipaul, and throughout he keeps his estimate of the man properly separate from his estimate of the writer, which is very high. But the achievement is partly Naipaul's. For he did not have to agree to these conditions, or speak to French so openly. He has chosen to submit himself to the truth-telling and ruthless objectivity that have always characterised his own work. In this respect, approving the publication, and asking for no changes in the typescript, may be seen as an act of self-lacerating honesty. And an act of remorse. For he accepts that his affair with Murray 'undid Pat's life', and that his publicly airing the fact that he had once been a 'great prostitute man' devastated her, and brought her cancer back after a period of remission – 'It could be said that I had killed her.' In the last glimpse we have of him, he is leaning against his car, tears streaming down his face, while his second wife, Nadira, whom he met and asked to marry him while Pat was dying, scatters Pat's ashes in a little wood.

Hergé: The Man Who Created Tintin
Pierre Assouline, translated by Charles Ruas, 2009

The Tintin books provide an alternative history of the twentieth century, from the Russian Revolution through to the space age, in which the innocent never get hurt. A fifteen-year-old boy and his talking dog emerge unscathed from a relentless sequence of plots, tyrannies, explosions and natural disasters. What kind of man did it take to create this joyful fantasy? A wise, kind idealist, surely, whose heart was torn by the sufferings of the real world and its children. Well, no. Pierre Assouline's biography shows that Tintin's creator was, in fact, an emotionally retarded workaholic who cared for nothing but his art, disliked children, and collaborated with the Nazis.

Georges Remi (his pen name Hergé was his reversed initials, RG, as pronounced in French) was born in 1907 in a Brussels suburb. His father worked in a sweet factory. Home life was uniformly 'grey', he recalled, but he was mad about drawing and covered his schoolbooks with sketches. The school, run by Catholic priests, had a scout troop, which was his other passion. He became leader of the Squirrel patrol and drew his first comic strip for a scouting magazine. One character in it later provided the model for Tintin who, though ostensibly a cub reporter, represented, for his creator, the perfect boy scout, helpful, chivalrous, brave and asexual.

On leaving school, Remi got a job on an ultra-Catholic paper that advocated authoritarian government as a bulwark against democracy. Its editor, Father Norbert Wallez, kept a signed photo of Mussolini in his office, dedicated to him personally as 'the friend of Italy and fascism'. This enterprising cleric became Remi's inspiration and spiritual director. 'I owe him everything,' he avowed. Wallez fixed him up with a wife, Germaine Kieckens, a slightly older woman who had been Wallez's secretary, and he also suggested the subject for the first Tintin story. Serialised in Wallez's paper (and drawn in black and white like all the early stories), *The Adventures of Tintin in the Land of the Soviets* gave a cautionary account of the famine, terror and repression rife under the atheist Bolsheviks.

Success was instant. In May 1930, to celebrate the story's publication in book form, thousands of fans converged on Brussels's Gare du Nord to greet a fifteen-year-old boy scout dressed up as Tintin, his hair gelled to give it the trademark quiff, and a lookalike Snowy on a lead. Accompanied by Remi, they were driven through cheering crowds to the paper's offices, where Tintin made a speech from the balcony. The follow-up was *Tintin in the Congo*, another of Wallez's ideas. The horrors and brutalities of Belgian colonisation in the Congo had inspired Conrad's nightmarish *Heart of Darkness*. But Wallez wanted to fire his young readers with missionary zeal, so Remi's Congo is a happy place. Its natives are childish and lazy, but friendly, and they revere Tintin as a great white medicine man.

Attacked in later years for the book's racist caricatures, Remi retorted that they were commonplace at the time. His aim was to catch the mood of the public, not give them moral or political instruction. What concerned him was the clarity of his line, and making his stories instantly intelligible. All this was probably true, Assouline reckons. Remi was not so much malign as thoughtless and shallow.

He was a perfectionist in his art, and seemingly did not stop to think that, by luring young readers to Wallez's paper with Tintin stories, he was also exposing them to editorials that justified Hitler's persecution of the Jews.

With the outbreak of the Second World War and the German occupation of Belgium, the paper Remi had published in was shut down, and he agreed to transfer Tintin to *Le Soir*, the leading Brussels French daily, which the Nazis had taken over as their mouthpiece. Whether he felt himself to be a traitor is not clear. He claimed that he was following the advice of King Léopold III to his people, which was to compromise and wait for better times. It was just a job, he insisted, with no political implications: 'I worked, period; that's all. Just like a miner works, or a streetcar ticket taker, or a baker.' To others it seemed that he was handing the occupying powers the endorsement of the most popular comic-strip hero in Belgium, and doing very well out of it. From 1940 to 1945 annual sales of Tintin books rose from 34,000 to 324,000.

Tintin's adventures during the war remained mostly fantastic and escapist. But one, *The Shooting Star*, reflected the prejudices of Remi's new masters. Its villain was a banker called Blumenstein, whose facial features replicated Nazi anti-semitic stereotypes. While the serial was being published, Assouline points out, anti-Jewish laws were being passed, and, six days after its final episode, it became mandatory for Belgian Jews to wear the yellow star.

At the liberation, resentment against collaborators was fierce. *Le Soir*'s editor was condemned to death. Many journalists were imprisoned. Remi was arrested four times, but released on each occasion. Incarcerating Tintin's creator, it was feared, would bring Belgium's young people out on the streets, and nobody was prepared to risk it. So he was merely banned from newspaper work for two years, and spent the time preparing colour versions of the black-and-white adventures. Then some former resistance fighters who had gone into publishing invited him to become the artistic director of a new *Tintin* weekly. It was such a hit that he had to take on other artists to help with the workload. From now on *Tintin* was a joint effort, though Remi always refused to allow anyone's name but his own to appear in the credits. By the mid-1960s, Tintin books were selling 1.5 million copies a year.

Despite this success, all was not well. Remi was shocked and hurt by the way he had been vilified after the war. In his eyes, he was the victim, and he remained incredulous when told of Nazi atrocities. He suffered several breakdowns and his marriage fell apart. Childless, he and Germaine had adopted a boy from an orphanage, but his presence irked Remi and he made Germaine send him back. He found a new, younger wife, and decided to reinvent himself. He could no longer stand the sight of Tintin, he said. Instead, he turned to Eastern philosophy – Zen and Taoism –, collected modern art, and tried to become an abstract painter, paying a professor of aesthetics to come and discuss art with him every Thursday at noon.

Assouline handles his difficult subject with objectivity and occasional distaste. He has interviewed Remi's closest surviving associates, including his wives, and is an expert on the stories and Remi's many later revisions. It is hard to imagine the job being better done. Yet it reads like the biography of a shadow. Remi, Assouline admits, is of no interest without Tintin. All that was worthwhile about him went into the books. As he explained in a letter to Germaine, 'Tintin has been for me the means to express myself, to project my desire for adventure and violence, the bravery and resourcefulness within me.' Leaf through any Tintin book, and within moments the imaginative vitality will captivate you, and the shabby compromises Assouline documents will be forgotten. That is why we need to be reminded of them.

The Last Englishman: The Double
Life of Arthur Ransome
Roland Chambers, 2009

Nearly all biographies contain lessons for parents – things to avoid lest you mark your child for life. The lesson, in Arthur Ransome's case, is that if you want to teach your small son to swim it is a bad idea to take him out on Coniston Water in a boat and throw him over the side. Ransome's father, an otherwise sensible professor of history, made this mistake, and the half-drowned child he eventually retrieved was, Roland Chambers believes, never the same again. It had planted in him a seed of hatred for the Victorian middle class, which his father represented. Other early ordeals helped the seed to grow. At his first boarding school, the headmaster, a boxing enthusiast, denounced him as a coward because he was too short-sighted to fight. Against the school's advice, his father put him in for a scholarship to Rugby, and he came bottom of the list of candidates. Despite this humiliation, he was sent to Rugby, where he showed no aptitude for any subject. In 1902, aged eighteen, he cut loose from the hated bourgeoisie, who had so clearly failed to appreciate his true value, and became a full-time bohemian, devoting himself to literature.

He worked hard, and published quantities of vapid Edwardian escapism. One book was called *Highways and Byways in Fairyland*. In 1909 he married a fellow bohemian, a mentally unstable young woman called Ivy, and their daughter Tabitha was born the next year. They went on family holidays in a Gypsy caravan painted with yellow roses and pulled by a donkey. Ivy indulged her husband's eccentricities, daily feeding and cleaning his large collection of mice. But she soon tired of this, and he of her. In 1913 he abandoned Ivy, Tabitha and the mice, and travelled to St Petersburg. Apart from occasional home visits, he stayed away for ten years, covering events in Russia for the *Daily News* and later for the *Manchester Guardian*.

These ten years occupy more than two-thirds of Chambers's biography, which, seeing that Ransome lived to be eighty-three, is wildly disproportionate. Yet it seems right, for they were years that changed the world. Ransome proved a brilliant reporter, alert to details that give a sense of place, from the dragonflies hovering over the summer streets in swampy St Petersburg to the candles flickering before icons of the tsar. The outbreak of war brought bursts of patriotism, and he watched German-made pianos cascading from the top storey of the city's premier department store. In March 1917, he witnessed the first days of the Revolution, ducking round corners to avoid bullets, and wondering at the sang-froid of women students who held ribbons of ammunition for the machine guns like bridesmaids carrying bridal trains.

The friends who had welcomed and looked after him in Russia were liberals, who wanted a constitutional monarchy. Ransome sided with them at first, but was increasingly attracted by the Bolsheviks. The Central Workers' Group invited him to attend a meeting of the soviet, and he felt he was living through a miracle. 'It was the first proletariat parliament in the world,' he wrote to his mother, 'and by Jove it was tremendous.' Both Lenin and Trotsky gave him private interviews (Lenin's 'joyous, happy temperament' quite won him over), and he fell in love with Trotsky's secretary, a 'tall, jolly girl' called Evgenia, who was to be his second wife. Trotsky's subordinate Karl Radek, a genial imp addicted to Shakespeare and Dickens, became a special friend. To Ransome they were not a bunch of mass killers but knights from chivalric romance. They had 'clean shields and clean hearts', and were writing a page in history 'as white as the snows of Russia'. Their mission, he explained to his readers, was to eradicate the bourgeoisie. Once that was done the old class divisions would magically disappear (and, although he did not add this, small boys would no longer be thrown into Coniston Water by their seemingly trustworthy parents).

The feeling that events in Russia were righting his personal wrongs allowed him to downplay their more fearsome aspects. Returning to St Petersburg after the Bolsheviks had seized power in November 1917, he reported that peace and order had been restored in the capital, but ignored, Chambers points out, the mass strikes and chronic food and fuel shortages that other commentators noted. The Red Terror, launched in 1918, which cost a quarter of a million lives, did not, in Ransome's account, really happen. Terror, he claimed, was merely a form of words, 'an integral part of the revolutionary vocabulary', not to be taken seriously. He ingratiated himself with the Cheka, the forerunner of the KGB, and made friends with its leader, Felix Dzerzhinsky. There was an obscure and sinister episode when Ransome apparently tried to elicit confidences from a British political prisoner while Dzerzhinsky lurked outside the cell.

At the same time, he was careful to maintain contact with the British authorities. He shared a hotel with a British mission that planned to overthrow the Soviet government and was enlisted by MI6 (his code name was S76) to report on the Bolshevik leaders. Nobody really trusted him. Trotsky suspected he was a British spy, and the War Office wanted him tried as a traitor. His MI5 file, released in 2005, shows that his letters home were routinely intercepted by British counter-intelligence. It has been claimed that this book reveals Ransome was a double agent. Chambers hesitates to go that far (though he thinks that files not yet released may tell us more). But he has uncovered a lot of damaging circumstantial evidence. When Ransome left Russia for Stockholm in 1918, for example, he smuggled out 3 million roubles of Soviet government money to fund Bolshevik activities abroad.

His anti-bourgeois convictions do not seem to have affected his own lifestyle. While awaiting divorce from Ivy he bought a yacht, the *Racundra*, and applied to join the exclusive Royal Cruising Club. Fearful that 'some swine' would blackball him, he 'sweated all over' at his interview, and rejoiced at his social rehabilitation when they let him in. The money he had to pay to support Ivy and Tabitha, as part of the divorce settlement, hurt him very much. He decided that Ivy was an 'incarnate devil', and wrote to Tabitha on her twenty-first birthday explaining that for her to take his money, which she had not earned, was 'theft', and that she was no better than 'a bug or a flea that sucks blood and gives nothing'.

No parent in *Swallows and Amazons* would write such a letter. But as Chambers emphasises, the point of Ransome's famous books for young readers was to put everything bad behind him. He settled with Evgenia in a cottage on Lake Windermere and wrote the first of the series in 1929, when he was 45. The world he invented is the opposite of the one he had lived in. Children trust their parents, all adventure is play, everyone behaves decently. His pared-down style, and the constant practical details – knots, flag signals, homing pigeons, charcoal burners – show how much he had learnt from journalism. Chambers's biography brings us nearer to Ransome than we have ever been before. The fact that the close-up is not wholly likeable has no bearing, of course, on the joy his books have given, and give. All the same, readers who, as children, could not swallow *Swallows and Amazons* may feel they were on to something.

Furious Interiors: Wales, R.S. Thomas and God
Justin Wintle, 1996

This is the most entertaining literary biography I have read in years – perhaps because a literary biography is not exactly what it is. You could call it an enormous detour, a round-the-houses, over-the-rooftops scramble to get past a slammed door. It all began in 1994 when Justin Wintle, an expert on South East Asia, decided his next book would be on the Welsh Nationalist priest and poet R.S. Thomas. He wrote to Thomas to tell him the good news, and request a meeting. The reply was courteous but curt: Wintle was unwelcome, his project unwanted. Two further, more ingratiating letters from Wintle to Thomas went unanswered.

Barred from the bard, Wintle decided to go it alone. He read everything he could lay his hands on about Wales, Welsh Nationalism and Anglo-Welsh poetry. He chatted with Thomas's ex-parishioners in a string of towns and villages across Wales. He lingered in bars sounding out the Welsh about Wales's most famous living poet. At the Hay-on-Wye Literary Festival he skulked in the audience while his quarry read poems in (Wintle noted with amazement) an upper-class English voice – 'like Alec Guinness reading late Eliot'.

The proceeds of all this research have been tipped into his book in a fantastic and often fascinating jumble. There are sections on Welsh literary clergymen of yesteryear, the history of Western philosophy, George Borrow (author of *Wild Wales*), Kierkegaard, Matthew Arnold's 'On the Study of Celtic Literature', and scores of other subjects that flit in and out of Wintle's head as he motors round the principality trying to pick up traces of Thomas without (a perennial dread) actually meeting him face-to-face.

The portrait he gradually assembles is of a man spurred to fury by self-contradiction. Thomas hates the English language, yet writes his poetry in it. He idolises Wales, yet despises the Welsh for their failure to shake off the English yoke, and their eagerness to sell their birthright for a mess of tourism.

His own fanatical nationalism, it turns out, was a midlife growth. As a boy in Holyhead he fell in love with the Welsh countryside, but showed no inclination to learn the language, and quickly forgot the little that was taught at school. His father, a merchant seaman, knew some Welsh, but his mother was of genteel anglicised stock, so English was spoken in the home. Thomas's way of putting this is that he sucked in an alien language with his mother's 'infected milk'. A slow developer, he got a poorish second-class degree in Latin at Bangor, and, still quite unstirred by ideas of any sort, was pushed into the church by his mother, who seems to have doubted his aptitude for anything else. In 1940, aged twenty-seven, he married an upper-middle-class English artist, Mildred Eldridge, whose feelings about his later contempt for her countrymen and culture Wintle does not record.

Thomas's enemies, keen to sniff out hypocrisy, note that his much-trumpeted Welshness did not prevent him sending his son to an English public school, Sherborne. Nor did the boy learn Welsh – though Thomas is so keen on everyone else doing so that he would not answer his parishioners if they addressed him in English. His refusal to condemn the torching of English-owned holiday cottages by Welsh extremists has also caused controversy. How, it is asked, can this square with his proclaimed pacifism and priestly office? 'I deplore killing,' he is quoted as saying, 'but what is the life of one English person compared to the destruction of a nation?' Whether he really said this seems doubtful. The malicious gossip that surrounds him is an index of the resentment he provokes among compatriots.

Why the Welsh should so distrust Welsh Nationalists Wintle seeks to elucidate in yet another billowing digression. From the outset, the movement was élitist. Saunders Lewis, first President of Plaid Cymru, dreamed of a 'new Welsh aristocracy', and saw the masses as a proletarian flood creeping greasily into chip shops. He wanted to deindustrialise South Wales and turn its people back into sturdy peasants. His idealisation of the 'folk' recalled, Wintle alleges, Nazi propaganda, and he opposed war against Hitler.

Some of this rubs off onto Thomas. He, too, has no time for the English-speaking South Welsh. Even the Welsh hill farmers, who attain almost Christ-like status in his poems, sound subhuman, with their 'half-witted grins' and clothes 'sour with years of sweat'. In hill-farming communities these tributes have not been well received. There is undoubtedly something austere and limited about his poetry, as well as about his view of people. It is the Welsh language, bubbling out of them like birdsong, that he venerates – its naturalness contrasting with his own Welsh which, acquired in adulthood, is stiff and academic (so Wintle's informants testify). Birds and people are always coalescing in his poetry, and bird-watching is one of his few relaxations, taking him as far afield as Norway and Alaska. He might have been happier, you feel, in a world of birds, provided they sang Welsh.

All the same, the figure you glimpse dimly through Wintle's feints and circlings comes across, in the end, as both heroic and tragic. His grief at seeing the Welsh landscape fouled by caravan sites ('an Elsan culture') and trampled by droves of English tourists is surely understandable. Why should he not feel rage when Welsh valleys are flooded to provide Liverpool and Birmingham with drinking water? His yearning for barren places beyond the 'human stain', and his detestation of towns, technology and machines in general, are already easy to share, and will be more so in the ruined, overcrowded world of the twenty-first century. In this respect he is a poet that the derelict future waits to welcome.

Like granite pebbles, his poems offer little lip or ledge for commentary to get a purchase on, and Wintle is not at his most effective in the critic's role. But their seriousness is unmistakeable and ennobling. They bespeak a man who has spent much of his life visiting the sick and dying. Asked by *The Oldie* magazine to predict what his own last words would be, he suggested: 'You again!' In 1991 his wife died, after a long illness, during which she went blind. A few days before her death, a parishioner told Wintle, Thomas brought her back from the hospital, and carried her upstairs, 'when he shouldn't have been lifting so much as an apple'. That is one of the sentences that stays in one's mind from this strangely satisfying book. Another is a tribute paid by a villager, remembering Thomas's retirement from his last parish: 'When someone like that leaves, a part of the landscape goes with him. There is one mountain less.'

LITERATURE

The Poet's Tale: Chaucer and the Year that Made the Canterbury Tales
Paul Strohm, 2015

Paul Strohm has written a brilliant book, and admirers of Geoffrey Chaucer may wish that he hadn't. His research reveals that Chaucer, though not exactly a criminal, was something arguably worse – a trusted civil servant who connived in the theft of huge sums of public money. Strohm, a professor emeritus at Columbia University, spins out his web of evidence at length, but the facts can be quickly summarised.

In 1374, a wealthy crook called Nicholas Brembre, who was soon to become mayor of London, managed to get himself appointed collector of customs duties in the wool trade. At the time, wool was the mainstay of the nation's economy, and Brembre proceeded to take full advantage of the opportunities for fraud that his position offered. However, the law required that a controller of customs should be appointed as a check on the collector's activities. For Brembre and his powerful cronies it was vital that the controller should be a stooge or cat's-paw who would not inquire too closely into their nefarious schemes. In Chaucer they found just the man they wanted.

He was appointed controller four months after Brembre became collector and continued to perform – or not perform – his duties for twelve years. The perks that went with the job included a daily pitcher of wine and a rent-free apartment over Aldgate, London's eastern gate. During his tenure, public outrage at the corruption that was bleeding the country of its wool revenue gradually mounted, and the scandal came to a head in the parliament of 1386. An inquiry into the 'great oppressions and extortions' perpetrated by controllers of customs was ordered, Brembre was discredited and, two years later, put on trial and hanged. Chaucer lost his job and his Aldgate flat, but he saw trouble coming and escaped to Kent, where he seems to have lived a wandering life for a while.

Why didn't he behave more responsibly as controller and bring the Brembre gang to justice? Strohm suspects he was afraid. Brembre and his associates were vastly superior to him in wealth and social authority, and things could have turned nasty if he had stepped out of line. That may be true. But it is also possible that he didn't think that the swindle, and the kind of men who enriched themselves from it, were of much importance compared with his own concerns. As he grew older he seems to have become more and more absorbed in himself and his poetry. Born in 1343, the son of a London vintner, he had been a courtier and soldier in his youth, fighting at the siege of Rheims in 1360, and travelling in France and Italy, sometimes on diplomatic business. At twenty-two, he married Philippa de Roet, a knight's daughter, and sister of Katherine Swynford who was soon to become the mistress of John of Gaunt, one of the nation's most powerful men.

Marriage to Chaucer was not socially advantageous to Philippa, and for his part he may have found family life an unwelcome distraction. So it seems that they agreed to live apart for most of their twenty-two-year marriage. Philippa and their three children joined Katherine at John of Gaunt's court, while Chaucer stayed in London, increasingly withdrawn from society. In a poem written while he was controller of the wool revenues, he jokes about the scholarly seclusion the job allows him. Each day after he has finished his 'reckonings' at the office he hurries home and buries himself in books until he is 'dazed' with reading.

In his poems he professes to scorn fame, and Strohm takes him at his word. But that seems questionable. Some time in the 1370s he finished his great epic of love and betrayal, *Troilus and Criseyde*. He wrote it in English, not the more established poetic languages of Latin or French, and at the end he worries about the diverse dialects and changeable nature of the English language. He wonders whether readers in the future, wherever they may be, will be able to understand what he has written, and whether they will get the metre right. He prays that they will, and sends his poem out into the world – 'Go, little book' – to take its chance.

It is an astonishing moment. In his lifetime (he died in 1400) few people knew that Chaucer was a poet at all. His poems, Strohm reckons, were read only by a group of friends and fellow scholars in London. Yet it is clear that at the end of *Troilus* he knows he has created a masterpiece and he seems to foresee, half a century before the invention of the printing press, that its readership will extend far beyond his own place and time. By comparison with that vision of poetic immortality the sordid, money-grubbing wangles of Brembre and his city slickers must have seemed scarcely worth notice.

His hasty departure for Kent in 1386 deprived him of even the few readers who had so far shown an interest in his poetry. His response, aptly seen by Strohm as a 'dazzling act of imagination', was to invent his own fictional readership by writing *The Canterbury Tales*. His pilgrims are both tellers and listeners, chattering among themselves and criticising one another's stories. He writes himself into the group, and relates a tale so boring that the host, Harry Bailey, cuts him short and pronounces it 'not worth a turd'.

The subterfuge – pretending he is no good at storytelling – is comparable with the subterfuge he showed as controller of the wool revenues, pretending he had not noticed the malpractices of the Brembre set. He was always fascinated by dissimulation. 'The smiler with the knife under the cloak' is one of his phrases that has passed into the language. Strohm's verdict on Chaucer's conduct as controller is that he was 'deeply ethically compromised'. No doubt that is so. But if his deceit gave him time to plan and write his poems we are hardly in a position to complain.

Shakespeare's Language
Frank Kermode, 2000

What is it that makes Shakespeare different? Is it his poetry? Or his characters? Or his invisibility, emptying the plays so entirely of his own views and opinions that they are infinitely re-interpretable, so never become obsolete? Sir Frank Kermode's new book, modestly disguised as an introduction to the plays for non-specialists, answers these questions with masterly directness. Something extraordinary, he argues, happened to Shakespeare in mid-career. Around 1600 he abandoned the formal rhetoric of the early plays and discovered a way of representing emotionally agitated thought that was unlike anything in previous world literature. Violently elliptical, and wildly improbable in its conjunctions of images, this new Shakespearean language is often too difficult for modern editors to decipher, and, Kermode suspects, could not have been fully understood even by the most intelligent in Shakespeare's original audience. But precisely because it bypasses coherent explanation the new language gives access to the confused possibilities and insoluble dilemmas that underlie rational thought. Modern critical emphasis on theatrical performance has, Kermode regrets, lost sight of the fact that Shakespeare was a thinker – not a thinker who dealt in fully formed ideas, like a philosopher, but one who portrayed thought happening.

As the theme unfolds, the book becomes a treasure hunt, with Kermode's critical intelligence spotting outcrops and quarries of the new language even in speeches by pre-1600 characters – the Bastard in King John, Hotspur in Henry IV Part I. But the true watershed is identified as *Hamlet*, a play that not only depicts thought processes with matchless depth, but also illustrates, as never before, a second feature of the new Shakespearean language – an obsessive, self-indulgent passion for the repetition and interchiming of particular words. In *Hamlet* this takes the form of a persistent rhetorical device that splits a single thought into two words or phrases (as in 'the slings and arrows of outrageous fortune'). All the play's passionate and moody broodings revert to this one-into-two pattern. In the great soliloquies it sanctions bizarre conjunctions of ideas – 'He took my father grossly, full of bread; / With all his crimes broad blown, as flush as May'. What can may blossom and bread-eating have in common? Why should they occur to a young man outraged by his father's murder? Our not being able to answer such questions is what makes the play new, unintelligible and, in Kermode's sense, Shakespearean.

The doublings and illicit couplings in the language of Hamlet spread out to produce pairs of characters (Rosencranz and Guildenstern) and duplex plot-motifs (incest, adultery, Hamlet's hesitation between alternative courses of action). It is as if Shakespeare's fascination with a particular word-pattern came first, and determined the kind of people he should invent and the deeds he should make them perform. So, too, in the other tragedies, the stubborn, convoluted repetition of key words – 'luck' and 'become' in *Antony and Cleopatra*, 'time', 'man' and 'done' in *Macbeth*, 'voice' and 'name' in *Coriolanus* – represents, as Kermode sees it, Shakespeare's deepest interest. It mattered more to him than plotting, at which he could be careless, and it preceded the formulation of characters. That a great poet should be absorbed in word permutations is hardly surprising. Yet with Shakespeare, Kermode argues, the obsession could become inhuman, like the fascination of a great mathematician with numbers.

King Lear particularly shocks him, by allowing a language pattern to irrupt into dramatic action, as the text's relentless emphasis on 'eyes' and 'seeing' culminates in the blinding of Gloucester. For Kermode – and it is hard to disagree – there is something sadistic about an author who could pursue his word games to such a conclusion.

True, Kermode's case is easily parodied. At its most extreme it turns Shakespeare into a mad wordsmith, pointlessly following the intricacies of a linguistic maze. The idea that the verbal patterns were primary, and plot and character secondary, is, after all, only speculative. Shakespeare's mind may not have worked like that. As for his sadism, the same charge could be laid against any writer of tragedy. All the same, Kermode's analyses of specific passages are so illuminating that distrust of his more general points tends to evaporate. He notices the constant, bewitching redundancy of Shakespeare's language, as in Cleopatra's 'Beneath the visiting moon' – why 'visiting'? He picks out amazingly powerful speeches squandered on minor characters – the shepherdess Phebe, in *As You Like It*, carrying on about 'The cicatrice and capable impressure' you might get from, of all things, resting your hand on a rush. Countless similar instances bear out the supremacy, for Shakespeare, of words over reason and probability. His passion for words was erudite as well as uncontrollable. Kermode's Shakespeare is learned in ways missed by previous commentators. He has read Augustine's *Confessions* and echoes them in *Macbeth*. Clarence's dream of the murdered boy in *Richard III* ('A shadow like an angel with bright hair / Dabbled in blood') suggests he has read Dante, or can out-Dante Dante without reading him.

Not that Kermode is an uncritical admirer. His outright views on Shakespeare's failings will alarm the timid. He is unsparingly funny about the early botches such as *Titus Andronicus*, and most of the comedies receive fairly cursory attention. He suggests that the 'tedious' repartee of Beatrice and Benedick in *Much Ado* was bettered by Restoration comedy. A 'dispassionate judge' would have to admit that Congreve excelled Shakespeare at this sort of sex-play. *All's Well* and *Timon of Athens* are written off as almost total failures. The second half of *Measure for Measure* is 'prosy and incredible'. *Cymbeline* is so ridiculous that it must have been a private joke between Shakespeare and his quicker-witted auditors. The later plays show the 'new language' running to seed. The manic convolutions continue, but there is often no pressure of thought behind them, so that we work out what is being said and wonder why it had to be said so obscurely. Despite scenes of acknowledged greatness in *The Winter's Tale* and *The Tempest*, it seems to Kermode that in these late years Shakespeare is simply defying his audience, not caring to have them as fellows in understanding.

The most refreshing feature of Kermode's book, compared with the generality of current criticism, is its concentration on Shakespeare's words. It does not switch attention to his imagined political views, his historical context or his failure to match us in postcolonial propriety. These evasions are understandably popular, because writing about the words is extremely difficult. Their meanings, as Kermode shows, are often multiple and unfixed, and their power is so evident it seems the critic can add nothing. Kermode's easy, urbane style belies a formidable achievement. He presents complex thoughts in simple language, which is the precise opposite of today's most approved critical practice. The result is at once the best available primer for beginners, and a book no specialist can afford to ignore.

Shakespeare's Wife
Germaine Greer, 2007

It is impossible to think of two minds more different than Germaine Greer's and Shakespeare's. The leading quality of Greer's mind is opinionatedness, whereas Shakespeare, so far as we can tell, had no opinions. He vanished into his plays, and trying to retrieve what he thought on any subject is like harvesting shadows.

This is frustrating for Greer, since her aim in her new book is to pin down Shakespeare's opinion about marriage, specifically his own. Only the barest facts are known for certain. When he married Ann Hathaway, a local farmer's daughter, in 1582, he was eighteen, she was twenty-six and three months pregnant. They married by special licence, which two of her father's friends obtained. Susanna, their first child, was born in May 1583, and twins, Judith and Hamnet, in February 1585. Before or soon after that Shakespeare probably left Stratford, and by 1592 he was already well known as an actor and dramatist in London, where he spent most of his married life. When he made his will in March 1616, a month before his death, his wife was not mentioned at all in the first draft, and a redraft left her his second-best bed.

Some scholars (most of them, Greer notes accusingly, male) have taken these facts to mean that Shakespeare was trapped into marriage by a designing older woman; that he was frogmarched to the altar by her family; that, like many women of her class, she was probably illiterate, and certainly unable to appreciate her husband's greatness; and that his insulting bequest signifies his lifelong alienation from her. Greer is convinced that, on the contrary, Shakespeare wooed Ann, not vice versa; that she proved a good, true wife, enjoying her husband's love and respect; and that she took a keen interest in his writing, and was quite possibly instrumental in getting the First Folio of his works printed after his death. Since there is little or no evidence to support these claims, their furtherance calls for considerable ingenuity on Greer's part.

She suggests that *The Comedy of Errors*, with its moving depiction of wifely loyalty, reveals Shakespeare's 'attitude to marriage', so he would be unlikely to have treated Ann in the way her denigrators allege. The weakness of such arguments is obvious – you might, with just as little cogency, select *The Taming of the Shrew* as showing Shakespeare's attitude to marriage – so most of Greer's book takes a different tack, and contends that Ann was a highly successful woman in her own right, so Shakespeare should have been proud of her, even if he was not, though he probably was. Exactly what she was successful at is difficult to decide. Greer thinks she might have been a successful moneylender. The one surviving document that may give a clue to her business activities, if she had any, is the will of the Hathaway family's shepherd, which says she owes him forty shillings. This does not sound like successful moneylending, but perhaps, Greer thinks, the shepherd entrusted the money to Ann's safekeeping, which could mean she was a successful banker. Alternatively, she might have been a farmer or a cheesemaker, a mercer or a haberdasher, a basket weaver or a lace maker or a stocking knitter. An official document records that New Place, the big house in Stratford that Shakespeare bought in 1597, contained malt for brewing, so probably, Greer reckons, Ann was in business as a brewer. Or maybe as a silk farmer. The mulberry tree that Shakespeare is supposed to have planted at New Place was, Greer suspects, the survivor of a plantation established by Ann to rear silkworms. Wherever Ann's success lay, she made enough money, Greer thinks, to bring up her family without her husband's help (though why he should not have helped her if she enjoyed his love and respect is not quite clear) and probably accumulated a lot more besides. Quite possibly, in Greer's view, Ann, not Shakespeare, bought New Place. It is true that no papers relating to Ann's remarkable career have come down to us. But then, Greer reminds us, paper was scarce, and old documents were used for all sorts of menial purposes, and there were a lot of mice about.

The uncertainty of the whole situation allows Greer to fill her book with vast amounts of extraneous material. There are lengthy digressions on Elizabethan farming, cheesemaking, haberdashery and Ann's other supposed occupations, packed with archival detail about the pigs, hens, household effects and genealogies of a great many people who, as Greer is perfectly willing to accept, may have nothing to do with Ann or Shakespeare at all. In the same spirit there are sections on Elizabethan cottages, in case the Shakespeares ever lived in one, though they probably did not, and a stomach-churning excursion on venereal disease and its treatment, on the off-chance that Shakespeare suffered from it, although there is no evidence he did. Threading this maze of blind alleys is the sort of reading experience that brings vividly to mind the many more useful and enjoyable things you might be doing.

Given Greer's interest in the denizens of Shakespeare's Stratford and the lives they lived, it is intriguing to speculate what they would have thought of her if some miraculous time warp had allowed her to materialise among them. They would have been terrified at first, of course, just as they would have been by the appearance of a jet fighter, or any other product of our advanced civilisation. Very likely they would have shut her away in a quiet room with some good man of the church, in an effort to restore her wits. But I think they would have soon perceived that she was perfectly harmless, and, indeed, that she had decent, conventional, Christian ideas about how people should treat each other. Before long they would have felt quite safe in bringing their little children to look at her.

What prompts this conclusion are the traces of Greer the romantic novelist that keep peeping out from behind her rigorous absorption in archives and statistics. She likes to think that William spent long hours teaching Ann to read as she watched her cows grazing on the common. She pictures him writing *Venus and Adonis* at the kitchen table and reading out passages to make her blush or laugh, and she imagines Ann 'enjoying the poem's lightness of touch, even as she shrank from its rampant sexuality'. When Shakespeare's sonnets were published, Ann, Greer fancies, would have read them with a 'grim little smile', recognising many of them as poems that, in their original versions, Will had written to her. 'Then she would have tucked the little book deep inside the coffer where she kept her own possessions, opened her Bible and prayed for them both.' She was sober, industrious, patient and loving to the end, and nursed her husband tenderly in his last illness. Fictitious though all this undeniably is, it seems reassuringly old-world and good-hearted, and should do something to correct Greer's reputation as a revolutionary thinker and disturber of the peace.

The Letters of Charles Dickens, Volume Eight: 1856–1858
edited by Graham Storey and Kathleen Tillotson, 1995

For readers of Dickens's letters the hardest thing is to imagine him asleep. What was he like when it all switched off – the gigantic good humour, the high spirits, the ferocious bouts of novel-writing, the cold baths, the ten-mile walks, the peacock waistcoats, the blaze of footlights, the glittering public dinners for this or that charity, with the Inimitable reducing throngs to tears by the force of his eloquence? Could he lie quiet afterwards? Or did he roar and twitch and boil even in his dreams?

Catherine, his wife, might have told us. But she was too busy bearing his nine children to leave any word, and by the time this new and momentous batch of the Pilgrim Edition of the letters begins, she has not much time left. Dickens did not expect more from his marriage partner than many other men. Eternal youth and ceaseless adulation would have been quite sufficient. But Catherine had never made any real effort to fulfil these requirements, and in the spring of 1858 his patience at last gave out. Amid howls of moral outrage from the popular press, he shunted her off to a separate establishment near Hyde Park, with a handsome allowance and a brougham, and began his relationship with the actress Ellen Ternan (seventeen years old to his forty-six) which was to last till his death.

The letters allow us to see these scandals from Dickens's viewpoint: how one thing led to another; how it all began with an act of selfless benevolence. It happened that the comic writer Douglas Jerrold died suddenly in June 1857. Dickens flung himself into fund-raising for the widow and children, and revived, for public performance, his friend Wilkie Collins's melodrama *The Frozen Deep*, which he and a group of amateurs had acted some months before. The revival was an enormous success: Queen Victoria commanded a special performance. But going public meant hiring professional actresses for the parts Dickens's daughters had played in the amateur production. The sisters Maria and Ellen Ternan were picked, and from that moment Dickens was lost.

Admittedly, he had felt discontented with his marriage before that. He had written to his confidant John Forster about the 'skeleton' in his 'domestic closet'. But if he had not met the Ternan girls he might have gone on satisfying his sexual needs with visits to high-class brothels under Collins's expert guidance. The Ternans were irresistible because in addition to youth and beauty they had innocence – or something very like it. Dickens wrote ecstatically to his old friend the banking heiress Miss Burdett Coutts about the touching distress Maria had shown when they played *The Frozen Deep* in Manchester. Kneeling over him in his death scene she had drenched him in genuine tears, repeatedly sobbing: 'Oh, it's so sad' despite his sotto voce instructions to calm herself. Perhaps Maria was acting better than he realised, and if her aim was to hook a wealthy and powerful patron for her family she succeeded admirably. Within a year Catherine had been sent packing, and the Ternan girls were ensconced in lodgings in Oxford Street under Dickens's protection.

But the letters give us an inkling, too, of how shattering it all was for Dickens. He was a pure-minded man, whatever his physical needs – he never shared the upper-class Thackeray's taste for smut – and he had a keen sense of the ridiculous. To find himself chasing after teenage flesh like some farcical sugar-daddy was a kind of nightmare. He had to pretend that none of it was his fault. Catherine had been a bad mother, unloved by her children, he assured his friends, quite untruthfully. In a letter leaked to the world's press he alleged she suffered from 'mental disorder'.

Driven frantic by unacknowledged guilt, and the need to keep his relations with Ellen secret, he was horrified to think he might lose the public's sympathy, which was his dearest possession. This, as much as his new financial burdens, led to the other crucial decision of these years, which was to give public readings from his works for his personal benefit. He had given readings for charity before, but the new idea risked seeming venal and ungentlemanly. Forster warned him against it. In the event, though, it gave him just the boost he needed. Packed houses wept, cheered and quaked with mirth at his bidding. He toured the British Isles, giving eighty-five readings, and sending home jubilant descriptions of crowds fighting for tickets, and box-office staff staggering bankwards under sacks of coin.

From the reader's angle it is a great relief to get Catherine and her troubles out of the way and return to the exultant bustle and humour in which Dickens's best letters are written. So long as he is feeling triumphant, even a note to his wine merchant ordering 'one dozen of the best gin' can acquire a special Dickensian brio. As always, foreign parts wonderfully revive him. There are rapturous letters from Paris where he wrote much of *Little Dorrit* in a flat overlooking the Champs Élysées, captivated, each time he looked up from the paper, by the fountains and the military bands and the red velvet carriages.

The Villa de Moulineaux, 'hidden in roses and geraniums' near Boulogne, where he takes his children for the summer, becomes, in letters to friends languishing in London, an elysium of comic misadventures. Local cats are suspected of designs on the Dickenses' canary; a manservant prowls the garden with a shotgun; young Dickenses hang in trees to direct his fire; tradesmen approach the house in terror, begging not to be shot.

The dynamism the letters convey is breathtaking. He sends detailed directions to his subeditor for every item in every issue of his periodical *Household Words*. He supervises Miss Coutts's home for fallen women. He buys and renovates Gad's Hill Place, the big house near Rochester he had wondered at as a child. He answers scores of begging letters. He arranges for his sixteen-year-old son Walter to go off to India with a commission in the East India Company – just in time, as it turns out, to take part in quelling the Mutiny.

News of the mutineers' slaughter of women and children at Cawnpore inflames Dickens's patriotism. If he were Commander-in-Chief, he tells Miss Coutts, he would exterminate the race responsible for such atrocities, 'blot it out of mankind and raze it off the face of the earth'. The outburst reminds us that Dickens wrote at a time when the English ruled the earth. The power and confidence of his work are, for good or bad, inseparable from that dominion. A Dickens in today's England would be unthinkable. He would stifle or explode.

Like its predecessors, this new volume of the Pilgrim Edition is a model of imaginative scholarship. It prints 1,324 letters, many previously unpublished, and it brings Dickens so close you can almost smell the cigar smoke. The magnificent footnotes (an absorbing read, even without the letters) unroll the whole cavalcade of contemporary life – the authors and actresses, clubmen and courtiers, statesmen, swindlers and sanitary reformers, who created the steam-driven, empire-ruling juggernaut that was Victorian England.

The New Annotated Sherlock Holmes, 2 vols
edited by Leslie S. Klinger, 2004

What do Sherlock Holmes and Father Christmas have in common? Answer: they make people want to believe they are real. In this luxury edition of the short stories Leslie S. Klinger lists 450 active Sherlockian societies (America and Japan have the most) who meet regularly to discuss the great detective, and add to the mountain of books and articles about him. The assumption behind their activities is that Holmes and Watson actually lived (or, some maintain, are still alive) and that their adventures truly happened. When fictional characters conquer our credulity to this extent, the likelihood is that they stand for some big idea that might, we think, make the world a better place. Holmes and Father Christmas both conform to this pattern. Father Christmas is total generosity; Holmes, total intelligence.

It matters, of course, that total intelligence, as represented by Holmes, is benign and decent, and implacably at odds with the other genius in the stories, satanic Professor Moriarty. Holmes is a democrat. He stands up for little, wronged men like the clerk Cadogan West in 'The Bruce-Partington Plans'. He champions the young American couple in 'The Noble Bachelor' when they incur the wrath of an English aristocrat, and he looks forward, he says, to the day when the Union Jack will be quartered with the Stars and Stripes. He curtly refuses a bribe from the mighty Duke of Holdernesse in 'The Priory School', and in 'The Three Garridebs' we learn that he has turned down a knighthood.

Despite his simulated dislike of women, he is clearly highly susceptible. He loses his heart to the opera singer Irene Adler in 'A Scandal in Bohemia', and behaves chivalrously with female clients, especially the pretty ones, taking tender note of the bruises left on their arms by brutal husbands or guardians. Wronging a woman is the unforgivable sin in Holmes's book. The blackmailer Charles Augustus Milverton, riddled with bullets by an avenging grande dame while Holmes looks on, and the serial seducer Baron Gruner, blinded with vitriol by a cast-off mistress whom Holmes brings to his house in 'The Illustrious Client', learn this to their cost. It matters, too, that Holmes's mind is not abstruse or mathematical. He notices ordinary things, as we all feel we could if we tried. He is total intelligence with a human face and a funny hat.

English readers will be able to skip at least half of Klinger's voluminous marginal notes that decode, for Americans, mysterious expressions such as 'Rugby football' or 'Scotland Yard'. But the remainder are useful, especially when they draw attention to inaccuracies. It has always been apparent that Conan Doyle was an astonishingly careless writer. He cannot even remember from story to story what Watson's first name is, or whether his war wound was in his arm or his leg. An early essay by Stephen Jay Gould (which must be the only relevant item omitted from Klinger's colossal bibliography) pointed out that almost every reference to science in the Holmes stories is wrong. But the blunders spread far beyond that, and make some of the most famous stories literally impossible. There is no such snake as the 'swamp adder', and if there were it would not be able to climb a rope or live in an unventilated safe, as the deadly reptile in 'The Speckled Band' does. In the same story, Holmes advises Watson to arm himself with his 'Eley's No 2', though Eley made ammunition not guns, and Dr Grimesby Roylott acquires a baboon from India, where there are no baboons. Roylott's stepdaughter could not possibly have got a train from Leatherhead to Waterloo and arrived at Holmes's Baker Street rooms by 7.15am, as the story says she did. Indeed, research into Bradshaw's Railway Guides proves that there is only one correct train time in the entire Holmes canon.

Sherlockians relish such mistakes because they provide an excuse for rewriting the stories, pointing out what must have 'really' happened. But, in fact, they just highlight the difference between Doyle and the folk hero he invented. Holmes was Doyle's opposite. Doyle is slapdash; Holmes, precise. Doyle became a fervent spiritualist and believed in fairies, Holmes is logical. Holmes reproves Watson for interspersing sober fact with grotesque details, but Doyle found them irresistible. The core of his stories is often a horror that defies reason. An inoffensive spinster in Croydon receives two freshly severed human ears through the post, packed in salt. A sister and her two brothers are found seated at a table where they have been playing cards, the sister dead from shock, the brothers raving mad. Holmes solves these mysteries, but he cannot disperse the hatred and terror that drive Doyle's plots.

What Holmes and his creator do share is an insatiable interest in people. The stories have one of the greatest casts of minor characters in literature. Imagine, Holmes says to Watson in 'A Case of Identity', being able to fly across London, removing the roofs and peering at the strange lives inside. His investigations have just that effect, and the trawl of weird individuals is phenomenal. Few are happy. They are haunted by criminal pasts, or fleeing from the tsarist police or the Ku Klux Klan, or locked in wretched relationships. They stew in resentment like Jonas Oldacre, the Norwood Builder, or sink beneath misfortune like courteous Harry Pinner in 'The Stockbroker's Clerk', who asks his guests to excuse him before stepping into the next room and quietly hanging himself. We long to know more about them. What becomes of the emaciated Colonel Lysander Stark, with his deadly hydraulic press, in 'The Engineer's Thumb'? Or Henry Baker in Doyle's matchless Christmas story 'The Blue Carbuncle', whose sad decline Holmes deciphers by close observation of his hat? When was pawnbroker Jabez Wilson in China, as Holmes deduces he was from the delicate pink fish tattooed on his wrist in 'The Red-Headed League'? Doyle seems to have enjoyed teasing his readers with hints of more and more bizarre characters waiting in the wings – Parker in 'The Empty House', 'a garrotter by trade, and a remarkable performer upon the Jew's harp', or Wilson 'the notorious canary-trainer' in 'The Adventure of Black Peter'.

With such personalities aboard, the danger was that the stories would float beyond the realm of probability altogether. Watson's flat style (avoiding fine turns of phrase and clever adjectives, as John le Carré notes in his Preface) helps to keep them realistic. For the original *Strand Magazine* readers, Sidney Paget's illustrations, reproduced in this edition, must have had the same effect. They are the dullest pictures ever to accompany a great narrative, consisting mostly of men in suits talking to each other. But their job was to be dull, and so make Doyle's fantastic imaginings believable. Fortunately, Klinger has also included some of the magnificent illustrations that Frederick Dorr Steele did for *Collier's* magazine in America. These may just tip the balance if you are minded to give a sumptuous present to a Sherlockian near to you.

The Short Sharp Life of T.E. Hulme
Robert Ferguson, 2002

T.E. Hulme was the brains behind the modernist movement in England, the founder, with Ezra Pound, of imagism, and the first English critic to defend abstract art. T.S. Eliot called him the forerunner of the twentieth-century mind. But he has always been a shadowy figure, and when he was killed in 1917, aged thirty-three, he left only a handful of essays and five brief poems. Robert Ferguson's admiring biography endorses his high reputation, but gets behind the legend to reveal a confused, belligerent young man who used philosophy to heal the rifts in his own chaotic nature. To many Edwardian aesthetes he must have seemed uncouth, even brutal. He believed you should fight for your opinions, and once hung Wyndham Lewis upside-down by his trouser turn-ups from the railings in Soho Square. His opposition to pacifism irked Bertrand Russell, who recalled him as 'an evil man who could have created nothing but evil'.

Satisfying the imperious demands of his libido caused him almost as many problems as his tussles with avant-garde thought. He once left a group of friends in the Café Royal, pleading an urgent appointment, and returned twenty minutes later complaining that the steel staircase of the emergency exit at Piccadilly tube station was the most uncomfortable site for sexual intercourse he had ever encountered. He came from Staffordshire, where his father was in the ceramics trade, and his coarse regional accent was another blemish from the viewpoint of London's literati. He had no formal training in philosophy. At school in Newcastle he studied mathematics, and won an exhibition to St John's College, Cambridge. But he soon realised he was miscast as a mathematician and reacted with mindless violence. As founder-member of a group of rowdies called the Discord Club he organised an undergraduate riot, then went to London on Boat Race night and assaulted two policemen. He was found guilty of being drunk and disorderly, although, in fact, he was a lifelong teetotaller and explained to the court that he had not been drunk but 'excited'.

After this it seemed best to get away, and he travelled steerage to Canada where he worked on railroads and in lumberjack camps. The landscapes awoke his interest in poetry, which seemed the only adequate response to their vastness. He read Rimbaud and Laforgue and became a convert to free verse. Poetry, he decided, should be anti-romantic, 'cheerful, dry and sophisticated', rather than perpetually 'moaning or whining'. But the traces of romantic wistfulness in his poems suggest that, like most of his ideas, this was an attempt to solve contradictions in himself. Back in Europe he taught at the Berlitz school in Brussels, and became interested in theoretical aspects of painting and sculpture. His mistress Dolly Kibblewhite had studied at the Slade, and her father's spacious house in Frith Street was a kind of arts and crafts centre where Hulme held regular Tuesday evening salons attended by all the more advanced artists and writers, including Henri Gaudier-Brzeska and Jacob Epstein, who became his close friends. Anxious for some academic credentials, he managed to get himself reinstated at Cambridge, but was sent down a second time – a rare distinction – for trying to seduce the underage daughter of the president of the Aristotelian Society. Her horrified father had come upon one of Hulme's love letters, couched in the surprisingly explicit language he favoured for such communications, and contacted his solicitors. Hulme left hastily for Germany, where he busied himself writing an essay on the German avant-garde.

Ferguson's book sorts out the development of Hulme's thought, which is obscured in the collection of his essays and fragments called *Speculations* compiled by Herbert Read in 1924. The problem that persistently dogged him, though in different guises, was the conflict between freedom and restraint. He started as a champion of freedom. A disciple of Henri Bergson, he believed that trust in human intuition could liberate men from science and its rigid laws, which turned them into machines. But he soon came to feel that any reliance on human capabilities was misplaced. Utopians like Wells and Shaw, with their faith in moral progress, struck him as deluded. Man was essentially limited, and prey to original sin, though he could be disciplined into 'something fairly decent'. Nothing, he proclaimed, was bad in itself, except disorder. Hierarchy and submission to authority were inherently good. His admiration for abstract art arose from the same kind of reasoning. It was pure and austere, like geometry, so it could function almost as an aesthetic redemption from original sin, lifting man 'out of the transience of the organic'.

The contrast between his cult of order and the way he conducted his life is obvious, and there was a similar mismatch between his conservative social views and his personal relations. He considered women unfit for rational discourse. Motherhood and domesticity were their proper roles; intelligent women were just 'misplaced whores'. Yet Dolly and Kate Lechmere, who replaced her as his mistress, were both independent-minded, cultured women (Kate had studied under Sickert) and Hulme lived all his adult life on an allowance from a bluestocking aunt who was a former headmistress. But consistency and correctness seem minor matters when compared to the vigour and sincerity of his thought. His aphorisms – 'All styles are only means of subduing the reader', 'All clear-cut ideas turn out to be wrong' – convey a lucid disillusionment reminiscent of Nietzsche. His mind, like his body, was intensely alive, and unshakably committed to his declared aim of making the new art intelligible to everyone.

When war broke out he enlisted within a week, and served in Flanders as an infantry private. His diary from the trenches, put together from letters he sent home, displays the discipline and self-control he had recommended in his philosophy. Bullets slapping into the sandbags above his head are 'irritating', but nothing more. With detached curiosity he watches seasoned tommies 'shaking all over and crying' under shellfire. But the letters he sent to Kate betray the other side of his nature with their passionate, animal cries for sexual stimulation, and their gasps of gratitude when the erotic artfulness of her letters brings him temporary physical release.

In April 1915, he received a bullet wound in the arm, and returned to England where he started work on a book about Epstein. He had had enough of the trenches, and, once recovered, was sent to help man the heavy guns of the Royal Marine Artillery on the Belgian coast. It was there on 28 September 1917 that he was hit by a shell from the German battery at Ostend and blown to pieces. Unlike his comrades, who had dived for cover, he had apparently not heard it coming, but remained upright as if lost in thought. It was not quite the last anyone saw of him. Just after the war, Kate, who never married, but remained dedicated to his memory, had a peculiarly vivid dream in which she saw him 'standing in the sun, looking happy'. Ferguson's book is exceptional in conjuring a flesh-and-blood figure from sparse and often abstruse materials. It is an unforgettable tribute to an unforgettable man.

Robert Graves and the White Goddess, 1940–1985
Richard Perceval Graves, 1995

Robert Graves: Life on the Edge
Miranda Seymour, 1995

Robert Graves: Collected Writings on Poetry
edited by Paul O'Prey, 1995

I remember walking down the Cornmarket in Oxford with Robert Graves one spring morning in 1973. We were out early – he had stayed the night with us – but there were already shoppers about, and heads turned. No wonder. Graves, at seventy-eight, was still a commanding sight – the ramrod back, the shaggy halo of grizzled curls, the haughty face with its broken nose, like a slightly battered Greek god. He looked, and was, every inch an officer and gentleman. Yet from his lips, in disconcertingly loud, upper-class tones, issued a bizarre stream of superstition and bogus history. The rings he was wearing were magic, and were, at that moment, helping to cure a distant friend; a stone he produced from his pocket was a meteorite, and had revealed amazing secrets under the microscope; the ancient Etruscans had discovered nuclear fission and used it to harden their clay pots.

For any biographer of Graves the problem is to reconcile these two beings: the old-fashioned, chivalrous Englishman and the crazy magician. How did they get inside the same body? His nephew R.P. Graves has laboured for ten years to clarify this, drawing on a vast archive of family papers. *Robert Graves and the White Goddess* triumphantly concludes a trilogy that embeds Graves's life in a microcosm of English social history. Miranda Seymour's *Robert Graves: Life on the Edge* is slighter, but sharper in focus. No one, she claims, has examined Graves's relations with women in any detail. This is shockingly unfair to R.P. Graves, who has examined everything in unsparing detail. But it is also the right line to take, for three things shaped Graves, and two of them were women.

The first was his mother, Amalia von Ranke, a pious German battleaxe who drilled her sons to be pure in heart and to win whatever the odds. A streak of callousness or stupidity allowed her and her overshadowed spouse, the Irish bard Alfred Perceval Graves, to send sixteen-year-old Robert back to Charterhouse, despite his disclosure of the bullying his German ancestry provoked. From Amalia he inherited shame about the physical side of sex, towering intellectual arrogance, and a masochistic identification of women as natural rulers.

The second thing that shaped him was the Great War. He went out to the trenches fresh from school, a patriotic young subaltern declaring: 'France is the only place for a gentleman now'. In the next four years he saw and heard things the civilised world of 1914 had never dreamed of. What could be described he described in his masterpiece *Goodbye to All That* (1929), now available with an introduction by R.P. Graves – its original, raw version, not the tidied-up 1957 rewrite familiar to modern readers. At the Battle of the Somme, a shell splinter entered his back and he was given up for dead. Amalia received his colonel's letter, announcing her son's loss, on his twenty-first birthday. In a way it was true, for the man who survived was not the same. For years after he was plagued by nightmares and the spectres of dead comrades. He no longer inhabited the world of the sane, and a sane remedy for his trauma would not suffice.

What he discovered instead was a myth, which transfigured his sufferings and gave them meaning. The first hint for it came from the psychologist William Rivers, who treated shell-shocked officers at Craiglockhart War Hospital. According to Rivers, early man had worshipped a Great Mother, later lamentably replaced by patriarchal deities. In Graves's imaginings she became the White Goddess, the sacred bride of young males who, after enjoying her embraces, were torn to pieces in frenzied Dionysian orgies. This prehistoric fantasy, backed up by tireless research into fertility rites and folk cultures, allowed Graves to fit together his overbearing mother, his sex-guilt, and the carnage on the Western Front. Better still, it proved his superiority to other, more successful poets – T.S. Eliot, W.B. Yeats, Ezra Pound – whom he despised and envied. For the White Goddess myth taught that no poet could hope to understand the nature of poetry unless he had, like Graves, been vouchsafed a vision of 'the Naked King crucified to the lopped oak', and of the wild women dancers, 'red-eyed from the acrid smoke of the sacrificial fires', chanting: 'Kill! kill! kill!' and 'Blood! blood! blood!'

But he still had to find his goddess, or her earthly embodiment. This happened when the young American poet Laura Riding, the third shaper of his destiny, arrived in England at Graves's invitation in 1926. That Laura was insane by normal standards seems clear. Her self-esteem was so gigantic it amounted to mental deficiency. She gave it out that time had stopped, and that she was 'finality'. Her acolytes, Graves included, worshipped her as the goddess Isis or as a reincarnation of Christ. When he set up house with her in the remote Majorcan village of Deyá, it meant abandoning his wife Nancy Nicholson, whom he had married in 1918, and their young family. The children's letters, reproaching him, are distressing to read even now. While they went hungry, he lavished jewels, gowns and real estate on his tyrannical paramour.

Did he, like other disaffected groupies in Deyá, come to see through Laura? It seems so. His historical novel *I, Claudius* (1934), a runaway success that helped to fund their island life-style, includes thinly disguised portraits of Laura as the 'abominable' Livia and the promiscuous Messalina. But if he realised she was a monster why did he submit? It was not out of sympathy with feminism. Early women's libbers who hailed him as a champion were way off target. He thought women less intelligent than men, and incapable of generous male love. He treated his consorts with the imperiousness of his class and era, selecting and discarding them at will. If they caused him pain, it was because he chose pain as the path to goddess-inspired poetry. Laura was succeeded by a procession of young female 'muses' whom Graves's long-suffering second wife Beryl was expected to welcome and befriend. He adored them, but warned that if they succumbed to other men (as they all did) they would instantly lose their magic and become common clay.

He was aware, as he aged, that these infatuations must seem ridiculous. But that was part of their appeal. He loved to feel he was defying a hostile world. It was not masochism, he insisted, 'or even stupidity', but 'the same endurance that sustains a soldier in the field'.

Sticking by Laura, till she dumped him in 1939, had been a similar heroic ordeal. In his non-fiction books this truculence shows up everywhere. He believed he had access to 'analeptic' thought, which enabled him to fill in the gaps where evidence was lacking, and come up with dazzling insights, unavailable to grubbing professors. In *The Nazarene Gospel Restored*, he claimed to have decoded the Christian gospels and heralded the end of the Christian era. Experts made merry, and the *Church Times* labelled it 'a farrago of rubbish'. But he did not learn. His reputation took another knock in 1972 when his version of the *Rubaiyat of Omar Khayyam*, purportedly based on an ancient Persian manuscript, was shown to be cribbed from a late-Victorian translation.

When he wrote about English poets, idol-toppling was at a premium. *Wife to Mr Milton* (1944) vilified the great Puritan for his alleged ill-treatment of women. R.P. Graves acutely suggests that Graves was holding up a mirror to his own soul, and that what the book truly condemns is his shameful treatment of Nancy. But there is no evidence this occurred to Graves, and joyful iconoclasm remains the keynote in *Robert Graves: Collected Writings on Poetry*, edited by Paul O'Prey. His belittlements can be so unfair as to diminish only himself, especially when he was playing to the gallery. The jibes at Yeats, or at 'sick, muddle-headed, sex-mad D.H. Lawrence', fall into this category. But against this can be set his marvellously funny exposure of Ezra Pound's ignorance of Latin, or his delicate responses to rhythm, cadence and word choice in the early essays. If there is a volume more sensitively intelligent about a wide range of English poetry, I do not know it.

That inevitably raises the question of his own poetic development, and the value of what he wrote under the White Goddess's influence. R.P. Graves and Miranda Seymour are biographers, not critics, and they seem not to notice the rhythmic flatness and stilted diction of the late love poetry they approvingly quote, nor its lack of wit and irony. Until Graves met Laura Riding, with her hatred of the masses and her cult of obscurity, he had it in him to be a great popular poet. The Claudius books and *Goodbye to All That* attest his closeness to the common reader. They will live, as the poetry, perhaps, will not.

Yet Graves was one of those figures – Samuel Johnson and George Orwell are others – who was greater than anything he wrote, and whose personal qualities are the true earnest of immortality. His magnanimity, his courage, his glamour, his unflinching loyalty to his ideals, seemed to set him on a plane above the human. Perhaps those rings were magic after all.

The Letters of Sylvia Plath, Volume 2: 1956–1963
edited by Peter K. Steinberg and Karen V. Kukil, 2018

In August 1961 Ted Hughes and Sylvia Plath bought a beautiful thatched house in Devon and put their London flat up for rent. Would-be tenants soon arrived at their door. There was a nice young couple that Hughes and Plath took to at once, and, bidding against them, a rather bossy older man they didn't much like. However, he was in a position to sit down and write a cheque straight off, so the young couple went away disappointed. Later that evening, though, Hughes and Plath changed their mind, tore the cheque up, notified the bossy man they were not moving after all, and offered the flat to the nice young couple.

There are several moments in this second volume of Plath's letters when you feel you are watching a Greek tragedy, but this is the most fateful. For the young couple were the Canadian poet David Wevill and his wife Assia. Within a year of tearing up their cheque Hughes had begun a passionate affair with Assia and walked out of his marriage to Plath, who committed suicide in February 1963. Six years later Assia killed herself and her daughter by Hughes, Shura.

In *Birthday Letters* (1998), published shortly before his own death, Hughes does not mention Assia by name. She becomes an anonymous woman, 'slightly filthy with erotic mystery', that Fate insinuates into the Hughes household. But that is far from how Plath recounts the episode in the passionate letters to her American psychiatrist Dr Ruth Beuscher, included in this volume. She represents Hughes as mocking, taunting, threatening and triumphant in his adultery. He asks her why she has not killed herself, and says Assia and he expected she would. Any criticism of his conduct makes him 'murderous', so she fears for her safety and that of the children, Frieda and Nicholas, aged respectively two-and-a-half years and nine months.

In his study she has found 'sheafs' of passionate love poems to Assia, 'describing their orgasms, her ivory body, her smell, her beauty, saying in a world of beauties he married a hag'. Many of them are 'fine poems', she concedes, but 'the knowledge that I am ugly and hateful kills me'. (The editors identify these unpublished poems as among those deposited in the Hughes archive at Emory University, Georgia.) In February 1961 Plath had suffered a miscarriage. At the time she told Dr Beuscher that the doctors did not know why, but a troublesome appendix, which she had out the following month, was perhaps the cause. Now she writes, 'Ted beat me up physically a couple of days before my miscarriage'.

In her Foreword to this book Frieda Hughes regrets that these private letters between a patient and her psychiatrist should ever have been published. She has, though, given permission for them to appear in full because damaging excerpts from them are already in the public domain. After Dr Beuscher's death, quotations from Plath's letters were put on the Internet by a dealer acting for an unnamed client, and were picked up and repeated in the press. Frieda is sure her father was not a wife-beater, reminding readers that 'exaggeration' is likely when two passionate people are 'fighting over their ending'. Readers who choose to believe otherwise may point to Plath's constant emphasis, in letters to her mother and friends, on what a 'saint' and 'angel' Hughes is, gladly taking on housework and caring for the children. This, they may suggest, looks suspiciously like an abused wife shielding her abuser. However, Frieda is the only person left alive who is qualified to give an opinion about what happened, and she has done so.

The feelings expressed in the Beuscher letters clearly lie behind poems such as 'Daddy' and 'Lady Lazarus' that, written by Plath in her final months, have won her global fame. Yet to regard the letters merely as raw material for poems undervalues them. They are astonishing in themselves, terrible in their intensity and as raw as freshly sliced meat. As a real-life depiction of a mind in agony they are, so far as I know, unmatched in literature.

The tragedy is intensified when you compare it with what happiness there might have been. They were two immensely gifted young poets who had found each other. At the start of this volume they have just married and Plath is in her final year at Cambridge. After she graduates they sail on the *Queen Elizabeth* to New York and find a flat in Boston. Plath teaches for a year at her old college, Smith, and in summer 1959 they drive across North America, camping out in the wild. Then they have two productive months in the writers' colony at Yaddo. Plath recounts all this in graphic, elated prose, and the question is, why did they return to England? She had been appalled by its lack of central heating, washing machines and modern dentistry, and had declared it no place to bring up children. But Hughes was homesick, so she gave way.

It was the fatal flaw that all Greek tragedies need. Writing to Beuscher she confesses she has been guilty of what the sociologist Erich Fromm calls (in a book Beuscher lent her) 'idolatrous love'. 'I lost myself in Ted rather than finding myself.' His career was partly of her making. She had sent his poems to magazines and publishers, undaunted by flurries of rejection slips, and had got secretarial jobs to help pay for his keep. She never doubted he was a great poet, as well as the 'most magnificent man ever'. But her stature depended on being his chosen woman, and finding she was not shattered her.

She fought against defeat, writing her greatest poems, and assuring her mother the next five years would be 'heavenly'. 'My dream is to sell a novel to the movies.' Setting herself impossible aims had always been part of her imaginative exuberance. In 1958 she had told her brother, Warren, 'Ted and I plan to educate ourselves in history, art, literature, language and philosophy this year'. When she and Hughes moved to the house in Devon she made eager plans to turn its two-and-a-half acres into a market garden. Then he left, and in her last letter, written to Dr Beuscher seven days before her death, she senses failure 'like an accusing wind'. She feels her 'madness' returning and is tempted by despair. 'I am scared to death I shall just pull up the psychic shroud & give up.'

Faulks on Fiction: The Secret Life of the Novel
Sebastian Faulks, 2011

F*aulks on Fiction* is not intended as a formal history of the British novel, but it is much more worthwhile and enjoyable than any history of the novel I have read. Early in the book Sebastian Faulks recalls meeting a university lecturer and asking her whether *Vanity Fair* and *Middlemarch* were popular with her students. She laughed and told him such books would never again be read by undergraduates: a single photocopied chapter was as much as they could manage. I do not think that is true in general, and it would be inane to laugh about it if it were. (It would, on the contrary, be a good reason for closing down some university English departments.) But if you happen to know any teenagers, undergraduate or not, who seem less than enthusiastic about their literary heritage, *Faulks on Fiction* might wake them from their torpor.

Written to accompany a four-part BBC Two documentary series, which begins on 5 February, it chooses twenty-eight characters from the timespan of British fiction, and divides them into four groups: heroes, lovers, snobs and villains. The mix is democratic – Sherlock Holmes, Jeeves and James Bond get as much attention as Heathcliff or Jane Austen's Emma – and Faulks's approach is pleasingly unfashionable. He treats fictional characters as if they were real people and tries to understand why they behave as they do.

It quickly becomes clear that he is no pushover as a critic. He distrusts the programme makers' categories. Heroes and villains are, he objects, out of place in novels: heroes belong in epic, villains in the theatre. Besides, most of the twenty-eight selected characters have, in his view, serious design faults. Of the so-called heroes, Defoe's Robinson Crusoe is not a character at all but merely a representative of *Homo sapiens*, ingenious at taming the wild. Fielding's Tom Jones has no inner being: protected from mishap by his indulgent author, he is just 'a jolly cork on a choppy sea'. Thackeray's Becky Sharp is a plucky survivor, but emotionally null. Clever, ruthless, selfish, a bad mother and ultimately a murderess, she might, Faulks reckons, have found a job in the financial sector if she were alive today. Literary criticism could hardly get more damning. As for John Self in *Money*, the 'continuing problem' of Martin Amis's fiction is that 'the style is the man and the man is always Martin Amis'.

Only Sherlock Holmes and Kingsley Amis's *Lucky Jim* Dixon eventually make the grade as heroes, and Faulks writes incisively about both. Dixon, by being so funny and so likeable, allows readers to relish his triumphs as if they were their own, which is the one inalienable duty of every hero. Holmes, like the heroes of old epics, is a 'demigod', and this explains the uncanny grip he still has on the public imagination worldwide.

Lovers fare even worse than heroes under Faulks's scourge. Darcy in *Pride and Prejudice* is 'a manipulative, hypocritical, self-centred depressive' who marries Elizabeth Bennet simply because she offers 'lifelong Prozac in an Empire-line dress'. Heathcliff in *Wuthering Heights* is a magnificent thunderstorm of passion, but reduces the rest of the novel to matchwood. Faulks particularly dislikes novels that twist character and plot to fit their authors' philosophical agendas. *Tess of the d'Urbervilles* falls into this category, with Thomas Hardy shouting and gesticulating behind the action like a 'clumsy chorus'. On second thoughts he withdraws this criticism, but he feels less nervous about applying it to Maurice Bendrix in *The End of the Affair*, who, he rightly insists, is little more than a 'conduit' for Graham Greene's cosmic pessimism. Worse still is Doris Lessing's *The Golden Notebook*. Faulks had not read it until he was obliged to while researching for this book, and he was aghast to find that its cast of sanctimonious women and horrible men had provided the prototype for all the 'Hampstead novels' he had groaned over in his fiction-reviewing days.

The one lover to survive more or less unscathed from this fusillade is Connie Chatterley in D.H. Lawrence's *Lady Chatterley's Lover*. Faulks concedes that the novel has its absurdities, and he is aware that feminist critics have condemned the virile gamekeeper Mellors's 'phallocratic' behaviour as politically retrograde. However, he contends, 'some women do enjoy what Mellors does to Connie', and political theory cannot alter neuronal preferences.

Predictably, the snobs come off best. As Faulks observes, the snob and the mainstream novel might almost have been made for one another. This is because in fiction snobbery is not necessarily stupid or wrong. Austen, in *Emma*, makes us all complicit in the fun of being snobbish when we laugh at vulgar Mrs Elton and her 'barouche landau' (the Chelsea tractor of its day, Faulkes suggests). Fictional snobs can be highly intelligent (Jeeves, Muriel Spark's Miss Brodie) or poignant and endearing (Pooter in *The Diary of a Nobody*, Chanu Ahmed in Monica Ali's *Brick Lane*). Despite this, Faulks believes that most novelists are 'instinctively democratic' in their views. That may be so, though some powerful exemplars (Flaubert, Proust, Waugh – and, indeed, Lawrence) seem to have successfully overcome their instincts.

With villains Faulks has some trouble, since they do not, or do not all, behave like sensible people as he rather feels characters should. He writes acutely about Barbara Covett in Zoe Heller's *Notes on a Scandal*, but she is an intellectual snob as well as a villain and even, to some extent, a hero, in that we identify with her acidic critique of her teaching colleagues. Ronald Merrick, the sadist and torturer in Paul Scott's *Raj Quartet*, fits Faulks's realistic criteria admirably, but Lovelace in Samuel Richardson's *Clarissa* is more worrying. Faulks sympathises, to an extent, with his aims ('Clarissa is a nice enough girl but can hardly remain a virgin for ever'), but he senses 'something diabolic' behind his behaviour. The 'demonic' Steerpike in Mervyn Peake's *Gormenghast* slips further from realism's grasp, and Fagin in *Oliver Twist* escapes it altogether, seeming to be 'almost part of a collective memory'. Dickens at his greatest is always like this, of course, and Faulks acknowledges the problem. 'It's difficult to write interestingly about Dickens. Sometimes it's hard to think of much to say beyond, "Isn't this unbelievably good?"'

Even saying that matters if you are a figure with Faulks's following. The most winning parts of his book are those where he describes his early encounters with literature. Reading George Orwell's 'A Hanging' when he was fourteen struck him with 'the force of revelation' and changed the way he looked at the world. *David Copperfield*, *Pride and Prejudice* and *Sons and Lovers,* read in the space of a single spring term when he was in the fifth form, convinced him that literature was the most important thing on earth. When he came to the bit where David Copperfield turns to the woman he loves – 'O Agnes, O my soul' – he found he was making 'strange snorting noises', caused by the fact that he was sobbing but trying to keep his eyes open so that he could go on reading. This is not the sort of recommendation literary criticism generally offers, and Faulks's relaxed, sharply observant book will no doubt be sneered at by academics. That is another reason for reading it.

The Good Soldier Švejk

Jaroslav Hašek, translated by Paul Selver, 1930

Jaroslav Hašek was a comic genius in the flesh as well as in fiction. As editor of a magazine called *Animal World* in pre-First World War Prague, he livened it up by introducing formerly unnoted animals. His discovery of a fossilised flea caused a sensation, and when he advertised a pair of thoroughbred werewolves for sale the office was flooded with applications. He seems to have decided that the best way of dealing with a world full of fanatics was to agree with them as eagerly as possible, since opposition would only make them worse. When war came, he joined the Austrian army, got himself captured by the Russians, became an ardent tsarist, and then, with the Bolshevik revolution, mutated into a commissar with the Red Army and editor of *Red Europe*.

A similar policy of non-resistance is adopted by his hero Švejk. When the novel starts in 1914 he has been discharged from the army for some years as a congenital idiot and is living peacefully in Prague attended by his charwoman, Mrs Muller. Her announcement that the Archduke Franz Ferdinand has been assassinated in Sarajevo in a car prompts a typical Švejkism: 'Well, there you have it, Mrs Muller; in a car. A gentleman like him can afford it.' Whether irony or stupidity predominates in such remarks is the question that soon perplexes the military authorities. For Švejk, re-entering the Austrian army with an alacrity rare among the Emperor's Czech subjects, finds himself confronting medical boards and courts of enquiry who earnestly enquire whether he is truly such a half-wit as he seems. 'Humbly report, sir, I am,' he invariably responds, beaming at them with his innocent blue eyes.

In encounters with superior officers he readily concurs with even their most insulting and bloodthirsty propositions. No one applauds pep-talks by the top brass more fervently. It would be glorious, he agrees, to be run through with a bayonet, and even grander to be blown to pieces by a shell. He is quick to reprove criticism of the army command, explaining, when confronted with some particularly gruesome military blunder, that 'Mistakes must occur'. His secret weapon is an enormous fund of irrelevant anecdote which reduces hearers, in extreme cases, to apoplexy and nervous breakdown.

Švejk's appointment as batman to a drunken and blasphemous regimental chaplain gives Hašek scope to satirise the Catholic church, which he detested almost as much as the Austro-Hungarian Empire. Švejk and his superior hold drumhead masses for the doomed troops, equipped with a folding field altar, on which the Son of God is depicted as a blithe young man 'with a handsome stomach, draped in something that looked like bathing drawers'. Another rich source of ridicule is official Austrian propaganda designed to inspire self-sacrifice in subject peoples. Placards depict feats of suicidal gallantry with cheerfully upbeat slogans. At railway stations ladies from the Society for the Reception of Heroes distribute boxes of mouthwash pastilles, inscribed 'For God and Fatherland', to battalions on their way to the front. A patriotic cadet in Švejk's regiment is engrossed in a treatise entitled 'Self-Education in Dying for the Emperor'.

There are gaps in the humour when Hašek lets us see the true atrocities. Manacled peasants, followed by carts bearing coffins, march to parade grounds to be shot for 'mutiny during call-up'. Photographs of executions carried out by the army in occupied territories show whole families strung up – children, mother and father – while soldiers with fixed bayonets guard the tree from which they hang. You might think it impossible, or indecent, to wring laughter from such situations. But that is the challenge Hašek faces with his blasts of sanity and scorn. Even a concentration camp is fair game. Švejk's charwoman Mrs Muller is arrested and court-martialled, but finding no evidence against her the authorities send her to a concentration camp, from which her family receive a card:

Dear Aninka, We are enjoying ourselves very much here. We are all well. The woman in the next bed to me has spotted – and also there are here people with small –. Otherwise everything is in order.

Hašek started writing *The Good Soldier Svejk* in 1921, and had to publish the first volume at his own expense because publishers were frightened off by his obscenity and truth-telling. He was half-way through the fourth and final volume when he died in 1923. Though unfinished, his work has rightly been classed with the comic epics of Cervantes and Rabelais and is funnier and more fearful than either. His message was that war is not merely cruel, unjust and obscene but ludicrous. Unfortunately, humans are programmed to believe otherwise.

BACK TO NATURE

Beatrix Potter: A Life in Nature
Linda Lear, 2006

Heroism might not be the first virtue you would expect to find in the author of *The Tale of Peter Rabbit*. But the Beatrix Potter depicted in Linda Lear's authoritative biography was undoubtedly heroic. Dauntless and public-spirited, she pitted herself against a world dominated by incompetent and obstructive men. Lear has discovered that, long before Beatrix began her famous series of 'little books' for children, she was a serious student of natural history, pursuing research unthought of by the established male scientists of her day.

The male scientists were very cross, of course, for she had no right to be so clever. Besides being a woman, she was virtually untaught and had never had access to a proper laboratory. Her rich, snobbish parents had not believed in sending girls to school or university, so she and her younger brother had assembled their own botanical collection, including frogs, lizards, rabbits, hedgehogs, bats, mice, a snake, a brilliant green lizard called Judy and a family of snails who, Beatrix remarked, had 'surprising differences of character'. When their animals died they were boiled and their skeletons measured, labelled and preserved.

As a young woman, her interest in plants and animals became all-absorbing. On family holidays in the Lake District she made friends with the local postman, who was also an amateur naturalist (he later became the model for Mr McGregor), and he encouraged her to study fungi. With the aid of a microscope she made beautiful, precise drawings and watercolours of their different varieties, learnt to germinate their spores and developed theories about their relationship to algae and lichen. With the help of her uncle, a well-known chemist, she eventually gained access to scientists at the Royal Botanical Gardens, Kew, and at the Linnaean Society – this was in 1896, when she was thirty – but they treated her ideas with undisguised contempt. Their ignorant prejudice cut short what might have been an epoch-making scientific career, for later research has proved her conclusions correct. In the 1940s, when news of the discovery of penicillin began to circulate, she was unsurprised, for she had observed the penicillium mould's antibacterial potential herself many years before while experimenting on moulds and fungi.

Painting and drawing were her other passions, so she turned her attention to them. The Peter Rabbit books began as illustrated letters and stories she sent to friends' children. She tried them out on half a dozen (male) publishers, but they were unimpressed, so she decided to publish herself. Her privately printed *Peter Rabbit* came out in time for Christmas 1901, and caught the attention of Norman Warne, younger partner at Frederick Warne & Co. In negotiation with Beatrix he evolved the little-book format, incorporating her coloured illustrations, and *The Tale of Peter Rabbit* appeared in October 1902. By the end of the year it had sold 23,000.

Warne & Co. was a timid, inefficient publisher. It failed to copyright *Peter Rabbit* in America, an enormously costly mistake, and had no idea how to exploit the book's success. Beatrix, by contrast, proved a shrewd businesswoman. Her Peter Rabbit doll, with signature blue coat and black shoes, was ready in time for Christmas 1903, and she registered it at the Patent Office. Other spin-offs followed – Peter Rabbit wallpaper, handkerchiefs, tea sets. But Beatrix was not just out to make money. She wanted her creations to be beautiful, and available to not-so-well-off children. She strove to get Peter's coat just the right blue, considering Harrods' rival rabbits 'very ugly', and she battled with Warne to keep the price of her books down.

There had been plenty of animal books for children before, but hers were the first to reflect accurate knowledge. Animal behaviour in her stories, though fantasised, is based on years of scientific investigation and hundreds of precise drawings. The insects who invade Mrs Tittlemouse's house could have come from a botanical textbook, and many of the leading animals – Peter and Benjamin Rabbit, Hunca Munca and Tom Thumb the bad mice, and Mrs Tiggy-Winkle the hedgehog – were her own pets, which she had studied and sketched endlessly. Pig-Wig, the little black pig who is rescued by Piggling Bland, had been a pet, too. She had kept him in a basket by her bed and bottle-fed him until he was able to survive by himself.

Beatrix and Norman Warne became engaged in July 1905, much to the outrage of her parents, who disdained him for being 'in trade' (though their own fortune derived from Beatrix's paternal grandfather who was a calico printer in Manchester). But barely a month later, Norman died of leukaemia. Beatrix surmounted the tragedy with characteristic energy. She and Norman had dreamt of farming in the Lake District, so in October 1905 she bought Hill Top Farm beside Esthwaite Water, and set about turning herself into a countrywoman.

As usual she met male opposition. She discovered she had paid twice what Hill Top was worth, because the owner considered a woman fair game, and the local stockmen and farmers scorned her chances of success, particularly when she decided to raise Herdwick sheep, a small, sturdy breed with all-black lambs, that had been a feature of fell farming for centuries. But she confounded the wiseacres. For two decades, her Herdwick ewes won top prizes at all the agricultural shows, and her straight-dealing and good-heartedness won the villagers over. She joked about their earlier suspicions. Her picture of Jemima Puddle-Duck dashing downhill, bonnet askew, was, she said, how she had appeared to the locals, always rushing about and quacking industriously.

She became Warnes' bestselling author, writing thirteen books over the next eight years, and using the proceeds to buy more farms and properties. William Heelis, a solicitor whom she married in 1913, was a great help with the conveyancing. Her unavailing attempts to extract financial statements from Warne & Co came to a head when Harold, Norman's elder brother, was found guilty of forgery and sent to prison. Beatrix buckled down to save her publisher from ruin, producing two quick books, though by this time farming and conservation had become her great enthusiasms.

Her plan was to protect the Lake District from development, so that walkers and holidaymakers could enjoy its unspoilt beauty. One of her oldest friends was Canon Rawnsley, a founder of the National Trust, and it was his example that inspired her gradual accumulation of land. When she died in 1943 she left 4,300 acres to the Trust, including fifteen farms, scores of cottages and 500 acres of woodland. Her will stipulated that the sheep stocks on her fell farms should maintain the 'pure Herdwick breed', and that Hill Top should be open to the public. It still attracts millions of pilgrims every year.

It is hard to imagine a better life, or a better use of wealth. Almost the most attractive thing about her was her hatred of publicity and self-advertisement. The day before she died she told her shepherd Tom Storey that she was to be cremated, and that he should scatter her ashes in the fields above Hill Top, where she had so often walked and sketched, but tell nobody where he had put them. 'I want it kept secret.'

Orchard: A Year in England's Eden
Benedict Macdonald and Nicholas Gates, 2020

Try to imagine an orchard. If the word suggests to you rows of fruit trees, evenly spaced, with the ground beneath them cleared to allow access, then you will have a precise idea of what Benedict Macdonald hates and despises about English orchards. His previous book, *Rebirding* (2019), took as its focus the Knepp Wildland in West Sussex, where large mammals such as bison have been introduced into the English countryside. The precise location of the orchard at the heart of this new book is not revealed, presumably to deter intruders. But it is somewhere in Herefordshire. Its owners, 'Nancy' and her son 'David', also remain shadowy.

At first it does not sound like an orchard at all. A line of ancient oaks cuts across the middle of it, and part of it is taken up by towering hedges of blackthorn and hazel, several metres high and correspondingly thick, to provide shelter for wild birds. Branches that drop off old trees are allowed to lie and rot, encrusted with fungi and covered in nettles, because they become a habitat for a huge variety of insects, spiders and worms. The dead wood also attracts woodpeckers, and the holes they bore in it are used as nesting places by many other species – dormice, toads, stoats, hornets, tawny owls.

This impression of complete wildness is modified later in the book. Nancy and David, it turns out, do not leave all the dead wood lying around, only chosen specimens that are judged most suitable for wildlife. The rest is burnt. Nettles and brambles would soon make the orchard impassable if left, so most are cleared. The few remaining brambles are woven into 'thorn-studded igloos' to shelter wrens and other small birds. The orchard has 700 trees, yielding 100 tonnes of fruit, and they are regularly pruned to encourage new growth and remove old. David markets a highly prized perry, or pear cider, and the room where the fruit is pressed is a hygienic sanctum of glass, plastic and polished metal. He also grafts new varieties on to old stock, producing 'a tidy rank of new trees'. This, on the last page, is the only place in the book where 'tidy' is used as a compliment.

For tidiness is Macdonald's bugbear, and he regards it as a vice peculiar to the English. It is this that impels them, he believes, to drench their fields with pesticides and to reduce their hedgerows to 'skinny, flailed relics'. In July he pays a visit to Hungary, which is like stepping back in history to what England used to be. In some villages the pavements are thick with purple emperor butterflies, and house martins abound to feed on them. Some villagers still use horse-and-cart transport, and the insect-rich dung the horses drop attracts hordes of birds. The dawn chorus is deafening. In the garden at night there are so many hedgehogs you can hear them going 'snuffle, shuffle' through the grass, and the gardens are miraculously free of slugs.

Curiously, it never occurs to Macdonald to check on comparative population figures, which are readily obtainable on the internet. The population of Britain is 1,010 people to the square mile, due to rise to 1,349 by 2056. The population of Hungary is 276 people to the square mile. The intensive English farming Macdonald derides as 'tidiness', and his mortifying tally of the enormous acreage of English orchards that have been grubbed up over the past century, quickly become explicable in the light of these figures. Without some practical notion of how population growth might be controlled, books such as *Orchard* seem ultimately evasive.

That said, *Orchard* has much to offer in its observation of wildlife. Macdonald and his co-author, Nicholas Gates, have been studying their 'adopted' orchard for eight years. They have remote cameras clamped high in the trees, so they can watch nests at a distance on screen. This produces one of the most harrowing episodes as they observe a great spotted woodpecker carrying off the tiny fledglings of a lesser spotted woodpecker, one by one, to feed to its young, and witness the parent lesser spotted returning agitatedly to their depleted brood, till all are gone. Less gruesomely, Gates sees on his monitor three robin chicks, no more than twenty-four hours old, with their eyes 'still glued firmly shut; oversized dark orbs hidden behind a fine layer of tissue-thin skin'. Writing as sensitive as that makes the book's colour plates, although excellent of their kind, seem flat and static.

The book is full of unexpected revelations. A vital capacity for a queen bumblebee, for example, is the ability to detect mouse urine. She needs this because an old mouse or vole nest, consisting of a narrow tunnel leading to a moss-lined chamber, is the ideal place for her to raise her family. Perhaps the book's most astonishing section is about the migration of painted lady butterflies. These delicate creatures start their journey in central Africa, cross the Sahara at a steady 30mph, wing their way up through the Mediterranean and arrive in Britain in July and August. In some years, such as 2009, as many as 11 million butterflies cross the Channel. Sometimes they push on as far as the Arctic Circle.

What impels them? No one knows. Macdonald does not go so far as to suggest that they plan their journeys intelligently. But he does detect intelligence elsewhere in the animal world. Wild boar, which arrive in the orchard in December, are, he says, 'hugely intelligent'. His grounds for believing this are that they eat large quantities of fruit and then excrete the seeds 'complete with fertiliser'. So they play a vital role in propagating the next generation of fruit trees. It seems a desperate argument, unless you drastically redefine 'intelligence'. As things stand, we seem to be the only intelligent beings, and, as *Orchard* vividly shows, our evolution has upset a perfectly balanced ecosystem.

Owl Sense
Miriam Darlington, 2018

Miriam Darlington's highly praised *Otter Country* (2012) recorded four years spent tracking otters across the British Isles. Her new book, *Owl Sense*, is just as vivid and engaging and more adventurous. It starts quietly. Intrigued by the ghoulish shrieks of tawny owls near her Devon home, she takes to patrolling the woods at dawn, leaving her husband, Rick, and their children, Jenny and Benji, still cosily in bed. Eager to learn more, she joins the Barn Owl Trust as a volunteer, and accompanies an expert on his tours of nest boxes, helping him weigh and ring owlets while the parent birds swoop and panic.

She hears on the owl grapevine that Serbia is the place to see them, so she books a flight, and it is a revelation. Being less developed agriculturally, Serbia is a paradise for wildlife. The hares are as big as cocker spaniels; the flocks of cranes darken the sky when they take flight. Some villages have more owls than people.

Her guide takes her to see long-eared and short-eared owls (in both species the 'ears' are really horn-like plumes, to scare predators) and the locals are so pleased to welcome owl tourists that they hold an owl festival each October. After that, there's no stopping her. She travels to Finland to see the Eurasian eagle-owl in the wild, then to the Vercors plateau in southeastern France to see a colony of pygmy owls that is seemingly a relic of the Ice Age, left behind in this high, remote region when the glaciers receded.

Behind all her activity is a nagging worry. Benji, a healthy teenager, starts to have mysterious, disabling seizures, eventually diagnosed, not very helpfully, as non-epileptic attack disorder. Prognosis is doubtful. This human tragedy, coupled with a bird story, might suggest a connection between *Owl Sense* and Helen Macdonald's *H is for Hawk*. In fact, the two books are completely different.

Darlington hates the idea of wild birds being used as pets or companions or human accessories. It is the savagery and remoteness of owls that attracts her – how they look right through you, how they refuse to be sucked into humankind's clammy, treacherous embrace. She hears with horror that, thanks to the popularity of J.K. Rowling's books and their friendly owls, Harry Potter fans now hire owls to deliver the wedding rings at their nuptials, and that the unfortunate birds tend to collide with stained-glass windows, damaging them and themselves.

You learn a great deal about owls from Darlington's book, almost without noticing it. Her skill is to make it seem she is learning, too. While working with the Barn Owl Trust she finds a dead owl, takes it home and examines it scrupulously, from its ferocious raptorial talons to its mask-like face, covered in hard feathers, 'as if starched like a choirboy's collar'.

The face, she explains, acts as a kind of satellite dish, channelling sounds to the owl's ears, which are the most sensitive in the animal kingdom, and are housed in great clefts at the side of its head. It has extra vertebrae and blood vessels that allow it to turn its facial disc through 270 degrees, and its ears are asymmetric so that it can triangulate and pinpoint the least sound. It can hear a mouse nibbling, pounce and kill it before it has time to squeak.

She discovers another owl secret when she runs her fingers over the super-soft, comb-like edges of her dead owl's wing feathers. These (known technically as 'fimbriae') are designed to break down air turbulence as it flows over the wing, and they are what makes an owl's flight terrifyingly silent, without the warning rush other raptors cause.

Owl digestion is another distinctive feature. The bits of its prey that are too dangerous to pass through its digestive tract are compacted into a tight pellet in the owl's gizzard and regurgitated. Reading this reminded me of a forgotten phase of my childhood, for when we lived in the country I used to collect owl pellets and take them apart, wondering at the tiny teeth, claws and bone fragments they contained. They reminded me of what I had heard about Egyptian mummies, and maybe these funerary bundles help to explain why, as Darlington finds, owls are linked with death in the folklore and poetry of many cultures. In Egyptian, Celtic and Hindu mythology they are guardians of the underworld.

Her style can seem pleasingly informal, but when focus is needed it acquires the power and precision of poetry. She is particularly good on things you might expect to go unnoticed, such as grass. In a Spanish nature reserve the autumnal grasslands 'appeared to be made of withered gold, a mass of crisp, sculptured grasses and filigree this-tles that fragmented underfoot'. In Finland, 'the reindeer moss and lichen crinkled and crunched, dry as biscuit beneath our feet'. This is an owl view of landscape, because it is on grassland creatures – voles, shrews, mice – that owls live.

By the book's end Benji seems a little better, but Darlington's last owl quest ends in failure. News comes through that a snowy owl has been sighted in Cornwall, and she and Rick bundle into the car and race off to find it. Snowy owls breed in the Arctic tundra, and they seem to have had a deep, ancient resonance for humans. Prehistoric cave paintings depict a snowy owl with her chicks, and a shaman with a wolf's tail, antlers on his head, and an owl's facial mask. However, no snowy owl is found in Cornwall.

In a way it is a fitting end, because it reminds us of the many fruitless hours of waiting, wet, cold and, as Darlington puts it, 'as quiet as ivy', that owl-watching entails. Besides, it means that there are still three European owl species – the hawk owl, the great grey owl and the snowy – that she has not seen, and it seems likely she will rise to the challenge. I hope she does, and writes a book about it.

The Spade as Mighty as the Sword: The Story of World War Two's Dig for Victory Campaign
Daniel Smith, 2011

Dig for Victory wasn't an organisation, like the Home Guard, nor just a slogan, such as Careless Talk Costs Lives, but some-thing in between. In October 1939, a month after the outbreak of war, the Ministry of Agriculture launched a campaign to step up home-food production. But its watchword, Grow More Food, failed to catch on, and it was Michael Foot, then a young leader writer for the *Evening Standard*, who came up with Dig for Victory. Churchill seized on it, and with his backing the idea swept the country like a wave of hope.

The need was real. In 1939, Britain imported 75 per cent of its food, and with German U-boats patrolling the shipping lanes that could not continue. But Dig for Victory was also a morale booster. At last civilians saw how they could help. Lawns, flowerbeds, playing fields and parks were dug up and planted with vegetables. Allotments appeared on railway sidings, in the moat of the Tower of London and in the grounds of royal palaces. A field of wheat, reputedly the largest in the country, flourished in Windsor Great Park. At the other end of the scale, the damp, dark interiors of government-issue Anderson shelters, although uninviting for humans, proved ideal for mushroom cultivation.

Daniel Smith's engaging, informed book traces the movement at every level, from government action to gardeners' diaries. By 1943, he estimates, the nation's gardens and allotments were producing more than 1 million tons of vegetables annually, and it was a triumph of publicity as well as horticulture. Chivvied by Churchill, the Ministry of Information organised gardening events and demonstrations countrywide and issued a series of helpful pamphlets (titles ranged from *How to Sow Seed* to *Jam and Jelly Making*). You could get a sign saying 'This Is a Victory Garden' to hang beside your vegetable patch, and there was a Dig for Victory anthem ('Dig! Dig! Dig! And your muscles will grow big'). Films with cartoon characters – Potato Pete, Doctor Carrot – extolled the virtues of root vegetables, and broadcasters offered advice in programmes such as *The Radio Allotment* (which the BBC, seemingly unaware of the point of allotments, criticised for 'covering much the same ground three years running'). Posters kept the campaign in the public eye – the most famous was a photograph showing a foot wearing a left boot pressing a spade into the ground. Eerily, there is no sign of the digger's right foot or leg, just a background of ethereal clouds. Perhaps it was this surreal aspect that gave the image its power.

Garden pests were regarded as enemy agents. The Ministry of Agriculture identified the house sparrow as 'Hitler's feathered friend', and recommended its extermination. In the same spirit, the *Daily Express* ran a story about rabbit damage under the heading 'Herr Rabbit: Fifth Columnist'. Humans who obstructed the war effort also received short shrift. Despite grumbles from the civil-liberties brigade, local authorities insisted on tennis courts and flower gardens being dug up and took defaulters to court. Theft from allotments was seen as a kind of treason and severely punished. A man from Penrhyn got two months' hard labour for stealing potatoes and onions from a railway-embankment plot.

Vegetable growers often kept livestock – hens, rabbits, pigs – and bees, all of which yielded astonishing quantities of food. In the course of the war, the quarter-acre smallholding of a school near Gloucester, run entirely by the pupils, grossed eight tons of bacon, 50,000 eggs, 250 kilos of rabbit meat and 250 kilos of honey. Pig clubs multiplied, not least because members could keep half the meat for themselves while handing over the rest to government-approved retailers. By 1943 there were 5,000 clubs tending 120,000 pigs. Even the royal household had one – the 1,000th to be registered. In the first months of the war a pioneering group of dustmen from Tottenham in north London fed their club's pigs on the food scraps they collected on their rounds. Soon pig bins appeared on street corners across the country and posters showed a gleeful pig proclaiming: 'We want your Kitchen Waste.' Pigs had to be slaughtered by a licensed butcher, but rabbits could be dispatched privately, which called for ingenuity in explaining to children why their pets kept disappearing.

The unwillingness of vegetables to grow in an orderly manner caused headaches among bureaucrats. When gluts occurred, allotment holders were naturally keen to market or give away their surplus rather than see it go to waste. But this alarmed the Ministry of Agriculture, who were fearful of antagonising commercial growers. Luckily the food minister, Lord Woolton (who lent his name to

Woolton pie, which contained carrots, parsnips, turnips and oatmeal under a potato topping, served with brown gravy), insisted that maximising food production was the top priority. The Women's Institute came to the rescue, setting up a network of 5,800 centres, equipped with canning machines, bottles and Kilner jars, and geared to collecting and preserving perishable fruit and vegetables and distributing them to schools and hospitals. It was, Smith ventures, perhaps the WI's finest hour.

The most heroic story comes from Bethnal Green in east London. Eighty tons of bombs fell on the area during the war, damaging or destroying 22,000 homes and killing at least 550 people. In April 1942, the survivors formed the Bethnal Green Bombed Sites Association, to clear the ruins and use the land for vegetables and farm animals. By the end of 1943 there were 300 thriving allotments, thousands of chickens and rabbits, ten pigs and nine goats. Queen Elizabeth was an admiring visitor, and the Christmas hecatomb of Bethnal Green poultry was celebrated in the national press.

Smith's book also points to a wider perspective. Besides staving off starvation, Dig for Victory and its accompanying publicity educated the British about nutrition and improved their health. A 1936 survey had shown that more than half the population was undernourished. Food rationing, introduced in January 1940, enforced a healthier diet, and by 1943 people were consuming 30 per cent less sugar and syrups and 30 per cent more milk and vegetables. Churchill and Woolton encouraged a canteen culture, serving nutritionally balanced meals in schools, factories and 'British Restaurants' – the name was Churchill's invention; bureaucrats had wanted to call them Community Feeding Centres. The results were measurable. Selecting the proportion of children dying in their first year of life as 'the most sensitive index of a nation's health', the chief medical officer reported at the end of 1944 that, whereas it had risen during the First World War, it had dropped steadily from 1941 to 1944, by when it was the lowest recorded. A 1946 Ministry of Health report concluded that children were bigger, more resistant to disease and better nourished than in pre-war years. Another benefit, less measurable, was the thousands of lives Dig for Victory transformed by reconnecting people with the natural world from which, since the Industrial Revolution, they had been increasingly estranged.

Smith's closing pages remind us of his book's modern relevance. The global population is expanding by a billion every ten or fifteen years. Half the world is already gripped by hunger, and it would be absurd to expect other nations to go on feeding us. The Dig for Victory story is as much a preparation for the future as a hymn to the past.

Bertie, May and Mrs Fish: Country Memories of Wartime
Xandra Bingley, 2005

Xandra Bingley was born in 1942 on a farm in the Cotswolds. Her father, Bertie, had gone off to the war, leaving her mother May in charge. To help her she had three elderly farm hands, and Mrs Fish who came in to do the washing. Around them stretches the usual Cotswold scenery – skylarks, dog roses, nettles, dragonflies, owls, drystone walls. But there is nothing usual about Bingley's story or her way of telling it. It is full of bright colours like a child's paintbox, and its short, present-tense sentences capture the unguarded immediacy of childhood experience.

May is the heroine. Nothing in her background has prepared her for the rigours of farm life. The daughter of a rather grand Anglo-Irish family, she had relished the pre-war whirl of house parties, dances and point-to-points, hunted with the Pytchley foxhounds, and won fame as a horsewoman. Her cups and trophies gleam from the farmhouse sideboard. Now she finds herself in command of a 2,000-acre farm, plus thirty cows that need hand milking twice a day. Little Bingley watches it all and stores it in her memory – the sapphire and ruby eternity rings glinting on her mother's chilblained fingers as she churns butter, or fills the paraffin stoves that they depend on for heat; the long white kid gloves wrapped around a leaky pipe in her bedroom.

There are accidents. Snow comes through the roof in winter and has to be shovelled out of the attic. Rats are a problem. A wire trap is rigged up that chops them almost in half, and their bodies are thrown into a paddock to rot among the yellow kingcups. One dreadful day, the milking herd strays into a neighbour's clover field, gorges itself, and collapses – thirty gasping brown-and-white humps – until May arrives and stabs their distended bellies with a knitting needle to let out the gas. Three are already dead. Cutting up apple boughs on a circular saw, a farm labourer manages to sever two fingers. Calm and authoritative, May staunches the bleeding and drives him to hospital, scrabbling first among gore and sawdust to retrieve the fingers in case they can be sewn back on.

Kindness to animals combines with what might strike tender-hearted townees as cruelty. Putting a ferret down a netted rabbit hole to eke out wartime rations, May talks to the struggling captive in baby language – 'Naughty mister bunny rabbit' – before smashing its head in with a stick. Driving home in the dark she hits a stray bull, and breaks its forelegs. All night she sits out on the road with its head on her lap, whispering comfort – 'Try to lie still, my darling' – until a milkman finds them in the dawn and fetches a kennelman with his gun. May, Bertie and their daughter all hunt with the Cotswold, are mad about horses, and treat them like human beings. 'Look where you are going. That was very silly,' May advises her chestnut mare after a stumble. She and her daughter bottle-rear a discarded foal on milk and Virol in the farmhouse kitchen as carefully as if it were a child. Yet when a favourite hunter is past his best, Xandra, now in her teens, strokes his neck and feeds him sugar lumps to distract him while a huntsman puts a stun gun between his big dark eyes and shoots him dead. She has been 'blooded' as a toddler,

the Master of foxhounds drawing red crosses on her cheeks after a
kill, as she sits perched on her roan Welsh pony.

She registers class differences with a child's fastidious objectivity.
The land girls, on loan from Wills Tobacco factory in Birmingham,
whinge and snivel, throwing her mother's patrician stoicism into
high relief. Coarse Mrs Fish, elbow-deep in soapsuds, terrorises
her employers' daughter into raiding their drink cabinet ('If you don't
get my gin I'll tie these sodding jodhpurs round your neck').
May, with little Xandra in tow, takes eggs and vegetables to a farm
labourer's wife whose son has been killed in the war, and they
learn about the sufferings of the rural poor in the early years of
the century – 'there were people starving then. On a baby's death
certificate they wrote consumption of the bowels ... that was what
they called starvation. Babies so frail they had to be carried on a
cushion'.

There is tragedy in their own family. Once a month, May collects
her brother Patrick from a lunatic asylum, and brings him home for
tea. He had a breakdown after Oxford, and has withdrawn into a
deep, autistic silence, nobody knows why. May forbids her daughter
to be alone in the room with him, but she disobeys and miaows,
barks and moos to arouse his attention, all to no avail. Later he
wanders out of the asylum at night and dies of pneumonia.

But it is her father Bertie who casts the deepest shadow, though it
takes time for us – and his daughter – to piece his character together.
A colonel in the 11th Hussars, he goes ashore with his armoured-car
battalion on Juno beach soon after D-Day, only to see it decimated by
American friendly fire. Home from the war, he shouts and rages in
his sleep. In waking life he is bluff, hearty, brave, extravagant, kind,
funny and untrustworthy with women. Mrs Fish's daughter Betty
closely resembles him facially, which is perhaps why Mrs Fish feels
entitled to be so free with his gin. Rumours of his infidelities reach
May during the war. Little Bingley overhears her on the phone: 'If
you prefer someone else then I do not want to be married.' When he

is home for good, things get worse. There are shaming episodes with choirgirls at church, and even some fumblings in his young daughter's direction. May makes a dignified exit ('I am afraid I do not make Daddy happy') and sets up home elsewhere.

The sad ending does not detract, though, from the joy and exuberance of the book. Everyone in it sings hymns in the most unlikely situations. Even Mrs Fish bawls 'For those in peril on the sea' over her washtub. It reflects a time, recent but now utterly vanished, when *Hymns Ancient & Modern* supplied a nationwide common culture. On the last page, as her mother lies dying, Bingley shares horse-and-pony memories with her and sings 'There is a green hill far away'.

Snapshots from the family album are scattered throughout. Usually illustrations enliven a text, but here, although they provide pleasing informality, the effect is the opposite. Surrounded by the vivid stream of Bingley's writing, they seem like black-and-white stills from a colour film. This is her first book – previously she has worked as a publisher and literary agent – but it instantly takes its place beside country classics such as *Lark Rise to Candleford* and *Cider with Rosie*. The kind of life it depicts has attracted the passionate loathing of anti-hunters and their mob following, and is now illegal, which makes it more important to learn what it was really like to live it.

Running for the Hills: A Family Story
Horatio Clare, 2006

In the late 1960s, Horatio Clare's parents, Jenny and Robert, threw up their promising London careers and bought a farm in Wales. They knew nothing about farms, but the drawbacks of this one must have been clear even to the untrained. It was halfway up a mountain at the end of a precipitous track. Its walls and floors oozed damp. There was no bathroom or running water, just a chemical loo in a shed. Its tilting acres held sheep, which Jenny and Robert knew nothing about either. On the other hand, it was undeniably embosomed in nature – indeed, reverting to it – and its mountain perch gave it an eagle's-eye-view of a vast green swatch of Wales.

Jenny fell in love with it, and her diary of their life there forms the nucleus of Clare's memoir. It is a wonderful source, at once romantic and down-to-earth. Tramping the woods and fields, winter and summer, she describes things even country-lovers have never seen – newly hatched owlets, or the 'greedy marigold eye' of a cuckoo spying out the nests of smaller birds. She is frank and funny about her mistakes. When she moved in, she spent hours pulling wedges of hay, rags and dirty newspaper out of cracks and crannies in floors and ceilings, only to shove them back when she discovered that they were a vital part of the insulation system, perfected over generations, and that their absence admitted a fusillade of vicious draughts. Her diary tells her son about the early years of the adventure, before he and his brother were born. But it also provides him with a model of how to write. The joy of *Running for the Hills* lies in its seemingly effortless richness and precision. No matter what Clare seizes on (ewes licking and snickering over their newborn lambs, or a clump of nettles, or a dead mole, or the 'gasmask faces' of wasps) he brings it to the page bursting with its own actuality. It is the prose equivalent of a collection of poems by Ted Hughes – or Wordsworth. One bit, about climbing up through mist into sunlight, is a presumably unconscious rewriting of a famous passage in *The Prelude*.

Growing up on the farm was the perfect education for a writer because of its deprivations. There was no television or commercial radio, so he and his brother knew nothing about pop culture except mysterious allusions on cereal packets. The house was full of books, and even before they could read Jenny told them the stories of Shakespeare's plays and other classics, and taught them the names of stars and wild flowers. There was no money for the sweets and crisps their schoolmates gorged on, so they made do with whatever was edible in the woods – whinberries, groundsel, the honeyed parts of honeysuckle.

They learnt give-and-take with other animals. A tame mouse nicknamed Vivian nibbled lentils in the kitchen at mealtimes, and his relatives lived noisily behind bulges in the bedroom wallpaper. Life was exciting, especially in winter. Once, after a night of blizzards, they opened the door to find a solid wall of snow, marked only by the imprint of the doorknob and knocker. Once, after Robert had installed an oil tank, the tanker-driver fractionally misjudged the track and managed to eject just before his tanker pirouetted daintily down the slope, dived through the fence and exploded in a stream far below.

Clare does not soft-pedal on what was cruel and horrible about their existence. Jenny and Robert soon discover that sheep provide sustenance for other creatures besides humans. Crows will peck out the eyes and tongues of lambs while they are still being born, and, even without marauders, lambing is a nightmare. Helpless ewes hide under hedges, straining to give birth to lambs that have their heads or legs askew. Day and night patrols are necessary, and frantic bouts of midwifery in rain, hail and snow. In summer, flies lay eggs round the tails of sheep and in any sores or cuts, and these become squirming nests of maggots that will eat an animal alive. The only solution is to scoop out disgusting handfuls and squash them on the grass. Jenny can manage this, though Robert quails. But her natural sympathy makes the basic routines of food production an agony for her. When the ewes have to be separated from their lambs at weaning time, she listens in torment to their bereaved bleatings. Taking the lambs to market, she feels like a murderer.

Among neighbouring farmers cruelty was more deliberate. At the time, the Common Agricultural Policy subsidy was calculated according to the number of sheep a farmer held, so it encouraged them to overstock, cramming the hillsides with starving animals. Tottering spectres cast yearning eyes on the hay Robert feeds to his flock, and he occasionally throws them a bale out of pity – a soft townee gesture that elicits grins from the canny owners. The idea that life in the city is more stressful than in the country is sharply contradicted by this book. The struggle to survive creates monsters. Robert catches one neighbour beating a horse in maniacal fury. Another, finding a stray sheep on his land, snaps its foreleg with his bare hands. When Clare is six, Robert can stand the strain no longer, and walks out on the family, never to return.

Clare is anxious not to blame him. The wish to recapture a time when his parents were happy together lies at the heart of the book. Yet for the reader Robert's inferiority is plain. He is ruled by male competitiveness, constantly trying to beat his own record for running up the mountain, and by male bravado. His silliest trick is bringing home two unexploded mortar bombs from an old army range. The prospect of bankruptcy terrifies him. Where Jenny has a vision, he has only a balance sheet. Some time after he had gone, she asked him to increase his maintenance payments, but he refused, and told his deserted sons of his decision with, Clare recalls, a cold, hostile face. Jenny, by contrast, adapts to poverty without fuss. Although she once lived in luxury and attracted affluent lovers by her brains and beauty, she accepts help without shame: 'Remember, you're getting free school meals, so eat as much as you possibly can. Gobble it all up! OK?' She begs marrowbones from the butcher and boils them for soup. Nobody is allowed to refuse food just because it is a bit mouldy: 'It's only penicillin.' Her spirit lights up the whole book.

Clare writes of their life on the farm as a leap backwards through time to the pre-modern world – and so it was. But it may also be the future. With global warming, rising sea levels and the end of fossil fuels, subsistence hill-farming will quite probably be the fate of our descendants, and sooner than we like to think. If this heartening, raw, tender, radiant first book has a lesson for that time, it is that women will manage better than men, and that their closer bond with nature may be our redemption.

MIND BENDERS

A Short Treatise of the Great Virtues: The Uses of Philosophy in Everyday Life
André Comte-Sponville, 1995

Ethics are in the spotlight just now. Since 9/11 politicians have taken to discoursing on the 'evil' and 'wickedness' that threaten us. But what the Twin Towers tragedy brought home was something even more alarming – the stark relativism of moral viewpoints. An act that seemed almost unthinkably cruel and vile was evidently, for other human beings, an occasion for laughter and celebration. Its perpetrators were, to their partisans, martyrs, dying in a holy assault on Western values. That is much more unnerving than any simple crime, not least because, looking around at what in the main seems to be valued in the West – money, celebrity, drink, drugs, sex – it is hard to think anyone would readily die in defence of those.

André Comte-Sponville, a professor of philosophy at the Sorbonne, wrote his book before September 11, but in some respects it prefigures the dilemmas that event raised. In his section on courage he hypothesises about terrorists who blow up airliners. Because courage is a virtue, he suggests, we despise a terrorist who plants a bomb and remains on the ground more than one who boards the plane and dies with his victims. That might seem to count in favour of the 11 September murderers. But the case is altered, he argues, if the terrorist is a religious fanatic, convinced his crime will gain him happiness in the afterlife. If he believes that, he is no longer courageous, but simply sacrificing innocent lives for his own benefit.

The elegance and trickiness of that dialectic typify Comte-Sponville's approach, and help to explain how a treatise on ethics has managed to stay on the French bestseller lists for fourteen months and get itself translated into twenty-four languages. He sticks, by and large, to the traditional moral message that self-love is the root of all evil but renovates it with unusual twists. Recommending humility, for example, he classifies pride less as vice than as ignorance, because it entails blindness to one's own limitations. Humour is promoted to one of his eighteen key virtues on the grounds that taking oneself completely seriously is incompatible with true intelligence. Prudence, one of the four cardinal virtues of the medieval church, is updated to confront contemporary problems. Carelessness about sex becomes lethally imprudent in the age of HIV and Aids. Ecology, demanding that we take thought for the future of the planet, confirms prudence as the one indisputably vital modern virtue.

Faith, another former cardinal virtue, is dropped. Comte-Sponville does not believe in God or gods or in the absolute and universal moral laws that religion used to ratify. Our fate in the twenty-first century, as he sees it, is that we must be moral though we no longer believe in the truth of morality. With the disappearance of religion, notions of the 'sanctity' of human life also become untenable. He does not oppose capital punishment, if it can be shown to be effective, and he holds that the terminally ill have a right to commit suicide.

Even the accredited virtues that he decides to retain begin to look shaky under the force of his analysis. He accepts that justice is a virtue, but finds it difficult to give it any meaning. If it means treating everyone as an equal, it is obviously ridiculous. What would we think of a teacher who gave the same grade to every student? But if it means recognising the differences between people, and giving each what he or she deserves, it is humanly impossible. Who is fit to judge what another deserves? Justice, it seems, is not so much a virtue but an illusion, though an illusion that we must pretend is real.

Tolerance, too, is a virtue that breaks up on examination. It seems a recipe for global harmony, until we ask whether tolerance can afford to tolerate the intolerant. Plainly it cannot, since they will destroy it. On the other hand, if it does not tolerate them it is no longer tolerance. So either way tolerance is self-destructive. Religious belief has always been the great adversary of tolerance, whether represented by the kind of fundamentalism that lay behind the 11 September massacres, or by Pope John Paul II's decree that all those who do not submit to the truth about moral good and evil as indicated in divine law live in sin. Comte-Sponville recommends that every believer, however convinced that he is right, must acknowledge that he cannot prove he is right, and must therefore tolerate those who believe otherwise. But supposing he refuses? Supposing he proclaims his intention of destroying unbelievers? Do we then destroy him in the name of tolerance? Although paradoxical, that seems the logic of the American assault on the Taliban, and it is for those who oppose it to explain how else tolerance can survive.

Since nearly all virtues can become vices (courage in a bad cause is bad; tolerance of evil is evil) ethicists have to decide what the aim of morality is before they can sort out true virtues from their spurious doubles. There seem, broadly speaking, to be two possible answers to this question. Either morality is meant to make you feel good, or it is meant to make things better for others. Of course, it may do both. Politeness, generosity, compassion and other Comte-Sponville virtues will give you a warm inner glow while advantaging those around you. So will temperance, which in his version means opting out of gluttonous consumerism and rediscovering the joy of frugality, while ceasing to claim an inequitable share of the world's resources.

His identification of the ego as the source of evil should dispose him, where there is a choice, to select virtues that benefit others rather than oneself. But in fact he wavers. Discussing marital fidelity he decides that it should not mean 'exclusive use of the other person's body'. Further, when a partner's sexual allure wanes, as it must, and alternative partners present themselves, we should be 'faithful to the truth of desire within ourselves', even if it means being false to our word. Being true to the 'grateful memory' of the times you have had together is more important than remaining faithful to your partner. This new definition of fidelity certainly has its attractions, although it makes it rather difficult to distinguish from old style infidelity.

Another puzzle is that Comte-Sponville says he has never been able to believe in the freedom of the will. He lets this slip while urging the virtue of mercy towards criminals, who since the will is not free are not responsible for their crimes. However, if we do not have free will, but act as our genes and education determine, then we are in effect machines, in which case Comte-Sponville's whole project collapses. It would be absurd to ascribe virtues and vices to machines let alone write a book in the hope of improving their behaviour. The ingenuity he commands elsewhere suggests he would be able to dig himself out of this hole, given time. But it remains, for the moment, a flaw in a glittering display of virtuous virtuosity.

The Human Touch: Our Part in the Creation of the Universe
Michael Frayn, 2006

Imagine you have a favourite clock that needs checking over, and you are introduced to a charming and affable craftsman who proceeds, while entertaining you with a stream of anecdote and reminiscence, to dismantle it, until it is scattered in tiny pieces all over his shop. Grateful but anxious, you inquire when he is going to put it together again, whereupon he replies with some asperity that he has no intention of doing so, since time is merely a human construct, and the idea of measuring it precisely is illusory. Besides, your belief that his dismantling your clock is the cause of its being in pieces suggests that you have an extremely crude and simplistic notion of causality, which is actually a far more elusive concept than you seem to suppose.

Michael Frayn's new book is rather like that, only on a much larger scale. For time and causality are by no means the only victims of his erudite, imaginative, funny and dazzlingly clever philosophical inquiry. He unbolts, chapter by chapter, the fabric of the universe. Things that most of us regard as certainties (the laws of science, the dependability of logic) vanish like smoke. It has become apparent, he contends, in the wake of quantum mechanics and the uncertainty principle, that scientific laws are human artefacts, with no real existence outside our statement of them. Logic is just a system we have made up, not an inherent condition of the natural world. The universe itself is our invention. All its characteristics exist only as figments of the human brain. Without us it would have no characteristics at all, and so would not exist.

The obvious objections to this position Frayn anticipates and dismisses with acrobatic agility. Mathematicians, for example, might protest that number must always have existed, irrespective of whether anyone was present to do the counting. On the contrary, Frayn responds, number is something we have imposed on the natural world. To claim that nature is 'doing mathematics' when particles combine or separate would be ridiculous, and to say that number must always have been present in principle, waiting to be discovered, would be like saying that bubble gum or the works of Shakespeare were always present in principle.

Besides, before you count anything – sheep, say – you must have decided they have enough in common to be grouped together for counting, and this depends on our human ability to see analogies, which has allowed us to invent an ordered world, and language in which to describe it. You cannot have a word 'sheep' until you see one sheep is like another. Of course, analogies are themselves just constructs, with no real existence. No sheep is identical with another sheep, and anything can be like anything else according to the pressure of our purposes. You may say I am a sheep (dimwitted, easily led) and the statement will become part of the enormous delusive fabric of metaphor that our analogy-making brains create. What we call understanding the world is really a haphazard game of imagined similarities.

A key component of Frayn's thought is the idea that everything is infinitely various. 'Open your eyes at random and you are looking at more than could be described in a thousand years and more than could be explained in a million.' Human perception reads meaning into what we see, and does so by deleting most of it. This is what Frayn has against causality. To claim one thing is the cause of another is to ignore the vast, expanding cone of other antecedent events, going right back to the Big Bang, which might equally be claimed as causes. To cram all this confusion into the simple 'guilty' or 'not guilty' of the courtroom is as insane as religious fundamentalism. People often cling to a vague idea that if every single antecedent event were known everything would be found to be locked together in a chain of cause and effect. But this, for Frayn, is mere superstition, like belief in a benevolent deity. Underlying all material existence is the behaviour of subatomic particles, which is random.

Randomness seems a more likely answer than order or design, in Frayn's view, to most of the big questions. Life itself has evolved through random mutation, and modern astrophysics sees the development of the galaxies as random events. Mental life, too, may be random. How do we have ideas or make decisions? Examination of his own thought processes leaves Frayn in the dark. He finds it impossible to watch himself having thoughts, or tell where they come from. 'My thoughts think themselves', it seems. Brain operation may depend on the random behaviour of single particles, so that what we call 'free will' may be free but cannot be will. Other people are, of course, even more difficult to observe than ourselves. To have any conception of them we have to reconstruct them as fictions. Fiction writers, Frayn fears, may have a lot to answer for in this respect, because in their stories other people's motives and intentions are knowable, which tempts us to think they are knowable in life, sometimes with lethal results.

Not that he seems deterred from fiction. No philosophical treatise, surely, has ever been so alive with stories as *The Human Touch*. Its hypotheses and thought experiments throw up shoals of characters who get impatient with being teaching-aids and set off refreshingly on adventures of their own. We keep diving, too, into Frayn's past – a horrific car crash he once witnessed; his student days in Moscow, where a friend rigged up an electric random-choice machine, which they gambled on in kopecks; a mad correspondent in his journalist days who wanted him to found a Universal Brotherhood of All Mankind Association, and so inadvertently gave Frayn the word 'uboama', meaning a grandiose illusion.

Grandiose illusions he demolishes in passing, with much hilarity and splinter-sharp intelligence, include Chomsky's theory, unquestioningly accepted by most linguists, that the human brain is 'hardwired' for language, the philosophical belief in parallel universes, and the possibility of developing computers with feelings and consciousness, indistinguishable from human beings. What, he pertinently asks, would be the point, since we can produce creatures indistinguishable from human beings with the rudimentary means already at our disposal?

He sometimes slips. Arguing the case for total subjectivity does not really permit him to say that quantum mechanics gives us 'a truer picture of the universe' than we had before, for true pictures of the universe are uboamas. His claim that humans create the universe – 'if we go, so will everything' – entails, he concedes, a contradiction, for the universe existed for 14 billion years before we arrived and will continue exactly as before after we have disappeared. But if, as he argues, our consciousness gives it all its characteristics, it must exist, after we have gone, without any characteristics, which seems a mystical state of affairs, although he rejects mysticism. However, this looks less like a mistake on Frayn's part than an illustration of the limit of human understanding – a topic never far from your conscious-ness in this mind-stretching book.

The Clock Mirage: Our Myth of Measured Time
Joseph Mazur, 2020

Imagine completely empty space. It has no boundaries but extends infinitely in every direction. Nothing moves in it because there is nothing to move. When you have imagined that, consider this question: Does time exist in that space?

After reading Joseph Mazur's mind-stretching book, I am uncer-tain about almost everything, including the answer to that question and the answer he would give. However, I believe he would say that if your answer is 'Yes' – if, that is, you believe that time would exist in that space – you are still living mentally in the seventeenth century. You believe, as Isaac Newton did, that time is absolute, irrespective of the observer. The advance in knowledge represented by Einstein's relativity theory has somehow passed you by. For Einstein, time is not absolute, but relative to the observer, and since in that notional space at the start of this review there was no observer, there would be no time.

Mazur's book is skilfully written in that it starts with the easy stuff. The opening section is a history of clocks. First came sundials, which were known to the Babylonians. Then came water clocks, which released water in small quantities and could be used to measure time at night. Finally mechanical clocks with escapements emerged, perhaps in the sixteenth century.

Early mechanical clocks had only one hand, for the hour. Minute hands came in with the Industrial Revolution, which brought with it the idea of punctuality – workers getting to the mill or factory on time – and the new notion of the weekend. Agricultural communities had no weekends, the crops grew and animals needed feeding all seven days. Mazur rounds out this pleasantly ambling section with an account of the Prague astronomical clock, built in 1410 and still (or until recently) drawing crowds of tourists with its hourly clockwork procession of the Apostles. Apparently, the fashion for mannequin clocks such as this came to Europe along the Silk Road from China.

With Mazur's second section, his most difficult, we plunge into a maelstrom of physics and philosophy, starting with Zeno's paradoxes. Zeno was a pre-Socratic philosopher about whom little is known except his paradoxes, all of which relate to the idea of motion. He mocked, for example, the apparently indisputable idea that you cannot run to the end of a path without running halfway first, by pointing out that you'd have to run a quarter before you ran a half, and an eighth before a quarter, and a sixteenth before an eighth and so on to infinity. So you'd never reach the end. Aristotle attempted to disprove this in his *Physics*, and some believe that Zeno made his paradox up as a kind of joke called a reductio ad absurdum or reduction to absurdity.

To philosophers, though, it was not a joke, and they have pondered the implications of it for centuries. What Zeno actually believed is hard to say. Apparently, he said that time and motion were both illusions, which does not seem helpful. But then Einstein said, equally unhelpfully: 'The distinction between past, present and future is only a stubbornly persistent illusion.'

Such sayings seem exorbitant until, Mazur suggests, we consider the question of colour. We all accept that colour does not 'really' inhere in the objects we see as coloured. It is an illusion created by our optic nerves and the wavelengths of light. Yet we happily accept it as part of reality. Maybe time is similar, and Zeno's seemingly jocular suggestion that motion is not smooth, but entails little hops, is in agreement, Mazur points out, with quantum theory, which teaches that energy comes in individual units, or quanta.

Mazur is not a physicist, but a mathematician and science journalist. However, he has evidently kept up with recent developments. He cites loop quantum gravitation theory, according to which space and time are both granular. 'Space-time might be built from specks of space-time dust, whatever they might be.' Time may consist of quanta called chronons, just as light quanta are called photons, and space, although it seems continuous to us, may be a 'flickering movie'.

Keeping up with Mazur at this level makes your head hurt. But he has considerately inserted human 'interludes' between the scientific sections. These are reported conversations about time with a wide range of people, including a twenty-one year old who has been sentenced to life imprisonment; one female and two male astronauts; a worker on an assembly line in China who inserts a single tiny screw into an unending stream of iPhones, twelve hours a day, six days a week, for $4 a day; a hedge fund manager who makes and loses millions in moments; and a group of long-haul truckers at a stopover in Massachusetts.

These conversations reveal that time means something different to every individual, and it is this variable, perhaps illusory, human meaning of time that Mazur's book increasingly inclines towards.

As humans, he stresses, we are inescapably earthlings. Our organisms are created and sustained by our planet's alternation of day and night. His final section tries to imagine life on a planet outside our solar system called Proxima Centauri b, but his heart does not seem to be in it. Surprisingly he seems to assume that living organisms on Proxima Centauri b, if they existed, would have a concept of number, or at least be able to count up to four. Perhaps that is a natural assumption for a professional mathematician, but it is questionable. Michael Frayn, in *The Human Touch*, argues that number is just a human invention and has no independent reality. To believe that number has always existed and was waiting for humans to discover it, says Frayn, is like believing that the works of Shakespeare have always existed, but were waiting for Shakespeare. It would be good to know Mazur's response to this. One thing is certain: it would not be dull.

Sapiens: A Brief History of Humankind
Yuval Noah Harari, 2014

Sapiens is the sort of book that sweeps the cobwebs out of your brain. Its author, Yuval Noah Harari, is a young Israeli academic and an intellectual acrobat whose logical leaps have you gasping with admiration. That said, the joy of reading him is not matched by any uplift in his message, which is relentlessly accusatory and dismaying. His book presents a brief history of life on earth, starting with the big bang and ending 1,000 years in the future, by which time, he predicts, *Homo sapiens* will be extinct, because science will have replaced us with genetically engineered immortals and 'super-cyborgs', part human, part machine, with faculties we can't even imagine.

The disappearance of old-style humans is not, it is clear, a prospect he much regrets, for on his reckoning we have proved the most destructive species ever to plague the planet. Almost all the facts in the human story are contested, but, as Harari tells it, our remote ancestors lived peacefully among the other animals for many millenniums until about 70,000 years ago when *Homo sapiens* developed superior cognitive powers and, crucially, invented language.

No one knows how we alone managed this, rather than the other human species, such as Neanderthals, that archaeology has discovered. But it was language that enabled us to co-operate, organise and become the dominant animal. From their African homeland prehistoric humans spread across the globe, colonising Australia 45,000 years ago, where they became the Indigenous Australians, then North and South America, where they became the Paleo-Indians. Wherever they went they spread destruction, hunting the larger mammals to extinction. All this happened while we were still primitive foragers. As Harari vividly puts it, we obliterated half the planet's large-mammal species even before we got round to inventing the wheel.

A second wave of devastation came with the invention of agriculture around 10,000 years ago. Clearing land for the cultivation of cereals meant destroying the habitats of countless animal, bird and plant species, and reinforced humanity's claim to be the deadliest organism ever. In Harari's view, agriculture was also a tragedy for humans. With agriculture came private property, social and sexual inequality, greed and exploitation. What had been close-knit, self-helping hunter-gatherer groups were replaced by a social system in which the majority were serfs or slaves, ruled by despots who owned the land. Worse still, agriculture supported far greater numbers of humans than foraging had, so it led eventually to the global population that is now spiralling out of control and can be sustained only by the obscenities of factory farming, described in this book with justified horror.

Harari does not claim to be original in identifying the invention of agriculture as a world-changing disaster, and, in fact, the credit for this idea seems to belong to Jean-Jacques Rousseau, whose *Discourse on the Origin of Inequality* put forward almost exactly the same argument in 1754. Since then, research has tended to confirm the disaster scenario. Quite apart from introducing social inequalities, agriculture, it seems, led to a steep decline in the standard of living, because it required full-time labour whereas hunter-gatherers, it is estimated, spent less than twenty hours a week getting food. They also had a healthier diet than farming communities, were less prone to vitamin deficiency, and lived longer.

Harari would like to believe that, in addition to their other advantages, hunter-gatherers were happier than we are. You can see why the thought attracts him. It would be a fitting payoff for our ecological mayhem. However, for once his argument stalls, and peters out in metaphysical niceties. Quantifying happiness seems a patently daft idea, which is no doubt why historians have steered clear of it, as Harari complains they have. Knowing whether those nearest and dearest to you are happy is difficult enough, without imagining that you can get inside the mind of some anonymous bushman who roamed the earth centuries ago.

Mostly, though, Harari's writing radiates power and clarity, making the world strange and new. His central argument is that language has not just made us top animal, it has also enmeshed us in fictions. Myths, gods and religions appeared with the advent of language, and though they do not really exist outside the stories that we make up, they are enormously strong. Fictions such as Christianity and nationalism can bind millions together in a common cause, and people die for them. Humans, Harari observes, are the only animals that believe in vastly powerful entities that they have never seen, touched or smelt, and that is language's fault.

Laws, justice and human rights are all myths or fictions from Harari's perspective, having no objective reality outside our imagination. Nothing resembling justice exists in the universe. There are no rights in biology. In a bravura passage he deconstructs the most famous lines in the American Declaration of Independence ('We hold these truths to be self-evident, that all men are created equal, that they are endowed by their Creator with certain inalienable rights ...') to show that they are a mishmash of fictions, from the creation myth to the absurd claim that humans are equal. Not that Harari dismisses such fictions as evil conspiracies or useless mirages. We believe in them, he argues, because they bind society together and allow us to co-operate effectively.

At the same time, because we half know that they are fictions, believing in them requires a degree of self-deception, for which Harari adopts the term 'cognitive dissonance', meaning the ability to hold contradictory beliefs and values. This is often considered a failure of the human psyche, but Harari applauds it. Had people been unable to hold contradictory beliefs and values, he suggests, it would have been impossible to establish human culture. However, since his book shows that the effect of human culture has been to devastate the world, perhaps the failure to establish it would have been no bad thing.

Harari has his own contradictions. He makes predictions while declaring that prediction is impossible. He argues that history is a 'chaos' while treating it as a system of cause and effect. But such blips should not deter readers from treating themselves to this mind-stirring book.

VEGETABLE GARDENING

Vegetable Gardening
John Carey, 1980

It's perverse, really, to write about gardening at all. Half the point of gardening is that it repairs that part of your brain which words and thinking are constantly threatening to destroy. That's one thing it has in common with music: it lies beyond the reach of words, and you wouldn't need it if it didn't. Still, you're forced to be articulate about it sometimes, particularly when under attack. The other day one of those acid young women you come across nowadays, who give you the impression that they're on temporary release from an Urban Guerrilla Training Camp, demanded in the course of a chat how I could justify spending time on gardening when, as an academic, I ought to be reading books.

It took some time to sort out the various kinds of rage with which this query filled me. But when I'd done so I realized that it was my puritanism which had taken the worst knock. Whatever other pleasures attach to gardening, they're all based on the assumption that it's a blameless, nay meritorious, occupation. That feeling must go back at least as far as the myth of Eden. And if, as I do, you stick to vegetables and don't grow flowers, your sense of self-approval naturally redoubles.

Quite right too: for you are, after all, producing food, which is one of the few obviously worthwhile human activities. True, someone else would produce it for you, probably more efficiently, if you didn't. But then, you could find someone to perform most of life's functions in your stead if you were sufficiently comatose. By growing what you eat, you keep in touch with economic realities which lie deeper than money. As for the argument about wasting time, it's nonsense. If you're efficient you can keep your family stocked with vegetables by spending about one Saturday in every two gardening. For half the year, from October to March, you have virtually nothing to do but gather the produce – sprouts, leeks, carrots, kale, broccoli, winter cabbages – all of which will stand out in the snow and ice obediently fattening themselves for your consumption.

But these practical considerations, though sound, are by no means the whole story. Like most puritan pleasures, vegetable gardening contains a strong element of submerged sensuousness. By that I don't mean simply that home-grown stuff tastes better than the plastic-shrouded organisms which pass themselves off as vegetables in supermarkets, alongside the disinfectants and washing-up liquids. Garden produce undeniably does have more intense and varied flavours than anything you can buy, but gardeners are austere people, and it would strike them as indecent to set too much store by the pleasures of the table. The sensuous gains they look for are more remote and devious.

Take parsnips, for instance. With the best will in the world it's difficult to pretend that the parsnip is really eatable, but it's an immense and exacting pleasure to grow. At the start of the season you grub out a row of pits with a trowel, and fill them, almost to the brim, with finely sieved soil. Then you poke into each soft dell about a dozen of the crisp wafers which are the parsnip's seeds, and pat earth over them. Come the summer, you pull out all but one of the seedlings from each cluster – pale gold pencils, with feathery tops, which it always gives you a pang to throw on to a compost heap, though there's nothing else to be done with them. Then, as the winter approaches, the great spreading leaves of the survivors rot and yellow, and the parsnips withdraw into their subterranean existence until, some time after Christmas, the time comes to crack the frosty crust over them and lug them out gross, whiskered and reeking, from their lairs.

Once you have done that, and have scraped the earth from their sweaty white sides with a sharp knife, the parsnip's capacity for giving pleasure is, in my view, pretty well exhausted. You can, of course, roast or boil them like potatoes, or you can put off the evil hour of trying to get them down your gullet by making them into wine, which takes several months to perfect, and is generally so vile in the end that it has mercifully to be tipped down the sink. However, these posthumous considerations don't affect the satisfactoriness of the parsnip during its lifetime. As a fellow creature, rather than a food, it is truly glorious.

Most of the rich experiences obtainable from the vegetable garden are similarly untainted by any thought of actual consumption. They feed, rather, your other senses in covert and delicate ways. To feel the damp fur inside a broad bean pod, and see how it grips its beans by their little umbilical cords, is a lot better than eating broad beans – good as that is. With onions, nothing that happens on the culinary side is more satisfying than the business of preparing them for winter storage, after they have been uprooted and dried off in the sun. You start with a tattered, mud-caked heap, and one by one you rub the papery outer skins away to reveal row upon row of gleaming amber bellies – the onion equivalent of a riviera beach scene. Then you string the sleek bulbs together by the necks and hang them in dangling swags from the wall of your garden shed, where they will swing and glow through the dark months.

Like all garden jobs, podding beans and storing onions are seasonal – part of a pattern ruled by sky and earth which non-gardeners lose touch with, or apprehend only dimly through vulgarised annual occurrences like power strikes or Easter eggs. But the gardener's annual pattern is also a personal one, giving coherence to his life. At each stage in his year he finds himself rediscovering vivid sensations which have a whole stream of dormant memories trailing behind them. Spend a quarter of an hour, for instance, pinching out the side shoots on a row of tomatoes, and you will find your thumb and forefinger stained a deep and pungent green, so concentratedly that when you put your hand in water the greenness comes off in clouds and fills the bowl. I can still remember my pleased surprise when that first happened to me – or rather, I suppose, I can remember re-remembering it through years of renewal. Agreed, few people would take up vegetable gardening just for the sake of a bowl of green water, but if your nose and eyes are still alive it's a thing you'll find intriguing.

Since the gardener's year is circular, with life always overlapping death, these private annual ceremonies take you into the future as well as the past. Gathering runner-bean seeds, for instance, is a late autumn job with an atmosphere all of its own, compounded of weak sunlight, and that sense of wet collapse which a dying garden exudes. But the bean stems, you find, are dry and brittle, like twigs, and the pods still hanging on them crunch between your fingers into tobacco-coloured flakes, leaving in your palm the chunky beads which will be next year's crop.

As vegetable gardeners aren't primarily concerned with eating they harbour, like librarians, a tidy-minded dislike of anyone who actually wants to use the commodities they're in charge of. To have to uproot cabbages, say, from a row, and hand them over for cooking, is always an annoyance. The gaps look unsightly, like snapped-off teeth. A stalwart, unbroken line of cabbages, on the other hand, with their hearts tight as fists and their purple outer leaves spread to catch the dew, raise your spirit every time you visit them. Among the current clichés I especially deplore is the one which refers to hospital patients kept alive by machines as 'cabbages'. This is both inaccurate and insulting to vegetables. For a cabbage is a sturdy, self-reliant being, and compared with an average specimen of twentieth-century manhood it has, when well grown, a positively athletic air.

That's not to deny that the gardener has his work cut out keeping his vegetables healthy. The only vegetable which no insect seems to attack is the leek. That makes it the easiest of all to grow, which is perhaps why it's favoured by the lyrical and carefree Welsh. All the rest are assailed by ingenious and tireless enemies, with no other purpose in life than to destroy what you have grown. Even your attempts to care for your plants draw down disaster upon them. When you weed out a row of carrots, the smell of crushed leaves brings carrot-flies flocking from far, and wide.

In this situation the only adequate response is to thank God for chemical pesticides, and use them liberally. Unfortunately the strongest and most effective ones keep being withdrawn from the market on the grounds that they have been found to damage the environment. So when you hit on a really lethal sort it's a good plan to buy in a large supply, which will allow you to go on using it after it has been outlawed. I did this for several seasons with a splendid product, now alas unobtainable, which wiped out everything from snails to flea beetles. It had no adverse effect on the bird population so far as I could see, though the neighbourhood cats did start to look a bit seedy. That, of course, was an advantage from my point of view, for cats are filthy, insanitary beasts, and a fearful nuisance to the gardener. One of the anomalies of English law is that whereas it would, as I understand it, be an offence to clamber over your neighbour's fence and defecate among his vegetables, you can send a feline accomplice on precisely the same errand with total impunity. It has always amazed me that manufacturers of slug bait, and other such garden aids, should proudly announce on the label that their product is 'harmless to pets'. A pesticide that could guarantee to cause pets irreparable damage would, I'd have thought, sell like hot cakes.

But though gardeners grumble about their battle with pests and marauders, it's really a challenge they wouldn't be without for anything. It gives them a heroic sense of being pitted against the universe, and makes them realise how precariously we maintain life on our planet in competition with the swarming species struggling to shove us off it. It also peps up your aggressive instincts. With a bucket of toxic chemicals you can spread death almost as effectively as you could with a flame thrower, and far more usefully.

A different kind of pest, and just as bothersome, at any rate to the novice, as slugs or vermin, are the people who write the descriptive paragraphs about different varieties of vegetable in seed catalogues. I'm sure they don't mean to mislead, but the fact is that what they omit is far more important than what they say, and it takes years to accustom yourself to deciphering their curiously oblique literary mode. For example, the phrase 'a sure winner on the show bench' actually means 'inedible'. If, unsuspectingly, you grow a runner bean, say, which has this legend attached, you will end up with beans a yard long which have the flavour and consistency of ballpoint pens. Let us suppose that, after this experience, you vow never to grow vegetables which are not specifically recommended for their eating qualities. Next year, accordingly, you choose a strain of lettuce which has sent the catalogue compiler into raptures by its crispness and succulence. Surely now you'll be safe. But no. For the one thing that matters about lettuces is whether or not they bolt in hot weather, and since your author has remained silent on this point it means that you will find your lettuces wagging in the breeze like pagodas after a couple of weeks of sunshine. And so it goes on. Next year you carefully avoid both the show-bench successes and the secret bolters, but you forget to look for the assurance that your selected varieties are resistant to disease. Should this clause be absent, your vegetables, though enthusiastically recommended, and quite hale-looking in the catalogue snapshots, will prove to be generous hosts to every known virus, and will topple into fungoid ruin long before you have a chance to harvest them.

Not that seed catalogues can't provide their own special pleasures, so long as you don't expect them to be helpful or informative. Learning to outwit the compilers is itself a heartening experience. There's also much amusement to be derived from those fancy catalogues which urge the simple-minded to sow aubergines, soya beans, melons and other ungrowable exotica. It's always good to see fools and their money being parted. A more poetic source of enjoyment are the names of the vegetable varieties that any catalogue contains: Chantenay Red Cored and Musselburgh, Winter Queen and Wheeler's Imperial, Amager Rearguard and Hopkin's Fenlander. They are full of mysterious evocations, like monuments of a lost culture. Who was Ailsa Craig, now immortalised as an onion? Who was Dr Mackintosh, before he became a potato? Who was the Lobjoit of Lobjoit's Green Cos? I imagine Lobjoit as a lean pioneer bent double on some windswept smallholding, surrounded by immature lettuce plants. No doubt research into horticultural history could provide definite answers. But knowledge on such matters would be quite useless, whereas ignorance is a source of inexhaustible fascination.

As with most pursuits, one of the leading pleasures of vegetable gardening is that it makes you feel superior to those who don't pursue it. The degeneracy of the pampered masses, propped half-conscious before their telly screens, becomes, as you toil on your lonely plot, a profoundly satisfying subject of meditation. But here, as in other ways, vegetable growing has an educative, balancing effect – for there is always someone better at it than you. Take a stroll round any village horticultural show, and you will find your self-esteem draining away with horrible rapidity. Onions the size of Christmas puddings, balanced proudly on their little beds of sand; luminous tomatoes, each competitor's group of six standing demurely apart from the rest and as exactly matched as billiard balls; leeks as thick as your arm, with their vast green manes combed and beribboned like show horses; aristocratic carrots, like furled orange umbrellas – how is such grandeur achieved? Naturally you try to console yourself, remembering your experience of seed catalogues, by reflecting that this exhibition stuff is probably useless for anything else. But somehow that thought carries little conviction. For even if it were true, the artistry that goes into these prodigious creations is still daunting and, you are sinkingly aware, far beyond your powers.

This tendency to elate and humble you in quick succession is one of the factors linking vegetable gardening with religion. It is also religious in the devotion it inspires and the elect band it admits you to. Like other religions it instils a set of values combatively out of key with modern trends. The promises dangled before the public by political leaders are likely to strike the vegetable gardener with indifference or dismay. Those rousing forecasts of intensified house-building programmes and greater industrial expansion – what kind of moron, the vegetable gardener wonders, are they supposed to attract? Who wants to see a greater and greater acreage disappearing under concrete and sewage pipes? Isn't it time we realised that, given our bulging populations, vegetables have now become more desirable inhabitants of the earth than people: less destructive, more peaceful, more serviceable for sustaining life? The day I see a row of houses being pulled down to make a vegetable plot, I shall feel that something sane and healthy has happened.